THE ECONOMICS OF INFORMATION COMMUNICATION AND ENTERTAINMENT
The Impacts of Digital Technology in the 21st Century

Series Editor:
Darcy Gerbarg
President, DVI, Ltd.
Senior Fellow
Columbia Institute for Tele-Information (CITI)
Columbia University Business School
New York, USA

For other titles published in this series, go to
http://www.springer.com/series/8276

Darcy Gerbarg

Editor

Television Goes Digital

 Springer

Editor
Darcy Gerbarg
President, DVI, Ltd.
Senior Fellow
Columbia Institute for Tele-Information
Columbia University Business School
New York, USA

ISBN: 978-0-387-79977-3   e-ISBN: 978-0-387-79978-0
DOI: 10.1007/978-0-387-79978-0

Library of Congress Control Number: 2008937469

Printed on acid-free paper

springer.com

Foreword: Digital Television

A. Michael Noll*

\

A Little History

The first regularly scheduled television broadcasting in the United States began in 1939 by NBC in three cities. After the war, the Federal Communications Commission (FCC) allocated 13 channels for television broadcasting in 1945, which is the generally accepted year for the beginning of commercial television in the United States. In 1952, the FCC allocated additional radio spectrum for television in the UHF band. The FCC adopted the NTSC color television standard in 1953.

Analog television broadcasting in the United States uses 525 interlaced scan lines, although an industrial standard of 1000 lines was also used in limited cases for closed-circuit television applications. High definition television (HDTV) for the home generally means about 1000 scan lines, which is double the current NTSC analog standard. The 525-line standard was chosen based on the acuity of human vision at a specified distance from the screen. However, HDTV looks better if the screen is substantially larger and is viewed from a closer distance.

The Japanese Broadcasting Corporation (NHK) introduced HDTV broadcasting to the home in the early 1980s in Japan with the MUSE system. MUSE is an analog system using compression of the TV signal. Both CBS and RCA also developed analog HDTV systems in the 1980s, and these systems were backwards compatible with the existing NTSC system. The United States TV industry then made the decision to leapfrog over analog and develop digital television. One reason was to stimulate television manufacturing in the United States and forestall Japanese domination. A Grand Alliance was formed within the television industry to agree upon a standard and to promote HDTV. The industry then lobbied the Congress and the FCC for legislation and rules to promote HDTV on behalf of the television broadcasters and set manufactures.

The Telecommunications Act of 1996 authorized the FCC to issue "…additional licenses for advanced television services…" on designated frequencies to the existing

---

*This material is updated and expanded from a live radio interview on August 2, 2001 on FM radio station KPFK in North Hollywood, CA.

broadcasters. At some time in the future, "...either the additional license or the original license [would]...be surrendered..."

The FCC Fifth Report and Order (adopted April 3, 1997) set the rules for advanced television services as legislated by the Telecommunications Act. The FCC Order called digital television "a technological breakthrough" and reaffirmed the national policy to "...preserve and promote universal, free, over-the-air television." The FCC considered a schedule of 15 years for adoption of a digital TV system, but decided on a more ambitious target date of 2006 for ceasing the broadcasting of analog television. The target date was subject to review every 2 years and was extended to 2009. A variety of objective standards for determining when to surrender one of the licenses is discussed in the FCC Order, such as the percentage of digital sets sold or the percentage of TV households relying on digital television.

What Is Digital TV?

Digital is a form of encoding in which the waveform of a signal is represented as a series of digits, which are then encoded as a sequence of binary "0s" and "1s," or as "ONs" and "OFFs." Since digits rather than an analog of the waveform are encoded, the digital representation allows near perfect storage and transmission. But these advantages are obtained at the expense of bandwidth, and digital requires considerably more bandwidth than analog. The solution is to compress the digital signal. For television, this compression is accomplished using the Motion Pictures Expert Group (MPEG) standard. VCR quality is possible at about 1 Mbps. DVD quality is possible at from 2 to 4 Mbps.

The term "digital TV" has many possible meanings. It can mean HDTV. But HDTV involves many factors, such as an increase in the number of scan lines (to about 1,000), a wide screen display, noninterlaced scanning with less flicker, and compression of the digital signal to conserve bandwidth when transmitted. Digital TV can also mean multicasting in which a number of conventional (but digitized) TV signals are sent in the space of a single channel. The multiple signals (usually about four) can be time-displaced versions of the same program, multiple different programs, or different camera shots of the same program.

The Internet can be used to access digital TV – what is sometimes called Internet TV. The term digital TV has also been used to mean some form of interactive television. The many different meanings of digital TV can be confusing to consumers. The definitions are also different for different segments of the television industry, depending on the advocacy of the segment at the present time. This only compounds the confusion as we wait for the dust to settle. Whatever digital TV might be, consumers watch television because of program content – not picture quality.

The Spectrum Wars

In the end, digital television is all about radio spectrum space. Radio spectrum space is a very valuable commodity. Once a chunk of it has been allocated in some geographic region, it cannot be used for other purposes. Whoever obtains a license to its use, in effect, "owns" valuable radio spectrum property.

Radio waves travel over distance and reach us wherever we might be. Thomas Alva Edison first observed radio waves in 1875. Radio waves were first used for wireless telegraphy and then for broadcasting music and news. Guglielmo Marconi sent the first radio waves across the Atlantic Ocean in 1901. Nikola Tesla envisioned radio as a mass medium for broadcasting. Edwin Howard Armstrong developed essential electronic circuitry and championed FM radio broadcasting. Today, radio waves are used for commercial AM and FM radio broadcasting, for VHF and UHF television broadcasting, for wireless cellular telecommunication, for communication satellites, for Internet access, and for a host of other applications. Each application utilizes its own unique band of radio frequencies within the radio spectrum.

Each television station in the United States broadcasts within a band of electromagnetic radio spectrum that is 6 MHz (6,000,000 Hz) wide. For digital television broadcasting, the FCC gave each broadcaster an additional 6 MHz in the UHF band. Thus, each television broadcaster controlled 12 MHz of spectrum space. One of the channels is to be returned when analog broadcasting ceases in 2009. If spectrum were abundant, the hogging of 12 MHz by each television broadcaster would not be a problem, but radio spectrum is a scarce commodity. The bandwidth released is in the UHF spectrum.

Radio should be used for valuable, needed services that cannot be delivered by other media. Wireless cellular telecommunication reaches us anyplace, anytime, anywhere. Radio is the only way such telecommunication can occur. The tremendous growth of wireless cellular and data services has created great demands for additional radio spectrum space. The frequencies that would be most useful are in the UHF band that was allocated for digital television.

The television broadcasters were given licenses for the additional 6 MHz for free. Wireless cellular providers are charged by the government for their spectrum space through an auction process. Thus, digital television has become the biggest giveaway ever, to a privileged industry. Television broadcasters have considerable political influence. But soon the additional spectrum will be returned to the government, which will then auction it away. Who will bid and obtain this valuable spectrum is not yet clear.

Over-the-Air Television Is Dying

In 1945 when television first began broadcasting over the current VHF channels, 100% of TV households obtained their television over the air. There were no alternatives. Today, television is obtained over a variety of media: over-the-air VHF and

UHF broadcasts, cable television (CATV), direct broadcast satellite (DBS), other forms of satellite broadcast, and physical media (such as tape and disk). In 1997, only 22% of TV households obtained their television directly over the air, and I am told that today that percentage is much less than 20%, and continuing to decline. Over-the-air television is dying!

People who still obtain their television directly over the air are most likely too poor to pay for cable or DBS. These are not the kinds of consumers who will lead the pack by investing in new digital television sets. Most are likely to obtain digital adaptors, which are being subsidized by the government through coupons. Thus, there is little market for over-the-air television – analog or digital.

Digital TV Is Already Here

Although over-the-air digital television might have a dismal future, digital television is already here in many ways and forms. Direct broadcast satellite television is sent digitally using compression, and DBS systems are already offering HDTV on some of their channels. The digital video disk (DVD) is digital and offers images with tremendous technical quality. Television studios are using digital to process and store television programs which are then sent in analog form over the air in anticipation of the conversion in 2009 to digital broadcast. Cable systems already use digital transmission, and the telephone companies are offering digital TV over either optical fiber to the home or switched video over copper twisted-pair.

Conclusion

The world of television has changed from the late 1980s when HDTV was hatched. The market for over-the-air digital television has evaporated, and perhaps really was little more than the result of fuzzy thinking and overpromotion. Today is a time when most people in the United States obtain their television over cable, when satellite dishes are appearing on the roofs of homes around the country, when almost everyone has a DVD player, along with high-speed Internet access. This is a new world of television, and over-the-air television has been left behind.

There will always be a few consumers for whom over-the-air, free broadcasting is their only source of television. But radio spectrum is too precious to allocate 6 MHz per television channel to serve this dwindling audience. One solution would be to require cable companies to offer free basic cable service. Another solution would be to require television broadcasters to compress their television signal to 1 MHz using digital technology and then provide inexpensive converters to those who watch over-the-air television. The future and ultimate fate of over-the-air television is a matter of public debate that will require careful thought by the FCC and by political leaders.

Additional Reading by Noll

Noll, A. M. (1988) Television Technology: Fundamentals and Future Prospects. Artech House, Norwood, MA.

Noll, A. M. (1991) High definition television (HDTV), in Berger, A. A. (ed.), Chapter 57 in Media USA (Second Edition). Longman, New York, pp. 431–438.

Noll, A. M. (1997) Highway of Dreams: A Critical Appraisal of the Communication Superhighway. Lawrence Erlbaum, Mahwah, NJ.

Noll, A. M. (1997) Digital television, analog consumers. Telecommunications 31(9):18.

Noll, A. M. (1999) The evolution of television technology, in Gerbarg, D. (ed.), The Economics, Technology and Content of Digital TV. Kluwer, Boston, pp. 3–17.

Noll, A. M. (1999) The impending death of over-the-air television. info 1(5):389–391.

Noll, A. M. (2001) Principles of Modern Communications Technology. Artech House, Norwood, MA.

Acknowledgments

In addition to the chapter authors, there are many people who contributed to this book. The CITI[1] staff provided support, first for the initial conference that generated many of the chapters in this book, and later by supplementing author research. John Haywood, Loy Phillips and Arian Rivera, in particular, fielded my endless requests and questions and directed student intern research. Bob Atkinson and the other directors as well as the visiting scholars contributed to the unique and stimulating intellectual environment at CITI in which many of the concepts and ideas for this book were generated, discussed and developed. A. Michael Noll has been a staunch supporter, making himself available to read and comment on the text. Thanks are also due to Roberta Tasley for all her help with CITI conferences.

I owe Eli Noam an immeasurable debt of gratitude. Since 1997, when he invited me to organize and manage my first Digital TV conference at CITI, he has supported my activities there. That early DTV conference generated papers which I collected and edited for my first book on this subject, *The Economics, Technology and Content of Digital TV*.[2] In 2002 I mounted another conference at CITI which generated papers for a second book, *Internet TV*.[3] Some of the topics covered in these earlier books are complemented by chapters in the current volume. This new book is not, however, an update of the earlier ones but rather addresses new topics and fills in areas, particularly on background technology, not covered by the first ones.

Eli deserves credit for all three books which include a number of academic papers collected from conferences mounted at CITI. Without Eli's prescient topic selection and speaker recommendations, the conferences would not have been as timely or as strong.

Finally, the editors at Springer have provided much needed assistance in the production of this book. Nicholas Philipson's enthusiastic support for this book and the new series comes at just the right time. Having Daniel Valen at Springer, making sure that all the pieces come together, frees me to work with the authors and focus on the book's content.

Darcy Gerbarg
New York, NY

Notes

1. Columbia Institute for Tele Information, Columbia University Business School.
2. D. Gerbarg, ed., The Economics, Technology and Content of Digital TV, Kluwer, Dordrecht, 1997.
3. D. Gerbarg, ed., *Internet TV*, Lawrence Erlbaum, Mahwah, NJ, 2003 (also ed. Noam, Groebel).

Contents

Part III   Content

Part IV   Legal and Regulatory Issues

Introduction: The Digital Evolution of Television

Darcy Gerbarg

Television has been evolving since the first black and white TV transmissions. Spurred by relentless technological developments and ultimately embraced by manufacturers, content producers and the business community, television today includes an ever broadening array of content offerings.

A little over 10 years ago, when I mounted my first Digital TV[1] conference at CITI,[2] we had difficulty specifying exactly what digital television was. What after all was digital television in 1996? There was no digital TV broadcast or digital content to speak of. The FCC[3] was holding their public hearings before making their SDTV[4] and HDTV[5] rulings and almost no one had broadband. In the United States broadcast television was- and until February 2009- remained primarily analog. Today vast majority of US consumers receive television programming via cable and satellite set top boxes; so most television viewers can already receive digital SD and HD programming.

This situation was quite different 10 years ago. At that time, Dr. Einav's research turned up a mere handful of companies that were producing videos for the Internet. Dr. Carey examined the position the computer was assuming in the television household and the idea of lean forward and lean back for viewing was articulated. Computer animation and special effects were becoming common in TV advertising and had been used for background TV News graphics for more than a decade. The BBC had experimented with a variety of interactive television program formats as well as the online world called The Mirror.[6] While some of these were fascinating, all proved too expensive to produce. In general; just because one could do something innovative with the new technology did not mean that one was going to be able to turn it into sustainable TV programming. None the less, digital technology was already becoming a disruptive change agent in the evolution of television.

Digitization of audio and video content, which began years before the FCC started its foray into specifying a DTV standard, has now made it practical for telephony to go wireless and television wired. Digital technology, increased network capacity and speed, along with the development of the World Wide Web. New network communications capabilities are responsible for changes occurring throughout the television industry.

D. Gerbarg (ed.), *Television Goes Digital*,
© Springer Science + Business Media, LLC 2009

With the widespread adoption of cable and the satellite, television programming was no longer the sole purview of the television broadcast industry. Because many households were outside the range of analog broadcast television and since many early cable operators sold television sets, the earliest cable operators started capturing networks' broadcast signals on very large antennas and providing this signal over cable to their customers' homes. Early on, Satellite up and down links, which originally provided broadcast content to cable head ends, went digital. Later satellite companies figured out how to beam broadcast content directly to receptor dishes set up in yards or on houses. In the early days of analog television NBC, ABC and CBS created programs which were often funded by consumer products companies. By converting film to analog video, movies became available for television viewing. Today there are both advertising supported networks and subscription supported cable companies that produce their own programming and license quality content for television distribution.

Traditional TV networks now see themselves as content creators and distributors rather than broadcast companies. They understand it is imperative to provide their content to viewers on a variety of platforms. From their perspective conversion to digital, SDTV and HDTV, is expensive with no immediate revenue increases to offset substantial cost to upgrade their technology. Local TV stations and affiliates also see digital conversion as necessary for survival.

While the computer industry has been talking about the convergence of computers and television for more then a dozen years; the time is finally here. Television content, now digital, is available for viewing on a multitude of devices including a variety of large and small television screens and monitors, via cable or fiber and wireless to laptop computers and mobile services. Not only is this video content being produced digitally with cheaper and better equipment (Moore's Law) but we can now create and upload content for distribution on the web or send it to mobile phones of people in their networks. To add to competition, telephone companies now provide digital television programming over their fiber optic networks and new players, via IPTV, bring digital media content from around the world to computer screens and TVs.

Digital innovation is not limited to broadcast, cable, satellite, telephone and computer industries. Gaming industry and electronics manufacturers all have a role in it. Low barriers to entry enable new entrants to create and distribute content. New interactive devices hook up to televisions and computer monitors as well as mobile devices. All compete for audience time.

Ten years ago no one was talking about user generated content. There was no You Tube and search had not taken off. Today we talk about creating and monetizing content on the internet, new advertising and subscription models along with new audience measurement tools for tracking consumer behavior. When it comes to content, today's mantra is "what, when, where you want it." New mass entertainment paradigms emerge on the horizon: including virtual worlds, holography, 3D TV and greater interactivity.

This book takes a broad look at the digital TV ecosystem. It examines evolving business models and outlines technologies that drive and support this digital evolution. New content types, consumer behavior and tracking mechanisms are being explored in the effort to build and maintain profitable digital television business. Monetizing content and services, while maintaining copyright protections, is a major challenge. Spectrum allocation and the use of 'White Space' will have a great impact on services of the future. Digital Rights Management (DRM) and preserving media content as analog media disintegrates are also important issues.

In the Foreword A. Michael Noll starts us off with a brief history of "Digital Television" from NBC's first analog efforts in 1939 through the FCC deliberations that have led to the February 2009 digital change over. He grounds us in what digital technology is and gives us a brief overview of how digital television has evolved in the US.

This book is divided into four parts. The first part is The Changing Television Business. In this section's first chapter, "TV or Not TV: Where Video is Going," Eli Noam provides an overview of the history of digital television in which he identifies four generations of television picture quality. In "TV on the Internet: The New Screen for Video," Jon Gibs provides a framework for understanding Internet video audiences and how Nielsen seeks to identify and measure new consumer behaviors. The in depth paper, "The End of Advertising As We Know It," from the IBM team of Saul J. Berman, Bill Battino, Louisa Shipnuck and Andreas Neus, dissects changes taking place in media advertising, providing insights and recommendations for the future. Finally, in "From the Marketers' Perspective: the Interactive Media Situation in Japan," we are treated by Satoshi Kono, to an insider's view into how a large advertising agency in Japan is retooling its approach to better align its strategy with current audience trends.

In the second part, Technology: Content Creation and Distribution, Kas Kalba provides both anecdotal and analytic information regarding content, devices and audience for mobile TV, in "Adopting Mobile TV: Technologies Seeking Consumers Seeking Content and Cool." This chapter is followed by "Television Via Satellite," which reviews the history, including technical underpinnings, of satellite television, by Stephen Dulac and John Godwin. In this section's final chapter, "Creation and Distribution of 4 K Content," Laurin Herr looks into the future of high end media content over networks. He shows us the next generation of digital 4 K movies and gives us a peek into how high end research laboratories, world wide, are already experimenting with huge media files over ultra fast fiber optic networks.

Part three, Content, first approaches the issue of digital content from the perspective of what is happening to traditional television. Gali Einav and John Carey pose the question: "Is TV Dead?" and then, by examining changing audience behavior proceed to look into this question from the point of view of content distributors and viewers. In this section's second chapter, Jeffrey Hart examines "Video on the Internet: The Content Question." He asks whether internet video content types will differ significantly from traditional TV content, who will produce it, and who will be the audience. Focusing on new internet companies, Liz Gannes explains how things have radically altered in the last 3 years and why "YouTube Changes Everything: The Online Video Revolution." Then, while all thoughts are about the future of television, video content, and new companies, Thomas Coughlin reminds us that our video legacy is in danger of disappearing. Many efforts are underway to preserve analog video content, and in "Digital Archiving in the Entertainment and Professional Media Market," Coughlin provides a roadmap for this digital conservation.

In the fourth and final part, Legal and Regulatory Issues, three authors address large societal issues facing the US. Ellen Goodman brings her expertise on "Spectrum Policy and the Public Interest," to bear on who will take decisions and how these will effect us all. She brings us up to date by providing a succinct overview of how spectrum has been allocated and regulated in the past so that we can appreciate how today's decisions will determine future outcomes. Then, in "Cognitive Radios in Television White Spaces," Monisha Ghosh provides the technical background needed to understand the importance of what has come to be called "White Space" and how technological innovation can enable better use of this spectrum. Finally, in "Digital Rights and Digital Television," Bill Rosenblatt takes on the topic of Digital Rights Management (DRM). With the adoption of digital technology and the Work Wide Web, it has become more difficult for content providers to manage copyrights and distribution to control rights usages. Digital rights management seeks to address this situation.

A couple of the chapters in this book are adaptations or reprints of previously published papers. Many of the chapters began as papers presented at the Digital Television: Beyond HD & DTV conference that I organized in November 2007 at CITI. Several of the chapters were written specifically for this book. While it is not possible to cover every topic on this subject in one volume, I hope this selection will be useful. For additional chapters on this topic please see my earlier publications: *The Economics, Technology and Content of Digital TV* and *Internet TV*.

Notes

1. Digital Television.
2. Columbia Institute for Tele-Information, Columbia University Business School.
3. Federal Communications Commission.
4. Standard Definition Digital Television.
5. High Definition Digital Television.
6. Graham Walker and Rodger Lea, The Mirror: reflections on inhabited TV, International Conference on Computer Graphics and Interactive Techniques archive, ACM SIGGRAPH 97 Visual Proceedings: The art and interdisciplinary programs of SIGGRAPH '97, http://portal. acm.org/citation.cfm?doid=259081.259284
7. Reprinted with permission from IBM.

Part I
The Changing Television Business

Chapter 1
TV or Not TV: Where Video Is Going

Eli Noam

Abstract Television used to be a simple affair: a technically highly standardized medium, with fairly similar organizational structure, content types, and business models across developed countries. It provided a nationwide, middle-of-the-road content delivered by national networks, distributed regionally by TV stations with some local programming thrown in, and with either advertising or governmental funding as its economic model. But now, TV is getting quite complicated and varied. And the question is, where is this taking us?

Four generations of television picture quality can be distinguished:

1. *Pre-TV*. In this exploratory stage of the TV experiments of the 1920s and 1930s by Baird, Zworykin, and Farnsworth, a crude picture was being projected. Baird's 1926 video image had 30 lines of picture resolution.
2. *Analog TV*. This regularly scheduled TV has 525 lines. Its content aims at the broad taste center of the population. In the USA there were on average seven broadcast channels operating. The typical spectrum "pipe" was thus 42 MHz (7 × 6 MHz) in the 1950s and 1960s. The flow of information was synchronous because it was scarce, meaning that it was shared and simultaneous.
3. *Digital TV*. After the 1970s, analog broadcast TV branched out and was distributed over cable and satellites. In time, they became digitalized. Broadcast TV, too, became digital in the late 1990s, with standard and high-definition TV emerging and entirely replacing analog transmission by 2009. Cable TV and satellite created alternative TV transmission infrastructures. Today, cable TV uses pipes of about 3 Gbps, about 75 times more than the actual typical terrestrial broadcast spectrum used in a locality. This extra transmission capacity was used first in a horizontal fashion of a "widening," or expansion, of traditional-quality channels. This led to a "narrowcasting" in terms of content and audiences. But after a while, digital technology was also extended to a vertical "deepening" of the channel. HDTV is an example. It displays twice the number of horizontal lines, as well as a wider line and more bits per pixel.
4. *Individualized TV*. This new generation of TV is presently emerging, and its main manifestations are Internet TV and mobile TV. They are dependent

D. Gerbarg (ed.), *Television Goes Digital*,
© Springer Science + Business Media, LLC 2009

on fiber, coax or wireless. Together they increase enormously the individual transmission capacity in both upstream and downstream directions. This raises the number of channels horizontally, but also enables individualized, asynchronous, and interactive TV. Mobile TV also creates a ubiquitous availability of such individualized content. Internet TV permits user-generated content, which leads to a greater networking among users. This led to two-way transmission, moving from narrowcasting to individual casting, and to user-generated content sites such as YouTube. In bit terms, such low-resolution content translates to about 300 Kbps – a very low quality. However, we are willing to accept such video if the content is noncommercial and community based.

At the same time and by the same logic, there is also a *deepening* of picture quality, because the transmission path is becoming more powerful, and because people have always moved to a richer media experience. The introduction of 4 K HD (also known as S-HD or S-HV) has proceeded from the direction of advanced electronic film exhibition. It provides a picture quality with 4,096 vertical lines (pixels) and 7,281 vertical pixels at an aspect ratio of 1:1.78. Pixels at film theaters are at an aspect ratio of between 1.85 and 2.35, which would translate to about 8,200 horizontal pixels. Also, color coding would be 36 bits, and after all of the additions, generation 4 K TV would be 35 Gbps, uncompressed. Further developments such as three-dimensionality (3-D) provide for a richer media experience but also require a larger transmission capacity of about 70 Gbps, or 400× the transmission requirement of an analog generation TV channel.

Thus, the overall transmission capacity increase from analog generation TV to individualized TV is immense, mainly because the individualized two-way consumption requires much more bandwidth than shared synchronous media, even if each user does not consume a huge channel by himself. When compression is utilized, requirements are reduced but are still high. Standard TV, can be compressed from 150 to 3.4.

With this in mind, can an economic case be made for such a prolific transmission? What exactly would one do with 4 K TV? There are four industries or categories that will be greatly impacted:

- *Film Theatrical Distribution*: Such distribution has been talked about for a long time, but the transition is difficult and will happen only when the cost of projection equipment has significantly dropped. Also, diversion away from home theaters will need to occur – this can happen if film theaters greatly surpass the home theater experience. And this is increasingly unlikely when viewers move to individualized, interactive, and immersive experiences, which are harder to do in large-group settings such as film theaters.
- *Specialized Applications*: Examples are marketing uses, billboards, or medical services.
- *Gaming*: High-resolution TV will allow for more interactive and immersive games. However, even interactive games do not use all that much transmission capacity – on average, for *Counterstrike*, about 40 Kbps is used. The reason for this is that the processing capacity on the central node is limited, so that each player's stream is limited. But this will presumably change.

- *Home Entertainment*: Going back to the earliest days of consumer electronics, each generation has persuaded itself, with the help of marketers, that it has life-like audio and video quality. This history has long contributed to the traditional short-sightedness of expectations. The question, in relevance to home entertainment, remains: what would be the use of Internet TV on the consumer level?

Analog and digital TV have a clear economics base, namely, advertising and some subscription. In contrast, Internet TV has not yet found an economic model. Low-definition TV, e.g., YouTube, is mostly given away, or interspersed with some ads. Interactive and immersive HD does not exist yet. The willingness to pay for such premium interactive and immersive content is probably high, but this requires strong security and encryption for the content. One could show dozens of regular channels so the revenue for a single premium channel or program would have to be as large as those of alternative channels and content.

What kind of impact will this issue have on content of higher and lower resolution TV? Is there a difference between the content style of films made for high resolution theatrical film, and for lower resolution? There is a relation between media technology and content, as summarized by Marshall McLuhan's dictum that the medium is the message. When films were silent they favored slapstick and physical styles. Sound added dialogue, and sophisticated comedy and drama; romance became possible. Animation and computer technology added highly sophisticated special effects. The impact of higher resolution on style is to enrich the content in terms of the sensory stimuli and signals. The two-way capabilities of Internet and mobile phones also create direct involvement possibilities for the user, i.e., dialog instead of monolog.

Also, there is a budgetary effect of higher resolution. On the one hand, technology and its dropping cost lower the costs of a given production. But it lowers the cost for everyone. There is still competition for attention, which will ratchet up other cost elements, and lead to an escalating budget for special effects. Also, a higher resolution requires that details have to be done better. When film moved to color it favored large spectacular shows, and when computer animation and editing emerged it favored special effects. Interactivity, 3-D, and immersion TV add further cost elements. It can therefore be concluded that next-generation TV will be more expensive for premium products that vie for mass audiences.

This diversity of television in terms of technical quality will have implications on standards and protocols. In the Internet TV environment fewer standards and protocols are needed. Different providers or provider groups can encode visual images in a variety of ways, and users' terminals can decode it, based on software and hardware cards they acquired. Standards and protocols can coexist and compete. In other cases, servers can store content in several ways, or be able to reformat them.

To conclude, TV is becoming too big, too advanced, and too important for a one-size-fits-all medium. Television, whatever that means anymore, will be diversifying horizontally and vertically. Horizontal diversification includes more standard quality programs and channels and more specialized "long-tail" content in standard quality. Vertical diversification means a variety of quality levels, from cheap low resolution to highly enriched, immersive, participatory TV. Viewers will also accept low-quality resolution from noncommercial sources. But for commercial content, despite the lowering of cost of a given technology, competition and user expectations will drive the production cost to ever-higher levels.

Such premium content will be increasingly interactive, immersive, and 3-D. The greater bandwidth of next-generation broadband transmission, together with the ability to store content for downloads rather than through synchronous transmission, will enable a much richer content in terms of bits or sensations per second. Multiple TV standards and protocols will coexist and compete. There will also be further diversification in terms of business models, media firms, and global providers.

As a result television will have many more legs to stand on. It will have a wide range of quality levels, content dimensions, technical dimensions, and policy treatments. The traditional looking TV content, as well as some standardizations, will still be around, but there will be coexisting multiple TVs.

So is it still "TV"? Yes … Let a hundred televisions bloom.

Chapter 2
The New Screen for Video

Jon Gibs*

Abstract In the following chapter we will discuss the coming of "TV on the Internet." We will begin by recounting how we arrived at where we are, and the development of online video. Next, we will move to the present, and understand who is presently consuming video online, and what they are watching. Finally, we will peer into our proverbial crystal ball and look into future trends – the possible reunification of the computer with television.

Introduction

Around the time the continents were falling into their current locations and the ice caps began to recede, cable TV was born. Or at least it feels that long ago today.

For the past 20 years, since the birth of AOL and Prodigy, since the birth of the World Wide Web, Internet gurus have been predicting how it would be the media of the future. It turns out they were right. Interactivity, information over Internet protocol, and digital rather than analog do appear to own the future. However, this does not mean that "TV" as a concept (rather than a device) is dying, in fact quite the opposite is happening – TV is going through a revolution.

As more and more "TV" is being shown on an Internet platform, how the media itself is being consumed and how individuals interact with it are changing radically. These changes will almost certainly change every part of the TV industry, from the business model to the creative process.

It will be a lot of fun to watch.

---

*Grateful acknowledgment to Nielsen Online, a service of The Nielsen Company.

History of Online Video: Up to This Point Everything Has Been Short and Grainy

As with all that functions well online, the birth of video on the Internet came about because of pornography. As long as the Internet has functioned, adult content has been one of the most pervasive forms of media. This fact is not hugely surprising. The anonymity of the Internet, as well as its convenience made it an ideal distribution platform for this form of media (pornography) that people both use and are embarrassed by. Initially, most adult content online was either the written word or photographs, but fairly quickly this changed to short-form video and supposedly live streams. As early as 1995 (and perhaps before), adult Web sites were offering video for stream and download. This, combined with other factors, has moved adult content into the relative mainstream.

It is easy to make light of adult content online; however, many of the design elements developed for the adult entertainment industry, such as prerolls, standard clip length, and video networks were later co-opted by many mainstream media outlets as standards for video distribution and monetization.

About the same time that adult content began to hit the mainstream, Yahoo and others introduced music videos. Their length and lack of other outlets (MTV had long since broadcast music videos consistently) made the Internet an excellent outlet for music videos. The genre of music videos also began to stretch the length of online video, from the 30-s clips of adult content to a more robust 3–3½min.

The success of music video opened the door for other clip length media. The traditional broadcast and cable networks began to see the possibility of leveraging their own existing TV content in short clips. CNN and ESPN as well as others began to integrate online video into their overall consumer experience. Entertainment networks followed, presenting promotional content or "webisodes," as well as clips of existing shows. The flood gates of Web video 1.0 were opened.

This seemed fine for a few years. Then came YouTube and everything changed a lot. In the 13 months leading up to April 2008, YouTube to increased its online reach from just under 30% to almost 45%, reaching levels previously held by only the largest and most well established sites (Fig. 2.1).

With the advent of consumer-generated media (CGM) the production of video content online was democratized. Suddenly everyone was a producer and the cost of production for sites dropped to relative zero. Soon, the value of consumer correspondents was realized by most major media networks. The value of online video became apparent, and with cell phones as miniature video cameras, networks had reporters everywhere. Although other networks bought this type of video occasionally, CNN set the standard by creating iReport, a service where consumers can upload their own news-worthy video and where the most pertinent clips are shown on the cable network.

Around the same time another significant change came to online: full TV programming. Either through TV network Web sites, or through alternative platforms such as Joost or Hulu, the most recent version of full-length versions of TV

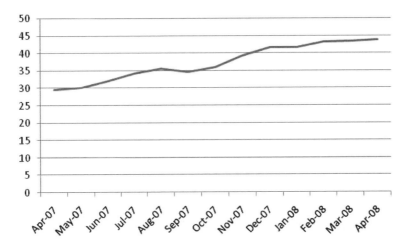

Fig. 2.1 Growth in YouTube viewership over 13 months

programs became available to stream. Initially hit TV shows led the way. Shows such as Heros and Desperate Housewives defined how long-form programming would be shown.

As broadcasters realized that there was interest in watching long-form video online, others began to take notice. Netflix and iTunes began to make full-length movies available online. Streaming video and video for download had begun to catch on. We were now moving into the era of "TV on the Internet," which brings us to the present.

Where We Are Today: An Overview

As we begin to discuss the present state of online video, it is important to under-stand a taxonomy of video types. There are primarily three types of video being broadcast online today: long- and short-form clips and consumer-generated video. Although we may be entering an era where CGM video ceases to be distinct, consumer-generated video is by far the largest category at this time. It is primarily made up of video shorts on sites such as YouTube; however, other news outlets, such as CNN and The Weather Channel, are increasingly using video shot by their own audiences. This advance has given them the ability to cover stories in a level of detail that was not possible in the past (Fig. 2.2).

Short-form videos are professionally made video shorts. Although these can be shortened versions of TV programming, such as ESPN and Comedy Central content, this also includes content developed directly for the Internet. This idea of webisodes helped support such TV efforts as NBC's "The Office" and Sci-Fi's "Battlestar Galactica."

Fig. 2.2 A taxonomy of online video

Table 2.1 Streaming audience – June 2008	Unique audience (000)	Streams (000)
YouTube	73,537	4,052,984
Yahoo!	22,179	221,600
Fox Interactive Media (MySpace etc.)	20,855	328,974
Google	11,054	58,411
MSN/Windows Live	9,873	149,684
AOL	9,331	38,849
Disney	7,219	93,649
MLB.com	6,940	51,213
Turner	6,513	81,586
Nick	6,323	151,828
ABC	5,857	60,786
CNN	5,681	84,782
ESPN	5,477	125,327
Comcast	4,383	53,761
NABBR	4,218	22,639
CBS	3,813	20,729
Dailymotion	3,766	48,897
Metacafe	3,658	18,205
NBC	3,553	61,447
Apple	3,535	14,627

Source: Nielsen Online VideoCensus

As the audience figures above show (Table 2.1), these forms of online video are both thriving.

Although the majority of the online audience presently view short-form professional or consumer-generated streams, we will spend the remainder of this chapter focusing on the relatively small but critical long-form audience.

Long-form programming, which accounts for a significant number of streams from ABC, CBS, Fox, and NBC, is programming that has, for the most part, been lifted directly from the TV airwaves and put on the Internet. Successes here have been Lost, Desperate Housewives, and Heros, but there are many others.

The reason this is of particular interest is that it has the ability to fundamentally change the way we consume TV programming. It allows consumers to view what they want, when they want, without presetting a digital video recorder (i.e. TiVo) or waiting for availability of DVDs or On-Demand.

When we first begin to think about consumption of this form of video content, it is important to consider where people are viewing it. Traditionally, a significant proportion of Internet video consumption has happened at work. This is not the case for long-form video.

A full 85% of long-form video consumption happens at home. This is most likely because people cannot generally give an hour of their time to watch programming while they are at work. It also suggests that online viewing has a very specialized audience: those with larger monitors, broadband access, and high-quality sound on their home computers.

As we further try to understand this unusual audience, it is useful to focus on their viewing preferences online and how it differs from TV. When Nielsen asked 2,200 long-form video viewers to rank order their preference in genres (i.e., drama, sit-com, reality programming) on both the Internet and television, their responses were basically the same. In general, consumers like watching the same programming on both media. This trend suggests that those consumers whom we identify as predominantly viewing this content at home see very little difference in the types of content they wish to watch. And although most would rather watch programming on TV than on the Internet, a sit-com on TV, in essence, is the same as a sit-com on the Internet.

Frequently, the next question that arises when we see these similarities is about cannibalization. Is watching long-form programming on the Internet eating into TV viewing? The majority of research done on the subject suggests that as of now, cannibalization is not a significant issue. Indeed, when we map TV consumption against Internet viewing consumption we see little correlation.

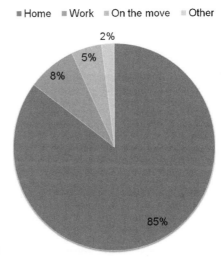

Fig. 2.3 Where consumers view video

Indeed, when we look closer at the relationship between TV consumption and Internet video consumption (see Fig. 2.4) we see little relationship. Although there may be pockets of use, there does not appear to be an overall consumption pattern. However, if you strip out the TV use data an interesting pattern begins to emerge.

Each point on Fig. 2.5 represents a person. The points are arranged in an order of high video consumption to low video consumption. The distribution that emerges suggests three different segments of the online video viewing population: a low-usage segment that accounts for most people, but relatively few streams, a mid-usage segment that is a much smaller slice of the population, with a moderate amount of consumption, and finally a high-usage segment that consumes the majority of the content, but is a tiny fraction of the population.

Viewing seconds, as shown above, is a good measure of video usage. But there are two other key measures to consider: the number of streams and the number of sites visited. The number of streams is important because a person can consume

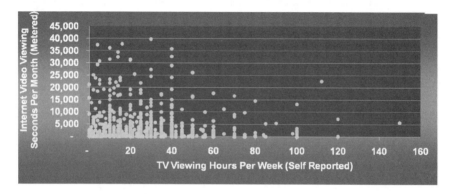

Fig. 2.4 TV and Internet video consumption

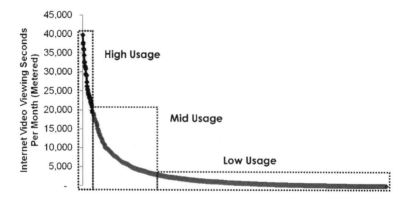

Fig. 2.5 Internet consumption distribution

relatively few streams, but generate a considerable amount of time (two, 2-h streaming movies is 14,400 s) or many streams on YouTube (which tend to be under 4 min) but still generate little time. This gets to the type of content being consumed, long form or short form.

The number of sites visited is an important metric because it gets to the variety of content consumed. Even if a person generates a significant amount of time, if this is only on one or two sites, that person is likely only consuming a fairly narrow band of content. If a person is consuming video on a high number of different sites it is likely they are consuming a variety of video formats and content types.

No, We Are Not All Alike; Some People View a Lot More Video than You Do

With these three metrics in minds, Nielsen has developed a segmentation to get a better understanding of the inner-workings of the online video viewing population. The segmentation was completed in January 2008, using a K-means segmentation on a sample of 2,200 video-viewing individuals. This sample was both surveyed and being metered by Nielsen software; so we were able to understand the relationship between actual behavior and attitudes.

The segmentation falls out much in the same way the overall distribution did in Fig. 2.6. About 83% of the overall population is in the low-consumption segment, about 12% is in the medium-consumption segment, and about 5% is in the high-consumption segment. As with many consumption models we see the 80/20 rule come into play here. About 20% of the population seems to be consuming about 80% of the content.

This distribution, while interesting, is not terribly meaningful. To get a better sense of who these segment are, it is useful to look closer at profiling data.

The low-consumption segment –"Average Joes" – generates few streams a month (110), for few minutes (9), and does not visit many domains (6). It does view

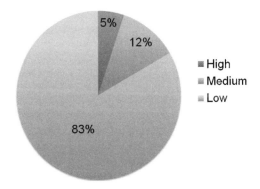

Fig. 2.6 Distribution of segments

about the national average of TV viewing, 24 h a week. The medium segment –
"Fast Followers" – generates considerably more streams (87) for a greater duration
(137 min) and significantly more domains (27). It too consumes about the national
average of TV viewing. The final and smallest segment – "Early Adopters", about
5% of the population, is the high-consumption group. This segment generates a
considerable number of streams a month (104), for a long duration (435 min) and
visits slightly more domains than does the Fast Followers segment.

This small difference between the Fast Followers and the Early Adopters segments in the number of domains visited may have more to do with the low number
of quality video viewing experiences presently offered online, than any constant
trait across both groups.

What is most noticeable between the three groups, however, is the fall off in the
number of TV hours generated. The first two segments are around the national average for TV consumption, while the Early Adopter segment consumes about 10 h less
a week on average than either of the other segments. This begs the question, does
higher use of online video, particularly long-form video, decrease TV viewing?

From this data, it seems unlikely. To get a better feeling for the dynamics behind
co-use of the medium, we must look at both demographics and psychographics.

For many in the TV industry this chart is very disturbing. A full 25% of the early
adopter segment is in the core 18–24 demographic. Beyond this, all of the other

Fig. 2.7 Media consumption by segment

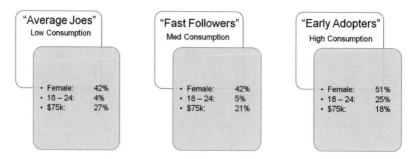

Fig. 2.8 Demographics by segment

demographics seem stable. Although, the Early Adopter segment does appear to be more female, this may be because one of the most popular long-form streaming programs at the time of this analysis was *Desperate Housewives*, which has a female skew in its demographics.

Even given the age and apparent lack of TV viewership of this Early Adopter segment, it does not seem that this should be a significant area of concern for TV networks. This is mainly due to two points. The first is that although a large proportion of this segment is 18–24, it is a very small segment and therefore does not represent the overall age cohort. The second is that the individuals in this segment do not appear to be representative of the overall population.

When comparing the 18–24 demographic overall to the general population, a couple of areas are important to focus on. First, Early Adopters only make up about 20% of the 18–24-year-old population. While this is a large percentage, two thirds of the demographic still fall into the Average Joe segment; so while large, this segment is certainly not representative of the overall demographic group. Second, there is only a 14-point difference when the high- and mid-consumption segments are compared from the 18–24-year-old group to the overall population.

This 14-point difference is clearly a defining factor, but there are other reasons why this demographic group would tend to fall into this segment. This population tends to have less TV viewing during the college years. Also, online video programming tends to be aimed at a younger market segment – YouTube specifically tends to be targeted younger. Both of these elements tend to be reversed as the population ages.

Beyond the demographic traits discussed above, there are also psychographic trends that suggest that this population is not representative of the 18–24 demographic group. In fact, this group might well have existed without the advent of online video.

When these segments are asked psychographic questions, a few elements seem to distinguish the groups. Average Joes and Fast Followers tend to have a higher degree of loyalty and they also tend to be slightly choosier about the programs they view.

The real differentiation happens on three key points: "I like to take video with me wherever I go," "I make sure to keep the TV off most of the time," and "I spend more time playing games on my TV than watching TV". In each of these three psychographic profiles Early Adopters are at least 10 points ahead of either of the other two segments.

P18 – 24 Video Viewing Population   **General Video Viewing Population**

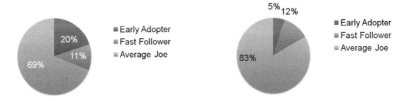

Fig. 2.9 Comparing age distribution: Early Adopter segment vs. overall population

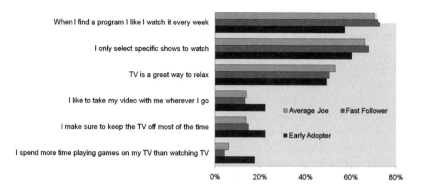

Fig. 2.10 Psychographic characteristics

The commonality that each of these three psychographic profile points is that they suggest that the Early Adopter segment has a dramatically different relationship with the television as an object than most other Americans. As a whole, Americans do not tend to view the television as an appliance; rather they tend to couple it with the programming that comes through it. For most Americans TV is a friend, another member of the household, a form of self-expression among other things.

This emotion does not appear to be the case with the Early Adopter segment. The fact that they like the idea of content mobility suggests that they have decoupled TV content from the physical object that is the TV. That they keep the TV off most of the time, rather than treating it as a constant companion, suggests that TV is only valuable for the content that comes through it, rather than being a constant stream of communication. Finally, that more video games are played through the TV speaks partially to the age of the segments, but also indicates that the TV is simply a screen for content to be viewed through, much as a computer monitor is.

The relationship between how the Early Adopter segment feels about the TV as an appliance and their viewership of online video is an important one. At a minimum it means that programming itself is important, while TV as an object is not. Therefore they are willing to view TV content on whatever platform (Internet, mobile, etc.) is most useful and convenient. The worst case, however, is that these individuals are not wed to the standard form of content development (TV networks producing TV programs) and are more likely to be open to alternate forms of development, such as consumer-generated media or webisodes made by either standard production houses, or alternate ones, such as *The Guild* or *Stranger Things*, short-form programs developed by independent producers specifically for distribution online either through streaming video or through video podcast for download.

Earlier in this chapter we stated that that there does not appear to be an overall relationship between increased Internet viewing consumption and TV viewing, but for the Early Adopter segment there does appears to be a relationship.

Although the Fast Follower segment has considerably more online video use than the Average Joe, their change in TV consumption, as shown in Fig. 2.12, appear to be the same across both segments. The percentage of both populations that plan to watch more TV and those that watch less TV tend to balance out. Additionally, about 57% of both populations believe that they will watch the same amount of TV next year that they will this year.

This difference is in contrast to the Early Adopter segment which is showing a 17-point net loss (those who plan to watch more minus those who plan to watch less) in viewership likelihood. However, it should be noted here that only marginally fewer people in the Early Adopter segment plan to maintain their TV viewership on the same levels than the other two segments.

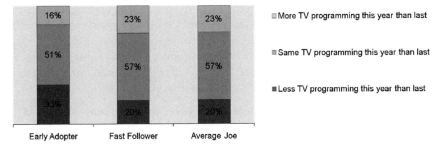

Fig. 2.11 Change in TV view by segment

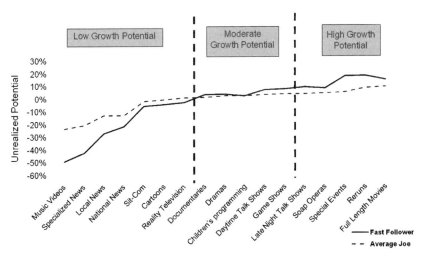

Fig. 2.12 Unrealized potential of genres by segment

Why Internet Video? The TV Was Working Out Just Fine

This brings up a logical question: Why are Early Adopters being drawn to online video? There seems to be three key drivers – convenience, additional programming to consume, and the NetFlix factor. Each of these factors seems to drive different subsegments of the Early Adopter segment.

Convenience can best be described as time and space portability. As one Early Adopter interviewed for this research said:

> I like online video because it means that I am able to watch videos in my bed or anywhere in my home, portable to my needs.

With the advent of cheap and easy wireless networking, streaming video means that the laptop becomes the portable device of choice within the house. Video on the laptop can be viewed in rooms without a TV or in concert with existing TV viewership. It basically untethers TV from the TV, onto a much lighter and more portable device – although with a smaller screen and in most cases a worse picture.

Additional programming is fairly self explanatory. As more programming is added to the Internet, there are more reasons for people to watch it. One Early Adopter put it as follows:

> Major networks offer episodes of most primetime shows online, and independent media outlets have improved both in quality and quantity of material.

This statement is telling a few points. First, the viewer included both network and independent content as growth drivers. Second, the consumer perceives that "most" primetime content is available online. As of early 2008, when these interviews were conducted, this was not the case. However, the majority of the most popular programming had been made available for either streaming or pay-per-download. Finally, the perception that independent media outlets have improved quality and quantity seem to be prevalent. Although few people debate that more content is available for free online (the popularity of YouTube suggests as much), there is some debate about the quality of the online-only content. Some programs have promise, but if long-term quality is to be sustained, a business model more robust than free downloads and per-roll advertising, will need to be established.

The last key driver of usage for the Early Adopter segment is what we call the NetFlix factor. In late 2007 NetFlix began allowing the free streaming of a select catalog of 10,000 full-length movies and TV shows available on DVD to their members. Shortly after this iTunes, Apple's download service for video and music began to provide a download rental service for its users. Both of these services have made it inexpensive to watch full-length films on PCs. They also come on the heels of years of illegal pirating of films via different online peer-to-peer networks. When characterizing the importance of these services, an Early Adopter stated:

> [There] are movies that I like to download from the internet, so I watch less television.

This simple statement sums up the role that full-length movie streaming/downloads have taken in the life of Early Adopters – they are a replacement for TV programming.

Given that tens of thousands of theatrical movie titles are available for free, pay, or theft online, the fact is that this group of consumers has no specific ties to TV, and so would chose to watch whatever they believed was best at the time, not simply what was being shown to them by a TV network.

The Genie Is Out of the Bottle … Now What?

Assuming that not all segments become the Early Adopter segment discussed earlier, two trends are inevitable. More consumers are watching long-form video online and therefore it is unlikely that content will stop being put online by networks, or stop being developed specifically by independent producers. With this said, how should the trends discussed impact the future strategy of online video providers?

To understand the impact of specific genres of programming, Nielsen uses an unrealized potential metric. This metric takes the interest in viewing a specific type of programming online and subtracts the existing penetration.

We then measure this unrealized potential for multiple genres measured as well across multiple segments. Up to zero growth potential are areas of little growth; 0–10% growth potential have moderate growth. Those areas that have higher than 10% growth potential have high growth.

Those areas with the highest growth potential online are the most likely to have long-form formats made available to them: specifically, late night talk shows, soap operas, special events, reruns, and full-length movies. Those areas with the lowest level of growth potential are those that tend to be more short form or clip based: specifically, news, cartoons, and music videos. While this metric does not guarantee success, it does point to where short-term growth should occur.

Since penetration is such a large part of this metric, overlaying the metric provides a means to narrow down those areas that have both the highest level of potential, and also high levels of existing penetration.

Figure 2.13 illustrates one effect of using penetration as part of the metric. Those genres that have the highest levels of penetration are also those that tend to have the lowest amount of unrealized potential. The goal, however, is not to show the success of any given genre, but rather its chance for strong growth in the future.

Of those areas that have both the highest growth potential and the highest penetration, reruns and full-length movies seem to have the most promise. We have discussed the trends in full-length movies in fairly great detail to this point; so we will focus the discussion here on reruns.

It is important to note that what is called "reruns" in the charts above we actually described as "reruns no longer available on TV" in the survey instrument that was used for this analysis. This fact is important, because consumers are stating that they want access to TV programs that they knew from the past, but are no longer available. This suggests that even though networks are concerned with cannibalization of their TV viewers, they could use this media as a way to monetize

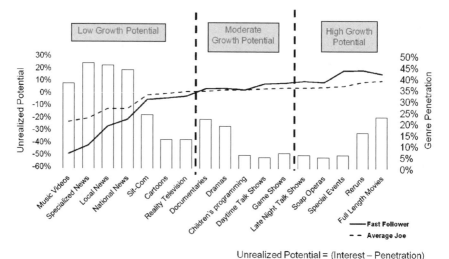

Unrealized Potential = (Interest − Penetration)

Fig. 2.13 Growth potential with penetration

content that is sitting on the shelf. At a time when video advertising inventory is limited, this demand for this deeper content could generate additional revenue for networks that are struggling in a time of increasingly lower ratings and fragmented programming.

Is All Programming Created Equal? No

Regardless of the success of any given genre, one thing is clear: Viewers are not interested in all genres being rendered the same way online. This statement is a conceptual departure from the way standard linear television is developed. Although programs vary in length, the way consumers interface with them is fairly standard: they sit back and watch. TV lacks the interactivity that would allow content producers to render different types of programming fundamentally differently; the Internet does not. Thus, content producers can feel free to render programming differently depending on what the consumers require.

Those areas that have the highest growth potential – late night talk shows, soap operas, special events, reruns, and full-length movies, all have different drivers of content usage, and therefore consumers are looking for producers to focus on specific areas in their development.

For full-length movies consumers are most interested in quality of the experience. This on its own is not a surprise. Consumers have gotten used to large, high-definition pictures for watching and listening to movies at home. They are looking for the same from their Internet video. Consumers are looking for high-quality sound and picture.

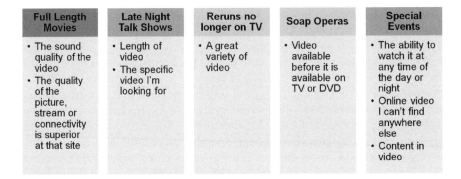

Full Length Movies	Late Night Talk Shows	Reruns no longer on TV	Soap Operas	Special Events
• The sound quality of the video • The quality of the picture, stream or connectivity is superior at that site	• Length of video • The specific video I'm looking for	• A great variety of video	• Video available before it is available on TV or DVD	• The ability to watch it at any time of the day or night • Online video I can't find anywhere else • Content in video

Fig. 2.14 Drivers of usage by genre type

Consumers will not have patience for pixilated images or grainy sound. They are looking to have the experience be like their current home theater viewing.

The drivers for late night talk shows are somewhat different. For this type of programming consumers are less concerned with the quality of the video itself and more concerned with controlling the experience to get the content they want. Specifically they are looking to have more, shorter length clips, most likely matching up to the segmented nature of late night talk show. They also want to make sure that they can view the piece of content they are looking for. For example, they might not be interested in listening to a Hollywood star promote a new movie, but they do want to be able to view the monologue at the beginning of the program, and the musical guest at the end. The ability to flexibly move between sections therefore is critical.

For reruns no longer available on TV variety is key. Variety, in this case, however, does not mean actual variety; it means the ability for the consumers to find the specific program they are looking for. For example, if a consumer is looking for the third episode of *The Barney Miller Show* and a site has every single program ever aired except that one, there will not be enough variety. However, if the same consumer is looking for the fifth episode from the third season of *The X-Files* and they are able to find it there is enough variety, even if that site has only episodes of *The X-Files*. This suggests that the current strategy of going very deep into the catalog of specific programs, and being clear with consumers as to what is available might be the best approach.

The soap opera audience is a bit of an unusual audience, although the lessons here might be applicable to any serialized programming. Viewers of soap operas are looking to "scoop" the program. They are looking to know what is going to happen on the program before it airs. While this type of programming is not main stream presently, that may be partially due to the day-time time slot. Many women (and some men) have spent specific times in their life becoming very involved in the ongoing narratives of specific soap opera. There is good reason to believe that if networks provided a way to watch this type of programming online, even in a weekly summary format, they may be able to increase their reach and their ad dollars, much in the same way they could by showing reruns no longer available on TV.

"Special events" is an unusual category since it is made up less of a specific type of programming, and more of a general format. These programs tend to be long, at times over 3 h, and because of the desire of networks to show them live, they tend to begin very early on the west coast and end very late on the east. Examples of special events would be award shows or important sporting events. Here, consumers want to be able to watch the events themselves, time shifted. Since the program might start very early or end very late, viewers want to be able to consume the content on their own time. They also want to be able to find video content they cannot find elsewhere. There is a feeling for many of these types of events that there is behind-the-scenes or extra content that does not make it to the TV program either because of niche interest or because it would be inappropriate for general viewership. Finally, viewers realize that not all special events are created equal. They have greater interest in watching the Oscars than perhaps the SAG awards. This selection of the specific content in the video is important to viewers of this type of content.

What Next?

There are two areas content producers need to be moving into in the next few years. First, what traps should they avoid? What are those myths that have been reported as being critical to online video viewership that turn out not to be the case. Second, assuming the Early Adopters are already generating a significant amount of video, and the Fast Followers are on their way, what is holding back the other 80% of the population, the Average Joes?

There are three myths that seem to have gained traction in the TV industry's practices which are moving long-form content online: content ownership, mobility between devices, and the idea of video networks that lie outside of the recognized TV networks.

- *Content Ownership:* Viewers seem to have little interest in owning a specific video and having it live natively on a PC. Rather they seem much more interested in being able to access the content they want, when they want it. A relic of ownership such as a file or a DVD is not necessary.
- *Content Mobility:* While it is clearly important to specific subsegments, consumers do not seem to be particularly interested in moving a video between a PC and a mobile device. There is good reason to believe, however, that there is a growing interest in streaming content directly to the television.
- *Online Networks:* Although there are good business reasons for the existence of services such as Veoh and Hulu (aggregations of different TV network's content), there does not seem to be a huge consumer desire for this format. Perhaps consumers find it confusing to go to Hulu to find Fox TV entertainment content when they could just go to Fox.com.

If these are the areas that content producers should avoid, what are the areas that they should focus on in order to move the Average Joes online? They are bandwidth and display. This is both good and bad news for content producers. The bad news is that it is unlikely that TV networks will be providing broadband access to consumers in order to accelerate their movement to watching video online. It is also unlikely that they will be buying flat panel monitors and high-end sound cards for consumers who are lagging on technology adoption.

Now for the good news: this is what is called an actuarial problem, one that time itself will take care of. We are reaching a point of near broadband ubiquity in the USA among Internet households. Therefore the bandwidth issue should be minimized over the next few years. The hardware issue should also be solved. The average PC replacement rate for US households is about 2 years. Technology such as flat-panel monitors and high-end sound cards are coming down precipitously in price. Nielsen believes that based on these two trends the consumption of video, both long-form and short-form, will increase over the next 18 months as hardware begins to be replaced and broadband penetration continues to increase.

Conclusions and Recommendations

Where does all of this leave us? In this chapter we have discussed segmentation, penetration, myths, and really just how big YouTube really is right now. There are many important trends discussed in this chapter. The important ones to focus on are the following:

- *The Relationship Between TV Viewing and the Internet:* Although there is plenty of research on both sides of this subject, our analysis seems to show that with the exception of one key segment, the Early Adopters, there does not appear to be a relationship between increased Internet video use and decreased TV viewing. We do believe, however, that the extra media time does come from somewhere – most likely from print media.
- *Early Adopters Do Not Signal the End of Linear TV:* The Early Adopter segment is young and does consume a significant amount of media. Indeed, they do appear to be watching less TV while watching more video elsewhere. It seems likely though that (1) this demographic is not representative of the overall youth demographic – there are just too few Early Adopters now, and (2) Early Adopters exhibit an unusual psychographic trait, not typically shared either by their age cohort or by most Americans; they decouple the programming of the TV from the TV appliance. Until we see an overall movement away from the fetishising of the television in the USA, TV as an institution is not going anywhere. Though it does remain to be seen how DVRs will impact this relationship.
- *Fast Followers Want Programming They Cannot Find on TV:* One of the more promising parts of our research suggests that Fast Followers, the segment that is most likely to be consuming more and more long-form online video, has a

significant interest not in shifting their TV viewing online, but rather using the Internet to find programming that would otherwise be unavailable. Programming such as reruns no longer available on TV and full-length movies seem to have the most promise here.

- *Forgot About Selling a Video:* Ownership of video seems to be becoming more of an outdated concept. As the industry moves away from physical DVD delivery to downloads, consumers increasingly have little need for physical ownership of the content. Instead, they are looking for a broad variety of programming available when they want it. And no, they do not seem to want liner notes and fancy packaging either.
- *Trust the Actuaries:* The missing pieces from moving the largest segment online are hardware and bandwidth. Both of these will be changing in the near future. Broadband is reaching near ubiquity, and the price of flat-panel monitors and high-end video/sound cards is coming down. Within the next 18 months we expect significant growth in the viewership of online video.

Finally, it is worth remembering, not all programming should be rendered the same way. Historically, TV as a platform has been a limiting factor for the development of video-based entertainment. It is, by its nature, a one-way medium. This is clearly not the case for the Internet. With this in mind, video publishers should remember to not simply take the content that they produced from the TV and slap it onto the Internet. In fact, each genre has its own idiosyncrasies. Although the guidelines provided earlier in this chapter are rough, they are meant as inspiration. Content producers will use the Internet to free themselves from the confines of linear programming. They will add value to both consumers and advertisers. Consumers will find themselves with the ability to interact with the video content in ways they could not on TV.

We have already begun to see this. Some networks have experimented with allowing consumers to mouse over parts of the video to get a back, or side story regarding what the character is talking about at that moment, even though that back or side story might have otherwise not been broadcast. This is just one experiment. Chat features and other forms of interactivity will allow community to build around programming in ways we are yet to see. The Internet will no longer be an isolating factor for TV viewing, but rather a unifying one.

Value will also be provided for advertisers. The 30-s spot is a concept wasted on the Internet. Creative advertising where the consumer can interact with the brand through gamming, or getting more information or seeing a full-length movie trailer rather than a 30-s spot is already a reality. In this mode advertisers do not have to preach to consumers; they can truly engage them. Indeed, they will be able to minimize advertising waste, through behavioral targeting and contextual placement. The movement online will bring about a new age of advertising.

We are about to enter a new era of online video. As I said at the beginning, it will be a lot of fun to watch.

Chapter 3
The End of Advertising As We Know It

Saul J. Berman, Bill Battino, Louisa Shipnuck, and Andreas Neus*

Abstract The next 5 years will hold more change for the advertising industry than the previous 50 did. Increasingly empowered consumers, more self-reliant advertisers, and ever-evolving technologies are redefining how advertising is sold, created, consumed, and tracked. Our research points to four evolving future scenarios, and the catalysts that will be driving them. Traditional advertising players – broadcasters, distributors, and advertising agencies – may get squeezed unless they can successfully implement consumer, business model and business design innovation.

A Glimpse into the Future of Advertising

Jim, the Chief Marketing Officer of a consumer products company, used to spend 60% of his marketing dollars on broadcast, free-to-air television – a significant portion of which was spent in upfronts. But he never knew exactly who he was reaching or how effective his advertising was.

Now, he has a very different approach and is more comfortable with the effectiveness of his marketing. Jim assesses all media channels (television, radio, mobile devices, print, interactive portals, and the like) neutrally to determine how best to allocate his marketing and advertising dollars. Recognizing that consumers have increasing control and choice over how they interact with, filter, and block marketing messages, it is more important than ever for Jim to know that his advertising is reaching individual consumers, not generic zip codes at the household level.

With the help of Cathy, the company's Chief Consumer Officer, he has gained a full understanding of who his target consumers are, where his consumers are going, and how to reach them on their terms across the plethora of media devices they interact with on a regular basis. As consumers move to 360-deg content and information experiences, marketing also personalizes its content to consumers' lifestyle, context, and location.

Previously, Jim bought broad-reaching spots, hoping to reach his target audience. But now, targeting, measuring, and analytical capabilities that previously were only available for Web advertising are available for all channels. Jim can

D. Gerbarg (ed.), *Television Goes Digital*,
© Springer Science + Business Media, LLC 2009

develop an interactive, integrated marketing plan tailored to his individual target consumer, and he pays based on actual impact rather than by cost per thousand (CPM) impressions. His marketing message follows those customers across content platforms to deliver a consistent experience.

His advertising includes a mix of creative spots and formats, such as special interest content, product placement, and self-published advertising that are tailored to his consumers' preferences, community affiliations, and devices. This enables his target consumers – be they traditional moms in Des Moines (Iowa), urban professionals in Berlin, or university students in South Korea – to better experience the value of his product. Jim created his advertising campaigns jointly with broadcasters, semiprofessionals, and avid product fans (or "influencers"), who develop creative at a significantly lower cost than his traditional agency did. Though Jim creates multiple versions of his advertising campaigns in order to appeal to numerous customer microsegments, his budget has not increased because of the decreased cost of developing creative campaigns. His ROI has also improved, because the advertising is more effective.

Because much of the budget is based on impact, he works closely with the Sales team, and a portion of the direct marketing budget has moved to advertising channels. He is now able to measure the effectiveness of his marketing campaigns through the use of marketing software packages that have centralized and standardized disparate data sources.

Jim's team can purchase much of its advertising space through an open, Web-based platform and manage its impact through a "dashboard" that delivers real-time metrics and analysis across all advertising platforms. Gone are the days of "hoping" advertising works. Jim is now in a world where he has full control of the effectiveness of his marketing spend.

Introduction

> We will see "neutral" evaluation of all media formats. There is no primary role for linear TV any more.
>
> Managing director, advertiser, Europe

The trends toward creative populism, personalized measurements, interactivity, open inventory platforms, and greater consumer control will generate more change over the next 5 years than the advertising industry has experienced in the last 50. This means that many of the skills and capabilities that were the mainstay of success in the past will need refinement, transformation, or even outright replacement.

Based on an IBM global survey of more than 2,400 consumers and feedback from 80 advertising executives worldwide collected in conjunction with Bonn University's Center for Evaluation and Methods,[2] we see four change drivers shifting control within the industry.

Attention

Consumers are increasingly exercising control of how they view, interact with and filter advertising in a multichannel world, as they continue to shift their attention away from linear TV and adopt ad-skipping, ad-sharing, and ad-rating tools.[3] Our survey suggests that personal PC time now rivals TV time, with 71% of respondents using the Internet more than 2h per day for personal use, vs. just 48% spending equivalent time watching TV. Among the heaviest users, 19% spend 6h or more a day on the PC vs. just 9% who watch a similar amount of TV.

Creativity

Thanks to technology, the rising popularity of user-generated and peer-delivered content, and new ad revenue-sharing models, amateurs and semiprofessionals are now creating lower-cost advertising content that is arguably as appealing to consumers as versions created by agencies. Our survey suggests that this trend will continue – user-generated content (UGC) sites were the top destination for viewing online video content, attracting 39% of respondents. Further, established players, such as magazine publishers and broadcasters, are partnering with advertisers to develop strategic marketing campaigns – taking on traditional agency functions and broadening creative roles.

Measurement

Advertisers are demanding more individual-specific and involvement-based measurements, putting pressure on the traditional mass-market model. Two thirds of the advertising executives IBM polled expect 20% of advertising revenue to shift from impression-based to impact-based formats within 3 years.

Advertising Inventories

New entrants are making ad space that once was proprietary available through open, efficient exchanges. As a result, more than half of the ad executives interviewed expect that open platforms will, within the next 5 years, take 30% of the revenue currently flowing to proprietary incumbents such as broadcasters.

To envision four possible scenarios for the industry in 2012, we juxtaposed two of the most uncertain change drivers – the propensity for consumers to watch, block, or participate in marketing campaigns; and the openness of advertising inventories. Because players across geographies and media formats will progress at differing rates, these scenarios will likely coexist for the foreseeable future. The four scenarios are as follows.

Continued Evolution

In this scenario, the one-to-many model still dominates, but the industry evolves in response to digital video recorder (DVR) penetration, the popularity of user-generated and peer-distributed content, and new measuring capabilities (albeit for "old" formats). Advertisers, therefore, allocate a greater portion of dollars traditionally spent on direct marketing to channels typically used for brand-oriented advertising.

Open Exchange

Here, the industry morphs behind the scenes, with little to no additional consumer influence. Advertising formats largely remain the same, but advertising inventory is increasingly bought and sold through efficient open exchanges, bypassing traditional intermediaries.

Consumer Choice

Tired of intrusions, consumers exert more control over the advertising they view and filter. Formats evolve to contextual, interactive, permission-based, and targeted messaging to retain attention.

Ad Marketplace

Consumers choose preferred ad types as part of self-programming their media choices and are more involved in ad development and distribution. Advertising is sold predominantly through open, dynamic exchanges, allowing virtually any advertiser (large or small) to reach any consumer. With new consumer-monitoring technologies in place, consumer action drives pricing.

As the advertising value chain reconfigures, broadcasters, advertising agencies, and media distributors in particular will need to make a number of "no regret" moves (necessary actions regardless of which scenario plays out in the future) to innovate in three key areas.

1. *Consumer innovation*: Drive greater creativity in traditional ads, while also pursuing new ad formats across media devices to attract and retain customers. For example, consider tactics such as campaign bleeds, microversioning, video ad flickers, pod management, and ad-supported content creation (embedded in the programming) to limit ad-skipping.[4] This also means making segmentation,

microsegmentation, and personalization paramount in marketing. Anyone who touches buyers and consumers needs to collect and analyze data to produce relevant and predictive insights.

2. *Business model innovation*: Pioneer changes in how advertising is sold, the structure and forms of partnerships, revenue models, advertising formats, and reporting metrics. For example, broadcasters, agencies, and distributors can pursue opportunities such as agency gain sharing, more sponsored shows, impact-based pricing models, user-generated advertising revenue-sharing models, and open inventory, cross-channel sales.

3. *Business design and infrastructure innovation*: Support consumer and business model innovation through redesigned organizational and operating capabilities across the advertising lifecycle – consumer analytics, channel planning, buying/selling, creation, delivery, and impact reporting.

We know that advertising remains integral to pop culture and media investment. But it also will need to morph into new formats and new channels and offer more intrinsic value to consumers to capture a meaningful share of fragmented audience attention.

There is no question that the future of advertising will look radically different from its past. The push for control of attention, creativity, measurements, and inventory will reshape the advertising value chain and shift the balance of power. For both incumbent and new players, it is imperative to plan for multiple consumer futures, craft agile strategies, and build new capabilities before advertising as we know it disappears.

Key questions to consider

- Will advertisers still need a traditional agency?
- If so, in what capacity?
- Will traditional programmers lose significant revenue to the Internet, mobile device providers, and interactive home portals?
- Will consumers reject outright the concept of interruption marketing in the future?
- Will consumer receptivity vary by medium (for example, mobile devices vs. home-oriented devices)?
- Will consumers see value in advertising as a trade-off for content?
- To what extent will advertising inventory be sold through open platforms?
- Do advertising industry players have the customer analytics needed to better understand and reach target customers?
- Are companies organized correctly to create, market, and distribute cross-platform content?

Industry Battles and Trends: Power Shifts

As advertising budgets shift to new formats and shape the future advertising market, control of marketing revenues and power will hinge on four key market drivers: *attention, creativity, measures, and advertising inventories.* This section will explore these changes and their economic impacts through 2012.

We expect overall ad spend to grow in line with the general health of the economy, but the composition of that spending will change. We have used an amalgamation of industry forecasts for our consensus view in Fig. 3.1. While this spending breakdown is helpful for highlighting the *direction* of change, the speed and magnitude of this kind of disruptive change tend to be underestimated by traditional forecasting methods. For example, our analysis shows that the actual growth of Internet advertising has outpaced forecasts by 25–40% over the past 2 years.[5]

But even in forecasts (in Fig. 3.l) – which may be too conservative – digital, mobile, and interactive formats are clearly the key to overall industry growth going forward. Mature channels such as print, traditional direct marketing, and TV have 2010 CAGR forecasts of low single digits, while the combined growth forecast for interactive advertising formats, such as Internet, interactive television promotions, mobile, and in-game advertising, is over 20%.[6]

Product placement is the only "traditional" marketing tool with comparable growth expectations – spurred by advertisers' desire to drive relevancy and reach for their advertising as consumer control over interruption advertising continues.

Although control of *attention, creativity, measurements,* and *advertising inventories* impacts all forms of advertising and content funding, we are focusing here on TV/video as an illustration of significant change.

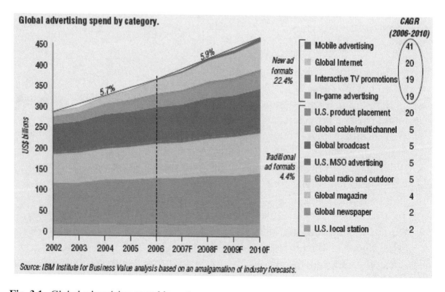

Fig. 3.1 Global advertising spend by category

Attention

> Consumers will continue to gain more power over content, but they will not "skip" all forms of advertising. Fewer will pay for all the content they want to consume; there will be new models to trade attention to advertising for content.
>
>   Account executive, full-service media agency, North America

As we predicted in our 2002 "Vying for Attention" paper, audiences continue to fragment.[7] Although this is not a new phenomenon, we are reaching a critical juncture where new platforms may soon have more impact than TV. Today, consumers have more options for visual entertainment than ever before – TV, PC, game consoles, mobile devices, and more. Studies from several countries have shown that, especially for young users, TV is increasingly becoming a secondary "background medium."[8] The primary focus of attention is elsewhere – surfing the Internet, chatting, or playing an online game. Our consumer survey showed that more respondents spend significant blocks of time on daily personal Internet usage than watching TV, especially among the heaviest users. This behavior is particularly prominent for younger audiences (ages 18–24) and "gadgetiers" (early adopter consumers who own at least four multimedia devices). Our survey also illustrates the ongoing fragmentation of consumer attention and the wide variations in adoption by age groups across content services (see Fig. 3.2). The only content service with mass adoption (greater than 50%) was Social Networking, and this was only among respondents under the age of 35. Younger audiences are far more willing to experiment with new content sources, though less willing to pay, particularly for online services. Older audiences had higher adoption of more traditional services, such as premium content for television and online newspaper subscriptions.

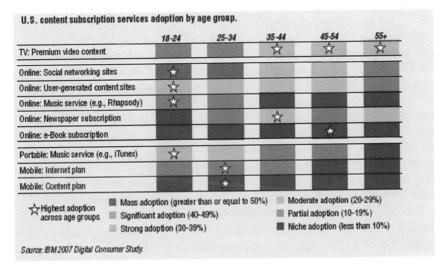

Fig. 3.2 US content subscription services adoption by age group

As users migrate to new screens for content and information, advertising and marketing will need to shift as well. It is more important than ever to reach consumers where they want, when they want, and how they want. And with advertising dollars funding a significant portion of entertainment around the world (sponsoring an estimated 50% of television in major markets, for example), the medium, content, and advertising spending must synch up.[9]

We are also witnessing the possible substitution of other visual media for TV viewing time. Though mobile video consumption is currently lower than PC video consumption among our respondents, 42% said they have already watched or want to watch video on a mobile device. In the United Kingdom, nearly one third of those who watch mobile TV had consequently reduced their standard TV viewing patterns.

In addition to preferring hot new devices and screens for entertainment, users are also enjoying and exploiting new control tools. With spam-blockers, "do-not-call," and "do not mail" lists in the United States, the DVR and peer distribution tools, marketers are being forced to rethink how to prevent buyers from tuning out.

For example, 25% of our US consumer respondents and 20% of our UK respondents already have a DVR. Given high customer satisfaction rates, forecasters project DVR penetration to reach close to 40% in the United States within the next 5 years, which poses a significant threat to the traditional TV advertising model.[10]

In our consumer survey, 53% of DVR owners in the United States report watching at least 50% of television content on replay, supplying them with the fast-forward capabilities that allow ad-skipping. As DVRs gain traction across demographic groups and consumer segments, traditional television advertising may be the first major casualty of changing media consumption habits. And though new commercial rating tools can now track viewership via DVR, industry debate continues about the true value of an ad if it is viewed after the initial, targeted broadcast period.

Multimedia devices are also proliferating, though adoption behaviors vary by country. For example, respondents from Germany appear to prefer portable devices and are far more likely to have MP3 players and Internet-enabled phones than any other country. Almost 70% of German respondents own an MP3 player, and almost 40% have an Internet-enabled phone, compared to global averages of 50% and 20%, respectively. In Japan, portable game player adoption is widespread, with almost 40% of respondents owning one, vs. between 15 and 23% in other countries. US respondents report higher adoption of living-room-related devices, such as DVRs, high-definition television sets, and game consoles, but have lower adoption rates for portable devices, such as MP3 players, Internet-enabled phones, and portable game players, than other countries. Finally, video on demand (VOD) habits vary, with close to 50% of UK and US respondents having already watched VOD, compared to less than 5% of German and Japanese respondents who have done so.

What do these trends mean for the industry's bottom line? Nearly half of the respondents in our advertising executive interviews expect a *significant* (i.e., greater than 10%) revenue shift away from the 30-s spot within the next 5 years, and almost 10% of respondents thought that there would be a *dramatic* (i.e., greater than 25%) shift.

Fig. 3.3 Index of US ad-spend growth: all television vs. consumer Internet

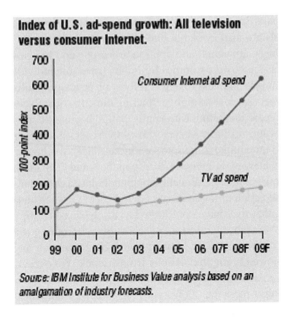

As consumers turn away from traditional television and toward new content sources, such as popular online sites (e.g., YouTube, MySpace and Facebook), games, mobile and other emerging entertainment platforms, the shift in attention will eventually be reflected in advertising, subscription, and transactional fees. This puts at risk the revenue base of incumbent, traditional content distributors and aggregators – especially for those who do not produce content or own rights to distribute content on these newer channels.

As shown in Fig. 3.3, growth in Internet advertising far exceeds that of traditional channels such as television. And while no evidence suggests a one-to-one correlation of advertising revenue with this audience migration to new channels, we believe that the current large discrepancy between advertising revenues and eyeballs will shrink significantly over the next 5 years.

The majority of the advertising executives we interviewed expect significant dollar shifts from traditional advertising vehicles to search, mobile, Internet protocol television (IPTV), VOD, and online video ads. Advertising industry incumbents could lose out entirely if they do not keep up with advertisers who are following their audiences into new channels.

Creativity

Consumer-created advertising will have all the appeal of anything crafted by the agencies, and will be Coopted' by the brands themselves.

CEO, advertiser, Asia Pacific

In addition to new tools for control of what consumers choose to view, lower cost tools are also available that allow new creative input from consumers, semiprofessionals, amateurs, and nontraditional players. Inexpensive video- and photo-editing tools create opportunities for hobby tribes and individual users to self-produce entertainment and advertising – a form of creative populism. At the same time, content owners are increasingly partnering directly with advertisers to develop innovative and strategic marketing campaigns that go beyond the traditional advertising formats.

Our consumer survey shows that users, particularly those in the United States and the United Kingdom, are increasingly willing to participate in social networking sites, with 26% of US respondents and 20% of UK respondents having already contributed content. And though not quite as popular yet, users are starting to create video content for UGC sites, with 9% of German and 7% of US respondents reporting that they have contributed to those sites (see Fig. 3.4).

We also see evidence of consumers becoming trusted influencers. When asked about how they find content on UGC sites such as YouTube, 32% said that they followed recommendations from friends. We expect the power of communities to grow, as tools for community-based recommendations improve. The "voice" delivering a message, along with its perceived authenticity, will become as powerful perhaps as the message or offer.

There are also other creative forces at play. In addition to users, other members of the value chain, such as content owners and broadcasters, are increasingly working directly with advertisers to drive nontraditional campaigns, bypassing the agency's

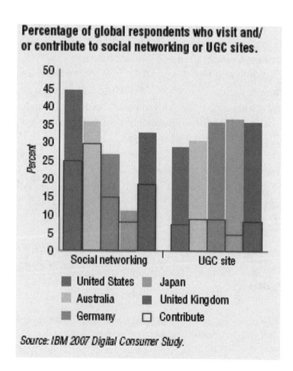

Fig. 3.4 Percentage of global respondents who visit and/or contribute to social networking or UGC sites

intermediary role as the cost of production declines and tools become generally accessible. For example, creating a professional video ad typically costs around US $100,000 to US $350,000 or more, which is prohibitive for most small businesses. However, cheaper tools and community-based or semiprofessional content creation can lower production costs to reasonable levels, making them affordable for small- and medium-sized businesses that cater to niche markets. Current TV, for example, pays US $1,000 for viewer-created advertisements (V-CAMs) that it chooses to air.[11]

Furthermore, content owners are broadening their creative roles, taking on responsibilities that previously belonged to agencies. There are already many examples of broadcast and publishing content owners who are displacing traditional ad agencies in creative and campaign planning. Companies such as Conde Nast's Media Group have creative units that work directly with advertisers to produce and distribute custom advertising programs often at lower prices than agencies by charging cost for creative services and making their money on the media.[12] Conde Nast trades on its ability to blend images, characters, and stories from content into relevant, marketing campaigns, relying on a panel of more than 100,000 consumers to evaluate the advertising.[13]

UGC impacts the industry through two primary avenues: content production and attention influence. We have already discussed the rise of semiprofessionals, user enthusiasts, and amateurs producing content. Now, let us link back to issues of attention, a circular topic of sorts. As new types of content are created, audience fragmentation increases. The advertising executives we interviewed expect a significant portion of content consumed on different devices to be user-generated within 5 years – nearly 15% of TV time and about 25% of PC time. This means that there is an opening for new aggregators and distributors – the likes of YouTube, Grouper, or Current TV – to capture a share of revenue that would have previously gone to traditional programmers or channels.

The majority of the respondents in our panel of advertising industry executives also indicated that UGC is not "hype" and is here to stay. They also felt that inexpensive video production tools will increase competition among professionals, amateurs, and semiprofessionals.

As a result, content owners, distributors, advertisers, and agencies are all becoming more creative about how to reach the target consumer. For example, broadcasters are making use of content bleeds in advertising pods – where characters become a part of the commercial message. On the flip side, product placement continues to become more popular as a way to integrate the marketing message directly into the program itself. There is also an everincreasing number of new ad formats to capture the consumer's attention, both on the TV screen and on the Web. Formats such as short-form video, flickers, bugs, banners, and pop-ups continue to evolve. Finally, players are doing a better job of matching the ad content with the programming content to drive relevancy. The recent results of an ongoing study by TiVo Inc. concluded that relevancy outweighs creativity in TV commercials.[14] The ads least likely to be skipped were well-tailored to their audience – they were often those ads that aired during the daytime on cable (where shows have smaller, niche audiences and it is easier to determine viewers' interests) or during prime time on directly relevant programs.[15]

With a wider group of content creators contributing to the mix, pieces of the creative value chain may commoditize or experience price pressure (similar to how independent films have lowered the cost of one echelon of filmmaking). The advertising value chain will therefore need to proactively integrate the more creative parts of its team, or others will do so from outside.

Measures

> It is becoming increasingly easy to measure actual viewership, engagement and response. Having that accurate information will greatly alter the way advertising is produced and disseminated and how it is ultimately paid for.
>
> Account Executive, full-service media agency, North America

Evolving technologies, coupled with advertisers' demands for improved targeting, accountability, and ROI, are driving changes in measurement and associated advertising business models. As consumer attention continues to fragment, measurements will only remain relevant if advertisers track finer segments and perhaps even individual viewers.

We therefore predict individual- and microtargeting becoming prevalent across all media formats. In addition to requiring new partnerships and investment, this kind of advertising will also necessitate a major increase in the number of creative spots and campaigns to reach targets with niche or specialized messages. More spots will likely mean lower average price points on creative. Companies such as Qmecom are allowing for customization with automation, so that hundreds of creative outputs take the place of the mere one, two, or five variations common in days past.[16]

Hardware (i.e., set-top-box-based, headend-based, portable device) and software technology advances are enabling improved targeting and response tracking capabilities across media formats. Companies such as TiVo and Nielsen are beginning to supply real-time, nonsampled measurements of ad-skipping, purchasing influence, and the like.[17] Other companies are moving toward providing targeted delivery capabilities across media platforms, based on a combination of user behavior and opt-in data.

Furthermore, a new breed of chief marketing officers, conversant with Internet metrics, is seeking more focused targeting and accountability (ROI) for marketing budgets across channels. As the first generation of professionals who have grown up with the Internet rises to positions of responsibility among advertisers, we are likely to see more experimentation and a greater readiness to adopt new platforms, especially if they can demonstrate effectiveness.

Two thirds of our global advertising industry executive panel expects 20% of advertising revenue to shift from impression-based to impact-based formats within 3 years (see Fig. 3.5). Targeting, measuring, and accountability capabilities will have to evolve to reflect new advertiser goals and demands. This shift will be

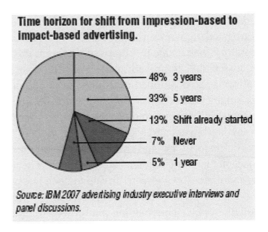

Fig. 3.5 Time horizon for shift from impression-based to impact-based advertising

particularly critical for traditional TV, as it is increasingly delivered digitally. New types of advertising, such as pod management, skip-resistant creative campaigns, greater creativity immersed within ads (to entice people not to skip), more dynamic product placements, and more, should produce greater impact.

Finally, although much of the current industry discussion is related to new measures for arguably "old," one-to-many advertising formats, the era of truly interactive, experience-based advertising is coming. For example, in virtual 3D worlds, audiences can use and interact with a brand, rather than just be "exposed" to it. And these new advertising experiences are marching forward largely without leadership from established broadcasters, agencies, and advertisers.

These trends imply that the boundaries between "local" and "national" advertising will blur. Media companies historically strong in local advertising (e.g., cable, newspapers) will have to improve their interactive capabilities, while national advertisers (e.g., Broadcast TV) and interactive players will have to improve upon their local targeting capabilities (meaning, know where the consumer is).

Advertising Inventories

> The U.S. television advertising upfronts are not likely to exist more than another few years.
>
> Executive, major online media aggregator, North America

Today, most inventory systems, such as the television upfronts in the United States, involve relatively few buyers and sellers, most of which are very large companies. For example, GroupM, of the London-based WPP Group, sealed the first major deal of the 2007 upfront season with a multiplatform, US $1 billion agreement with NBC Universal.[18]

New platform players are offering advertisers the ability to purchase ads via aggregated networks. These capabilities provide key benefits such as improved inventory management, improved pricing transparency, streamlined buying/selling processes, and improved analysis and reporting capabilities. These new entrants/platforms are positioned to capture an important part of the future advertising and marketing value chain. Going forward, we anticipate that inventory management systems will become more open and transparent and will involve a larger number of smaller buyers and sellers.

The majority of our advertising industry executives agreed with this directional trend. In fact, they predict a significant shift in control of advertising revenues, with more dollars flowing from private to open markets over the next 5 years. The panel also expects 30% of advertising revenues to shift from traditional proprietary sales models to placement/auction platforms within the next 5 years. However, changes to back-end platforms, along with the increased willingness of suppliers to sell both remnant and premium inventory through these open systems, will be required in order for this revenue shuffle to occur.

The reason for this trend? As revenues shift in response to consumer fragmentation, it will no longer be efficient to have dedicated platforms for each channel. Market forces will move the industry to open, dynamic platforms capable of following a customer by serving messaging across multiple channels. This is a natural progression caused by the shift of advertising dollars across channels, which, in turn, is driven by advertisers seeking to follow their customers' interests as content is increasingly divorced from devices.

Internet players have shown themselves to be more adept at extending their predominantly online platforms into other channels. Google, for example, is leveraging its tracking capabilities and matching algorithms for both new and traditional channels, such as radio, TV, and print through its acquisition of dMarc, partnerships with EchoStar and Astound Cable, and the launch of Google Print Ads.[19] This is a shift in focus to adjacent growth opportunities from Google's initial focus on paid search.

Investments in the traditional advertising space by new entrants may pose a threat to current value-chain incumbents. As fragmentation becomes a permanent fixture within media and entertainment, advertisers will be forced to move to more efficient and dynamic platforms capable of managing inventory, planning, delivering, tracking, and measuring effectiveness of advertising *across* multiple channels and in real time.

Future Scenarios: Scenarios of Disruption

To assess the degree and depth of change expected, we used a process called scenario envisioning. In this process, the most disruptive and uncertain variables are combined to create and articulate a variety of extreme outcomes for the year 2012.

Our scenarios are based on the following two variables, which we believe will be the most disruptive over the next 5 years:

- *Marketing control*: The propensity of the consumer to control, interact with, filter and block marketing messages
- *Advertising inventory system control*: The degree of movement from controlled, impression-based ad inventory systems to open auction or exchange platforms for advertising spots

In Fig. 3.6, the *x*-axis illustrates how the control of media consumption is shifting from providers to consumers. As we move to the right along the *x*-axis, consumers wrestle more and more control over their media experiences from providers. The *y*-axis illustrates the change from closed inventory to open auctions. As we move up the *y*-axis, more television, print, and interactive advertising deals become accessible to smaller, independent buyers and sellers.

Based on these two variables, four scenarios emerge.

Continued Evolution is arguably the least disruptive scenario, though it still involves rapid change from today's one-to-many advertising model. Control, in large part, remains with content owners and distributors, but growing consumer demand for control forces some progressive adjustments. The industry cannot ignore the implications of the current DVR penetration level and the associated ad-skipping behavior it enables, the explosive growth in popularity of UGC and related advertising opportunities, or the measuring capabilities now available to track ad viewership. These factors imply a bifurcated market – one in which a portion of consumers can still be addressed through traditional advertising models, while others must be attracted through interactive and innovative strategies. Increasingly sophisticated targeting, measurement, and accountability tools enable advertisers to continue to allocate a greater portion of dollars traditionally spent on direct marketing to channels historically reserved for brand-oriented advertising. Traditional agencies will continue consolidating in their efforts to respond to advertisers' demands for seamlessly integrated, cross-platform planning, buying, delivery and measurement services. Similarly, broadcasters and distributors will continue to focus on horizontal advertising opportunities for advertisers.

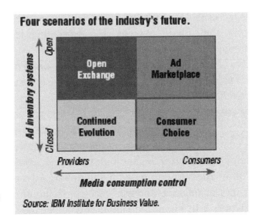

Fig. 3.6 Four scenarios of the industry's future

Open Exchange represents a scenario in which the industry changes behind the scenes, primarily driven by distributors – traditional players such as multiple systems operators (MSOs) and Telcos, as well as newer technology players – with little to no additional consumer-driven change. In other words, marketing stays the same as what was described in Continued Evolution, but the process of buying, selling, and delivering becomes more efficient. Also, similar to the Continued Evolution scenario, majority control remains with content owners and distributors rather than with consumers, and a majority of consumers continue to passively ingest marketing messages without a great deal of interference or proactivity. However, efficiency efforts – largely driven by new entrants – shuffle profits and power within the industry. A significant portion of advertising inventory that was proprietary is now "open" – sold through exchanges, as a result bypassing traditional intermediaries. New exchanges take major share in all advertising categories, and inventory that was once exclusively available to large advertisers – including historically proprietary national television spots – is now available to smaller buyers.

Consumer Choice is a scenario in which advertising formats change at the behest of consumers who are tired of interruption or intrusive marketing. Consumers exhibit more control and choice over the types of advertising that they choose to view and filter. Advertising formats, therefore, evolve to contextual, interactive, permission-based, and targeted messaging to retain consumers' attention and to help minimize both irritation and "tuning out." To remain relevant, distributors offer consumers choices – in some cases, enabling the consumer to select the appropriate advertising "packages" that are most appealing or relevant. For example, a consumer might request that advertising be confined to automotive, male-oriented consumer products, travel, and leisure. At times, these choices will act as currency, with consumers opting in for messaging in exchange for content. In other cases, relevancy is determined by combining opt-in information with behavior analysis of television, the Web, mobile and beyond. New measuring capabilities and consumer rating tools become a crucial component of any advertising deal.

Ad Marketplace, compared to all other scenarios, is the most disruptive. Significant change in back-end systems and consumer-facing marketing enable new entrants to emerge across the value chain. In this scenario, consumers reject traditional advertising and instead choose their preferred ad types as part of self-programming their media choices. The user-generated and peer-delivered content trend explodes, and consumers become much more involved in ad development and buzz/viral distribution of brand information. Furthermore, back-end players revamp the process behind the scenes. Because this scenario involves a truly open, dynamic exchange, virtually any advertiser can reach any individual consumer across any advertising platform – as long as the advertising is relevant and appealing. Consumers have significant choice over the types of advertising they choose to see – and can decide the specific content and form of their advertising. And with new consumer-monitoring technologies in place, consumer action directly impacts the price of an ad – driving bids up and down. Advertisers can know immediately whether a spot or interactive experience is producing anticipated results. Likewise, media networks will know immediately whether they have increased or decreased reach – with prices calibrating elastically. The definitions of "reach," "effective-ness," and even "marketing" itself change entirely.

Scenario Evolution

On the basis of their legacy assets and ability to develop new media capabilities, players across the value chain will take different evolutionary paths (see Fig. 3.7). Though we believe that the industry will eventually become an "Ad Marketplace," multiple scenarios will likely coexist for the near term.

Signs of this evolution are already evident in the marketplace. Examples of Open Exchange initiatives are currently limited to niche areas, but they illustrate what the future could look like.

- Google
  - Google Online: AdSense – offers online media publishers enhanced revenue opportunities by placing contextual advertising sold by Google on their Web sites[20]
  - Cable/Satellite: Astound Me, EchoStar – leverages Google online capabili-ties to sell, deliver, and measure targeted advertising on cable (Astound Me) and satellite (EchoStar) based on consumer behavior patterns[21]
  - Radio: dMarc – acquisition made in 2006 enables Google to offer its adver-tising capabilities to the radio industry[22]
  - Newspaper: Print Ads – 2007 initiative by Google to streamline the buying/selling process for the newspaper industry[23]

- NextMedium – Platform to sell, deliver, and track product placement for film and TV[24]

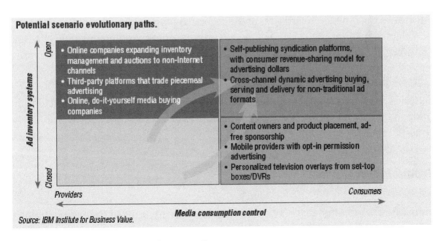

Fig. 3.7 Potential scenario evolutionary paths

- BlackArrow – Ad platform for the cable industry that aggregates inventory into a network and focuses on delivering targeted traditional and advanced advertising formats[25]

The following present-day examples of Consumer Choice illustrate experiments in new formats and marketing themes – in reaction to consumers driving change.

- TiVo's interactive advertising technology enables pop-up messages while consumers are watching programs, as well as while they are fast-forwarding through programming.[26]
- Aerie Tuesdays is a partnership between American Eagle and The CW Television Network to target teenage girls in more innovative ways, by developing unique content programming related to two Tuesday night prime-time programs.[27]
- Sugar Mama from Virgin Mobile pays subscribers 1 min of free air time for every minute spent interacting with ads. One year after launch, Virgin had given away 9 million free air-time minutes and was experiencing high response rates of around 5%.[28]
- NBC Direct announced that its 2007 programs will be available for free online for 1 week after initial broadcast. The content must be viewed on NBC proprietary technology, which prevents ad-skipping.[29]

Marketplace platforms that trade completely new marketing formats through an open exchange are still in the experimental phase. But we are beginning to see examples of how the Ad Marketplace scenario could play out in the UGC segment of the industry through evolving business models such as those of Revver, Narrowstep, Brightcove, and YouTube.

Value Chain Impacts

Given consumer and supplier changes, we believe that mid-term economic shifts will favor consumers, advertisers, and interactive players over the other players in the value chain (see Fig. 3.8). And as advertisers, Internet/interactive players, and consumers gain power, traditional agencies and broadcasters must evolve or risk being disintermediated.

We believe that looming changes and shifts in advertising revenue and industry control will affect a number of players in the industry value chain, in particular the following.

Broadcasters

Arguably, broadcasters that rely on linear television advertising to fund operational and content costs are at risk in a world of increasing consumer control, niche content, and fragmented attention. And yet, broadcasters have the opportunity to

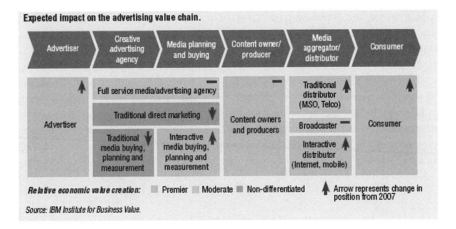

Fig. 3.8   Expected impact on the advertising value chain

leverage their current mindshare with customers, while transforming their operations to embrace the plethora of new digital content distribution opportunities. By delivering integrated, cross-platform advertising programs tied to their programming assets, they can migrate into a successful future model.

Distributors

Both traditional distributors (multiple systems operators and Telcos) and newer interactive players (Internet and mobile providers) have a small share of the estimated US $550 billion 2007 global advertising market.[30] Slowly but surely, incumbents are introducing the new platforms and formats needed to defend their positions in the value chain. They are developing new advertising capabilities (such as interactive and VOD advertising), integrating advertising across in-home video, mobile, and Internet channels, and focusing on local advertising delivery opportunities. By opening their inventories through dynamic platforms, distributors create an aggregated inventory view that makes it easier for advertisers to see the full reach and volume a distributor can offer, helping distributors capture a greater share of advertising revenues. The race is on to deliver cross-platform integration. Telcos and multiple systems operators currently have a window in which they could take the lead on integrating wireless, broadband, and video campaigns.

Advertising Agencies

Naturally, agencies would like to protect their creative and analytical positions as intermediaries and consultants. To do that, agencies will need to guard against increasing commoditization of their services by experimenting heavily with creative advertising content. If the rise of user-generated advertising seems "outlandish," consider how far-fetched the idea of a consumer-generated encyclopedia was only a few years ago. Agencies need to become the masters of 5-, 10-, and 30-s ads that are not tied to linear formats – be the vanguard of testing new alternatives. Agencies can mitigate the risk of the open inventory trend by offering robust planning and analytical capabilities – helping their clients analyze massive amounts of customer data and plan the optimal, integrated advertising strategy across the ever-increasing platforms, formats, and pricing models available to them.

Recommendations: Refashioning Success

How can advertising value chain participants prepare for the implications of these scenarios? Broadcasters, traditional ad agencies, and media distributors, in particular, will need to make strategic, operating, and organizational changes now to succeed in a world with more fragmented communication channels and new media interaction and consumption habits. We believe that there are a number of "no regret" moves for industry participants to work toward, regardless of how scenarios evolve (see Fig. 3.9):

1. *Consumer innovation*: making segmentation, microsegmentation, communities, and personalization paramount in marketing
2. *Business model innovation*: developing new revenue-sharing, distribution, and pricing strategies, radically shifting the dynamics in the industry
3. *Business design and infrastructure innovation*: improving horizontal organizational capabilities and adjusting operations to enable consumer and business model innovation.

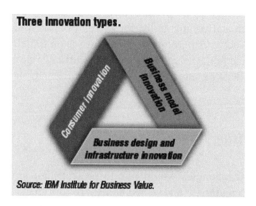

Fig. 3.9 Three innovation types

Consumer Innovation

For all players, consumer innovation means making marketing more interactive – bringing users and semiprofessionals into the content development, delivery, and response measurement processes to make the content innovative and relevant for consumers.

Building upon our recommendations for media companies in the "The End of Television As We Know It," we believe that the advertising industry will also have to address a bifurcated market of avant-garde, fashion-forward consumers who we call *Gadgetiers* and *Kool Kids*, as well as the large traditional segment we refer to as *Massive Passives*.[31] These vastly different markets mean companies need to adopt a dual strategy, focusing on both traditional and emerging digital business to address audiences. Regardless of the advertising vehicle, microsegmentation and targeting are necessary to drive relevancy for consumers. For example, *Kool Kids* and *Gadgetiers* will likely demand less intrusion, fewer interruptions, and a new interactive customer experience, while *Massive Passives* may still require a more traditional approach to advertising.

For *broadcasters*, these shifts imply the need to create relevant campaign content and marketing opportunities for diverse segments. Retaining audiences will also require innovative marketing tactics such as campaign bleeds (in which advertising capitalizes on well-known characters and programming), pod management during commercial breaks (focusing on the order and length of commercial breaks), cross-platform integrated messaging and promotions and innovative ad-supported content creation that limits ad-skipping. These capabilities are part of an ongoing cycle of "attention (re)invention," which can help generate increased affinity for broadcasters' brands. Broadcasters can develop their own enhanced, integrated brand marketing around television content franchises to drive viewership of television shows across media devices. Finally, broadcasters who reach out directly to consumers on the Web or contract with new suppliers, such as mobile providers, are better positioned to gather consumer data on their own or through partners. This allows them to mine aggregated consumer data for insights that can lead to improved content and advertising relevancy.

In this kind of market, *distributors* will need to differentiate by delivering location-specific, relevant content to consumers. This can be achieved in part by marrying set-top box and opt-in data with user behavior analysis. Distributors must also integrate new platforms (video, Web, mobile, and beyond), allowing advertisers to deliver fluid, follow-me content and marketing programs. Finally, the explosive growth in UGC will necessitate new distribution channels for delivering self-published videos and associated advertising messages across devices – PC, mobile phone, and TV. Recent partnerships between media distributors and UGC sites provide an example of how distributors can exploit the explosive growth in UGC to capture an increasing share of advertising revenues.

For their part, *agencies* should embrace the ability to reach consumers, regardless of their device preferences, and welcome consumers as part of the traditional, agency-driven processes by bringing users and semiprofessionals into the creative dialogue. They should also consider investing in differentiated creative development to drive advertising relevancy (microversioning). Agencies can combine their creative and analytical capabilities to develop multiple versions of an advertisement for various customer segments, and deliver the appropriate version based on a consumer profile. Agencies are also well-positioned to be "insight brokers" – aggregating the required information to enable integrated, cross-platform, targeted marketing campaigns – across the advertising planning, buying, and analysis/optimization functions. All of this implies the need for strong customer-data analytical capabilities, as well as the increased importance of the media planning role.

Agencies are developing new approaches to put consumers at the center of marketing programs. Niche-focused consumer research panels are increasingly used to test concepts and develop ongoing dialogues with target segments. Efforts to target online influencers or "magnets" are underway to fuel peer distribution of messages. Microversioning delivery concepts are being developed by combining consumer segmentation and analytics with low-cost creative development processes and dynamic ad-serving capabilities.

Business Model Innovation

All players must work toward differentiated business models that can address the changing business demands of advertisers. Innovation related to how and where advertising inventory is sold, the structure and forms of partnerships, revenue models, and advertising formats are all applicable.

Broadcasters must diversify their traditional focus to take on broader roles in driving relevancy and creativity in advertising. They are in a position to strike strategic partnerships directly with advertisers. By combining consumer insights with their creative knowledge, they can develop relevant, integrated, and innovative creative content (both short and long form) and campaigns that span media device platforms. Broadcasters can also expand their advertiser buyer base, by opening up select inventories through media platforms. They will also need to think through how to compensate broadcast affiliates as content ubiquity continues. Finally, they need to assess the alternative go-to-market options available to them for new distribution opportunities – whether that be by linking more closely with peers (e.g., NewsCorp and NBC) or with platforms (e.g., Google, Joost, Apple).

Distributors can drive persuasion and personalization by combining opt-in, permission-based information, click-stream analysis, and data on existing customer relationships. Distributors have a distinct advantage: the information they already have about their customers. This allows them to deliver relevant, contextual advertising to consumers and, thus, strong ROI for advertisers. It also allows them to deliver truly personalized portals of content and marketing across media devices. Distributors can also offer advertisers the ability to more accurately assess ROI through targeting, measurement, and analytics, as well as response-based advertising and impact-based pricing models. Advertisers are increasingly interested in having these kinds of capabilities (which are typically missing in today's world of television advertising) across advertising channels.

Agencies can leverage their current stronghold positions in traditional advertising and creative aspects of the business to capture revenues from the broader marketing communications industry, such as market research, media planning, and customer relationship management. For example, conversations with Sir Martin Sorrell, CEO of WPP, confirm goals to continue to diversify WPP's revenue streams and grow revenues from nontraditional advertising sources, such as consulting and customer relationship management, to two thirds of overall revenues in the next 10 years.[32] Agencies also need to be fearless in pursuing new formats and platforms, particularly integrated, cross-platform advertising opportunities. Finally, agencies need to seamlessly integrate new digital businesses and develop strategies to avoid conflict between traditional and digital ad buying and ad placement.

Distributors are piloting new models for advertisers related to targeting, mobility, and interactivity across platforms. Online advertising platforms are being developed to support the sales, delivery, and analysis of traditional and advanced advertising formats. Initiatives are underway to enable content and associated advertising portability across TV, Web, and mobile devices. Finally, distributors are increasingly expanding UGC and social networking tools beyond the PC.

Business Design and Infrastructure Innovation

For most industry players, significant shifts in current business design and infrastructure will be required to enable horizontal (meaning cross-platform) customer communications.

Broadcasters must move from departmental silos to a more integrated structure that enables horizontal content development and distribution, while also investing in "open platform" capabilities and operating systems to make portions of their advertising inventories available to larger buyer bases. They must also assess their current operating and organizational structures to determine whether they have the right resources and appropriate capacity to handle increased marketing promotions and integrated advertising sales across distribution platforms.

Distributors must continue their focus on behavioral analytics, but expand to measure outcomes holistically across platforms. They should also continue to invest in commerce and community tools that enable the delivery of interactive and response-based advertising. By working collectively across the industry, distributors can establish standards for emerging advertising capabilities – and sidestep the barrier that has historically impeded growth in the early stages of other new advertising formats, such as Internet advertising.

Finally, *agencies* must work across media platforms by integrating, or consolidating their currently siloed agencies – this is particularly relevant in areas such as horizontal customer analytics. Agencies have a wealth of data; however, much of this information cannot be turned into insights because of disparate data sources and incompatible underlying data infrastructures. To fund advanced and innovative advertising formats, agencies will need to drive cross-unit efficiencies, for example, connecting and standardizing the back-offices of all of their boutiques through the use of shared-services or off-shoring.

Broadcasters are realizing that the rapid expansion of nonlinear distribution opportunities has resulted in a dramatic increase in both the number and variety of promotions materials. The processes have become increasingly difficult to manage with existing, often manual, processes and disparate tools. Consequently, companies are investing in tools to digitally transform their internal content management, creative development, production, and sign-off processes. Digital Asset Management and Marketing Resource Management applications are being implemented to automate processes, store creative assets, and facilitate approval processes. The resulting time and cost savings can be substantial.

Industry Outlook

There is no question that the future of advertising will look radically different from its past. The struggle for control of attention, creativity, measurements, and platforms will reshape the advertising value chain and shift the balance of power.

As we have witnessed in previous disruptive cycles, the future cannot be extrapolated from the past. With incumbent and new players in the advertising space, each attempting to turn the tide in its favor, it is imperative to plan for different future scenarios and build competitive capabilities for all of them.

Regardless of their positions in the advertising value chain, participants will need to cover the three key bases of innovation – consumer, business model, and business design and infrastructure – to make sure they keep up with the industry changes underway.

To learn more about this study, please contact us at iibv@usibm.com.

Related Publications

Please e-mail iibv@us.ibm.com to request a copy of any of the following publications or visit our Web site at ibm.com/iibv

- Navigating the media divide: Innovating and enabling new business models
- The end of television as we know it: A future industry perspective
- Media and entertainment 2010 – Open on the inside, open on the outside: The open media company of the future
- Vying for attention: The future of competing in media and entertainment
- Beyond access: Raising the value of information in a cluttered environment
- Profiting from convergence: Defining growth paths for telecom service providers
- Paths for telecom service providers

Contributing Authors

Steve Abraham, IBM Global Business Services, Global Media and Entertainment Industry Leader; Dick Anderson, IBM General Manager, Global Media and Entertainment, Communications Sector; Steve Canepa, IBM Vice President, Global Media and Entertainment Industry, Sales and Distribution, Communications Sector; Karen Feldman, IBM Institute for Business Value Media and Entertainment Leader; Steve Mannel, IBM Cable and Broadband Solutions Executive; Ekow Nelson, IBM Institute for Business Value Global Communications Sector Leader.

About IBM Global Business Services

With business experts in more than 160 countries, IBM Global Business Services provides clients with deep business process and industry expertise across 17 industries, using innovation to identify, create, and deliver value faster. We draw on the full breadth of IBM capabilities, standing behind our advice to help clients innovate and implement solutions designed to deliver business outcomes with far-reaching impact and sustainable results.

Notes

* IBM Global Business Services, through the IBM Institute for Business Value, develops fact-based strategic insights for senior executives around critical public and private sector issues. This executive brief is based on an in-depth study by the Institute's research team. It is part of an ongoing commitment by IBM Global Business Services to provide analysis and viewpoints that help companies realize business value. You may contact the authors or send an e-mail to iibv@us.ibm.com for more information.

names may be trademarks or service marks of others. References in this publication to IBM products and services do not imply that IBM intends to make them available in all countries in which IBM operates.

1. IBM surveyed more than 2,400 consumers across five countries: Australia, Germany, Japan, the United Kingdom, and the United States. Questions covered a range of topics, including consumer preferences and adoption of multimedia devices and content, impact to date on traditional content consumption and preferred pricing models for new digital content offerings.

2. Our interviews and panel discussions primarily involved executives from the advertising buy-side, including representatives from advertising agencies and major advertising companies across key advertising segments.

3. By "linear TV" we mean historical television programming that is not interactive and is available to viewers at a particular time on a particular channel. The broadcaster is in control of when and where the content is viewed. DVRs and VOD offer the opposite environment – the viewer is in control.

4. *Campaign bleeds* combine programming content with advertising to make the advertising more relevant to the program; *microversioning* means developing thousands of versions of an advertisement to make messaging more personalized and targeted to consumers, based on preferences, demographics, and location; *video ad flickers* are advertisements that are displayed for a very brief period of time; and by *pod management*, we mean determining the appropriate number of advertisements to include within a commercial break "pod" and paying careful attention to the ordering of the commercials.

5. IBM Institute for Business Value analysis.

6. Ibid.

7. Berman, Saul J. "Vying for Attention: The Future of Competing in Media and Entertainment." IBM Institute for Business Value, 2002.

8. Neus, A., P. Scherf, and F Porschmann. "Media Study 2005 (Germany): Consumption versus Interaction." IBM Global Business Services, 2005.

9. "The Global Entertainment and Media Outlook: 2005–2009." PricewaterhouseCoopers, June 2005. Not for further distribution without the prior written permission of Pricewaterhouse-Coopers LLP.

10. "The Global Entertainment and Media Outlook: 2007–2011." PricewaterhouseCoopers, June 2007. Not for further distribution without the prior written permission of Pricewaterhouse-Coopers LLP.

11. "Do you still pay for content?" Current TV. http://current.com/s/faq.htm#faq35

12. Story, Louise. "Publishers Creating Their Own In-house Ad Agencies." *The New York Times*, June 4, 2007.

13. Ibid.

14. Helm, Burt. "Which Ads Don't Get Skipped?" *Business Week*. September 3, 2007.

15. Ibid.

16. "What is Qmecom?" QDC Technologies. http://www.qdc.net.au/

17. Benkoil, Dorian. "TiVo, Nielsen Adding New TV and Video Measurement Tools." *Media Village*, August 15, 2007. http://www.mediavillage.com/jmr/2007/08/15/jmr-08-15-07/

18. "NBC, Group M Ink $1 Billion Upfront Deal." *MediaBuyerPlanner*, June 14, 2007. http://www.mediabuyerplanner.com/2007/06/14/nbc-group-m-ink-1-billion-upfront-deal/

19. Kane, Margaret. "Google to Buy Radio Ad Company." *CNET News*, January 17, 2006. http://www.news.com/Google-to-buy-radioad-company/2100-1024_3-6027499.html; "Google Announces TV Ads Trial." Google Press Release, April 2, 2007. http://www. google.com/intl/en/press/annc/tv_ads_trial. html; "What is Google Print Ads?" Google. http://www.google.com/adwords/printads/

20. "Google AdSense." http://www.google.com/adsense

21. Zimmermann, Kate. "Google Announces TV Ad Partnership with DISH Network and Astound Cable." *Reprise Media*, April 3, 2007. http://www.searchviews.com/index.php/archives/2007/04/google-announces-tv-ad-partnership-withdish-network-and-astound-cable.php

22. "dMarc from Google." http://www.dmarc.net/

23. "What is Google Print Ads?" http://www.google.com/adwords/printads/

24. "NextMedium." http://www.nextmedium.com/

25. "BlackArrow." http://www.blackarrow.tv

26. "TiVo Launches New Interactive Advertising Technology." TiVo Press Release, July 18, 2005. http://www.tivo.com/abouttivo/pressroom/pressreleases/2005/pr2005-07- 18.html

27. "Aerie Tuesdays, Simple and Brilliant Concept." *BrandNoise.* October 5, 2006. http://brand-noise.typepad.com/brand_ noise/2006/10/aerie_tuesdays_html

28. "Sugar Mama." http://www.virginmobileusa. com/stuff/sugarmama.do

29. "NBC.com to Offer Users Free, Ad-Supported Downloads of Popular Shows." NBC Universal Media Village press release, September 19, 2007. http://nbcumv. com/release_detail.nbc/ entertainment20070919000000-nbc46comtooffer.html

30. IBM Institute for Business Value analysis.

31. Berman, Saul J., Niall Duffy, and Louisa A. Shipnuck. "The End of Television As We Know It: A Future Industry Perspective." IBM Institute for Business Value, January 2006. In this previous IBM study, we segmented the video market into three categories: *Massive Passives*, who are generally content with traditional, "lean back" television experiences; *Gadgetiers*, who are drawn to the latest devices and are interested in participating and controlling the time and place of their media experiences; and *Kool Kids*, who also prefer interactive and mobile media experiences and rely heavily on content sharing and social interaction. It is these last two groups of consumers, the Gadgetiers and Kool Kids, that will likely lead the way with multichannel entertainment consumption.

32. Correspondence with Sir Martin Sorrell, October 24, 2007.

Chapter 4
From the Marketers' Perspective: The Interactive Media Situation in Japan

Satoshi Kono

Abstract This chapter provides insights into the Japanese interactive media situation from the marketers' point of view. In this field, because most service companies rely on advertising revenue models, understanding the marketers' perspective is one of the keys to success. For a background, I will begin by explaining some unique facts about the Japanese media situation, compared to the US market. Then I will describe the "AISAS®" framework advocated by Dentsu, Inc., which will clarify the marketers' point of view. Finally, I will conclude with a presentation of some interesting IPTV and user-generated content companies in Japan.

The Japanese Market: Some Unique Points

Thanks to Softbank, ADSL service competition started in 2001 in Japan. Since then its average price has decreased dramatically. Consequently, as of June 2007, 26.44 million households (54%) of 49.06 million total households in Japan had broadband access. About 13.79 million households (28%) had ADSL access and 9.66 million households (20%) were served FTTH.[1]

Broadband connection via cable was present in just 3.69 million households (7.5%), which is quite different from the situation in the US market. Cable service in general has much less presence in Japan than in USA.

On the contrary, mobile phone service has advanced far more quickly in the Japanese market. As of February 2008, 101.3 million people subscribed to mobile phone service and 87.45 million (86%) of them are able to use WAP (wireless application protocol), to access the Internet via mobile devices. As of 2006, 69.9 million subscribers' bandwidths (72.3%) were 3 G.[2]

According to a Video Research media contact report, from 2002, when broadband penetration started increasing, Internet usage surpassed radio, newspaper, and magazine consumption and was second only to TV in terms of media exposure time. As a result, Internet advertising expenditure has significantly expanded in the Japanese market, surpassing magazine advertising expenditure in 2007.[3] The 2007 advertising sales ranking of the top five were TV ($19.98 bn), newspaper ($9.46 bn), Internet ($6.0 bn), magazine ($4.59 bn), and radio ($1.67 bn).[4]

D. Gerbarg (ed.), *Television Goes Digital*,
© Springer Science + Business Media, LLC 2009

The "AISAS®" Framework Advocated by Dentsu, Inc.

The purchase model "AIDMA" was invented in the 1920s and had been useful in planning advertising campaigns. This model uses the following process: Capturing the targets' *a*ttention, arousing their *i*nterest, increasing their *d*esire to buy, having them *m*emorize the product, and leading to *a*ctions such as purchasing. To make customers follow these "linear" steps, campaigns were designed with mass media at their core. The "memory" becomes the key here. In a conventional media environment, there was a gap of time and location, between media contact and purchase. Therefore, the key function of advertisements was to have the customers "remember" the product or service.

The diffusion caused by the Internet has changed this purchase behavior substantially. One of the big changes is the act to "search." When consumers find interesting products or services through various media or friends, they immediately search for its information on the Internet. It has become much easier than ever before to get detailed information about products.

The second change is that information is now dispatched by the consumer himself. Each one of the consumers can easily put up personal reviews of a product on a blog or an SNS (Social Network Service). This customer review is then browsed by potential users and becomes an important source of information for decision-making.

The third is the change in purchase behavior. Now consumers can find product information on the Internet, and if they like it, they can jump to the EC (e-commerce) site and purchase it immediately. Even if the consumer decides to purchase from an actual store, information of the nearest store as well can be found on the Internet.

These changes have caused a shift in the traditional consumer purchase model used by advertising from AIDMA to AISAS®. This new purchase model was originated at Dentsu. The desire, memory, action (DMA) of the old model has changed into search, action, and share (SAS) in the new model.

- **"Search" becomes the new next step**

As mentioned earlier, consumers immediately search on the Internet for intriguing products they see in advertisements, TV programs, newspapers, and magazines. Therefore, effectively promoting this "search," and providing accurate information when searched, becomes crucial.

- **Then "Action"**

Conventional advertising campaigns required "memory," to maintain consumers' desire, until the time of purchase. Now Internet consumers can search for detailed information right away and, if they like it, they can purchase the product online immediately. In other words, AISAS® allows advertising to influence consumer purchase more directly than does conventional advertising.

- **The last step is "Share"**

When consumers consider buying a product, they often focus on the information dispatched by actual users on blogs or SNS. Reviews and voices of the actual customers are becoming an important trigger influencing customer decisions.

The consumers' voice about a product is often searched by potential consumers when they are considering a new purchase. This creates a cycle which expands "WOM" (word of mouth) on the Internet. The conventional AIDMA was a one-way process. AISAS® is characterized by the creation of a "Search" and "Share" cycle.

By using the AISAS® framework, marketers want to control everything, including WOM, CGM (consumer-generated media), SNS, and buzz.

IPTV and User-Generated Content Service Offerings in Japan

The following are examples of IPTV and user-generated content services in Japan.

- GyaO – http://www.gyao.jp/ – is the name of the IPTV service held by USEN Co. from April 2005. It provides free content: news, sports, bikini, movies, animation, drama, etc. As of July 5, 2007, they had 15 million subscribers.
- Nico Nico Douga – http://www.nicovideo.jp/ – is a modified movie Web site. It is more popular than YouTube in Japan. A company named Niwango executes advertisements and EC on it. They won the Japanese Good Design Award in 2007. On this Web site users can upload, view, and share video clips in the same way as on YouTube. Users can also overlay their comments directly onto the videos, which is an original feature of Nico Nico Douga, so that users can feel like they are watching the same movie at the same time with other people.
- Mixi – http://mixi.jp/ – is the largest SNS in Japan. It had 10 million subscribers, as of May 21, 2007. Gree – http://gree.jp/ – is the second largest SNS in Japan. It had 2 million subscribers, as of August 17, 2007. These two major SNSs are increasing their subscribers by utilizing video and mobile. Mixi started the function of uploading video and they increased their subscribers dramatically. Gree's joint project with KDDI, the second largest mobile operator in Japan, recently enabled it to increase its subscriber base by 1 million.
- Mobage-Town – http://www.mbga.jp/ – is a mobile-based, free game site which also provides SNS. Since most Japanese SNSs permit only 18-year-olds or older to enter, high school boys and girls had no chance to use SNS before this site opened, in February 2006. This site was created with users 18 years and younger in mind. As of June 2007, Mobage-Town has attracted 6 million subscribers, including young teenagers.

Notes

1. Ministry of Internal Affairs and Communications. http://www.soumu.go.jp/s-news/2007/070918_4.html
2. Telecommunications Carriers Association (TCA). http://www.tca.or.jp/eng/database/daisu/yymm/0802matu.html
3. Dentsu Inc. Advertising Expenditures in Japan. http://www.dentsu.com/news/2008/pdf/2008009-0220.pdf
4. Assuming $1 = ¥100

Part II
Technology: Content Creation
and Distribution

Chapter 5
Adopting Mobile TV: Technologies Seeking Consumers Seeking Content and Cool

Kas Kalba

Abstract This chapter will examine how mobile TV is likely to be used and whether and how the early usage could stimulate widespread adoption. It will also look at how mobile TV's antecedent technologies – television and mobile phones – developed in response to market forces and user adoption issues, and what lessons can be learned from this. The chapter will address several aspects of adoption that are likely to affect the evolution of mobile TV in the USA and internationally, using Everett Rogers' *innovation attributes* as a framework.[1] Finally, it will suggest how interactions between technology, user environment, content options, and service development will shape the new medium, often in ways unanticipated by the initial developers and promoters of mobile TV.

Eyeballing (Not So Clear) Mobile TV

When the advent of mobile TV was first announced a few years ago the health planners in New Zealand were jubilant. It was in New Zealand that the most recent research associating obesity with TV viewing had been completed,[2] and now there was a solution in sight – a form of TV viewing that kept the body moving, even if only at a slow pedestrian pace.

Then came the news from one of the early deployments in Europe that many of the mobile TV viewing sessions were indoors – and lasted 20–25 min rather than a few fleeting moments when changing buses or waiting in line at the grocery store.[3] Unless these longer indoor sessions involved the concurrent use of an exercycle, the possibility that mobile TV promoted physical lethargy could not be dismissed. With mobile TV we could watch television or videos wherever we were in a house or apartment – without even having to walk to the TV room or to search for and pick up the remote. Mobile TV could render us virtually immobile.

This chapter will not investigate the health implications of mobile TV. Still the literally opposite ways in which mobile TV could be used – on the go during short snippets of time or in a slow sedentary manner – reflects the difficult choices that technology developers, service operators, and content providers face in rolling out this new communications medium. These choices involve not only technical issues and options – for example, which of several terrestrial mobile TV networks (DVB-H, MediaFLO, T-DMB, or DAP-IP) to rollout – but also issues of adoption, usage, and media evolution.

The chapter will illustrate how technology choices are intertwined with behavioral, economic, and programming ones. As a case in point; will the average viewing session last 40 min, 4 min, or 40 s? There is conflicting evidence, depending on where one looks. Research on early users in the USA and Finland found that most of the viewing sessions were short (and occurred mostly outdoors),[4] while UK, Swedish, and Australian trial results[5] reflected long sessions (many indoors). In Singapore the evidence points to short indoor viewing sessions, mirroring the location of most mobile callers in Asia and, increasingly, in most of the world. Similarly, in Germany much of the early viewing, according to an industry source, lasted less than 5 min.[6] In Japan, where commutes to work are often by train and can last 2 h, a lot of the viewing may be neither indoor nor outdoor.[7]

So does the mobile TV service provider install a network capable of covering the "uncovered" areas of a city or country, so that consumers can have access to television, videos, and video-mail when they are outside of home and office or one that can penetrate buildings, including offices, elevators, and suburban homes, not to mention airports and restaurants?[8] Does the service operator try to mimic or directly retransmit conventional multichannel TV, which users with 40 min to spare may be looking for, or to aggregate video clips through agreements with LiveVideo and YouTube? Does the content provider assume a world of user-generated "programming," soap-opera *mobisodes*, or conventional movies, which the mobile TV viewer will be able to "bookmark" (mixed metaphor, apologies), search, and even re-edit using new handset storage and image manipulation capabilities? Will the top source of mobile video content be *Desperate Housewives* or disparate housewives and other P2P users?

Illustrations of Media Innovation

In fostering mobile TV adoption, technology developers have been very aware of video quality and channel-switching latency issues. Similarly, content providers are beginning to develop new forms of programming that respond to how they believe the new medium will be used. Yet, as the following examples illustrate, despite the best efforts of technology and content developers, the process by which a new media, such as mobile video, is adopted on a widespread basis is not always straightforward.

Early Adoptions of TV and Video

Although new TV transmission technology is continually improving the array of products and services available to consumers, notably (in recent years) HDTV, the impact of such developmental advances are often over-rated as influences on consumer decisions. For example, NTSC, the oldest and technically the weakest of the TV broadcast standards, nonetheless manages to attract more eyeballs world-wide than do transmissions using technically superior standards such as PAL and SECAM.[9]

There are several possible explanations for the popularity of NTSC, including its legacy status, the more pervasive presence of advertising-supported television (and TV viewing) in NTSC-based economies and cultures, the greater channel and, arguably, greater programming choices available in NTSC markets, and, possibly, the role of large mono-linguistic audiences in the major NTSC markets (notably the USA and Japan). Another possible factor is the number of TV sets available in households in different countries, which can range from one in the living room to one in every bedroom plus living room, den, and kitchen.

There is also an alternative explanation of the relationship between NTSC's poor resolution quality and viewer involvement. It is based on Marshall McLuhan's theory of media development – and of the cycle of *hot* and *cool* media.[10] Lack of definition or poor resolution, according to this perspective, is a core feature of cool media such as television (presumably the NTSC version); this in turn fosters viewer involvement. This type of explanation has not been widely accepted but cannot be overlooked as a source of researchable ideas. The appeal of early mobile phones with limited-resolution cameras and involvement-stimulating procedural challenges (such as figuring out how to store a photo once taken), particularly among young users, provides another example of the theory's potential applicability.

There is another hypothesis that the fewer the number of sets, the greater the viewing of mobile TV indoors, but this does not seem to bear out, as the UK has one of the highest TV set per household ratios.[11] Possibly, the convenience of three or four sets generates a demand for omnipresent TV reception, which only mobile or portable TV can satisfy.

The programming level of TV innovation can also be disruptive and perplexing. Now that Web-based sites such as YouTube and LiveVideo are offering hundreds of thousands of content generators the opportunity to distribute their video clips (whether home- or studio-made or both), the concept of niche programming is gaining currency. But will this be what mobile TV viewers want? When VCRs were introduced in the late 1970s the buzz was that specialty programs – music videos, how-to, documentaries, etc. – would now flourish, as viewers would no longer be shackled by the "lowest common denominator" scheduling of the mass audience networks. Yet for nearly a decade feature films, primarily major studio releases, dominated the video rental market. The economics of early VCR adoption (i.e., a small base of deployed recorders) called for even *more* common denominator programming than did the prime-time TV schedule.[12]

At the same time, the advent of a new TV viewing generation can sometimes be so revolutionary that it effectively determines the next form that the medium takes – and the next business model underlying the medium's evolution. This is what happened at the birth of pay cable TV. The risks of launching Home Box Office (now known as HBO) have been long forgotten but cannot be minimized. After $40 million of investment in the 1970s (equivalent to about $400 million today), HBO was on the verge of being closed down before it became clear that this would be one of the most successful TV businesses of all time.[13]

Once made available nationally by means of satellite distribution, the service rode the wave of "Yuppies" (young upwardly mobile professionals) who happened to be part of an even larger demographic wave – the Baby Boomers. As these young professionals reached their thirties, married, and had young children, a home-based way to enjoy recent movies well before they appeared on ad-supported television became an essential part of their lifestyles, allowing them most of the benefits of movie theater attendance without the hassles of organizing and paying for babysitting (provided by a younger smaller demographic group) and incurring the costs of two tickets, parking, and sodas and popcorn. Could mobile TV's adoption be driven by a similarly cohesive and growing demographic burst?

Lessons from the Mobile Phone

Mobile phone adoption is equally instructive. Similar to the VCR, which was first used for time shifting and TV program recoding and only later for playback of rented cassettes, mobile phones have gone through several stages of adoption and usage. Initially they were bought by car owners for use during commutes to work and only later became tools of pedestrian communication – on the street and in subways, restaurants, and nearly-landed airplanes. Still later the prepaid formula, along with data and other new applications, allowed a new range of users, from children to migrant workers to anonymity-seeking vendors, to adopt mobile phones. Machine use of mobiles and the transfer of funds in the form of air minutes that can be cashed in, represent a further evolution of the medium.

The adoption of mobile phones was affected not only by the income level of a market but also by the degree of income inequality. Early adoption markets have generally been "vertical" societies, whether the USA, Hong Kong, or Venezuela. Inequality means there is a high-end group that is willing to pay a premium for a new service such as mobile communications. At a later stage of mobile adoption, with prepaid mobile available, more egalitarian markets have achieved widespread adoption – for example, the 100%+ penetration levels in Eastern European countries, their aging populations notwithstanding. By contrast, vertical Latin American markets, despite their large youth populations, have fallen significantly behind.[14]

Another lesson is that price appears to affect usage more than basic adoption. The USA, with the lowest average usage rates in the developed world, has the highest usage.[15] An average mobile subscriber consumes about 1,000 min of air time per month, followed by users in Hong Kong, Finland, and Israel. Still another lesson is that usage is not primarily determined by culture. Heterogeneous Americans, talkative Cantonese and Israelis, and laconic Finns all manage to be high users. On the other hand, some countries where mobile phones are not subsidized, such as Italy and Sweden, have achieved very high mobile adoption rates, while others, such as the USA and Canada, where aggressive handset subsidies prevail, have below average adoption levels.[16]

There have been some other surprises with mobile phone adoption. One has to do with the possible role of climate – specifically, extreme climate – as an adoption driver. When countries such as Italy, Israel, Singapore, and, more recently, the United Arab Emirates achieved very high mobile penetration rates, the first reaction was that this proved that the role of climate was negligible if not nonexistent. After all, the early market leaders read like the winning entrants in the winter Olympics (Canada, Denmark, Finland, the Netherlands, Norway, Sweden, and the United States); so mobile came to be thought of as a northern communications medium, especially in Scandinavia. Yet the real driver has been *extreme* climate, not just cold climates. In early mobile days drivers could instinctively sense the advantages of mobile phones (over searching – and possibly queuing up – for a payphone) in equatorial heat as well as Nordic permafrost.[17] As suggested below, the adoption of mobile TV may be driven by environmental influences too, though different ones than climate.

Finally, to the extent that TV and video are just applications *piggybacking* on mobile phones, the lessons of "3G" mobile should not be overlooked. When 3G spectrum was first being auctioned in the UK and Germany in 2001 the business models assumed that there would be a dozen data and multimedia apps, multiple "killers" – from music downloading and Intranet access to video calls and location-based social networking. downloading videos on demand and video e-mail were occasionally assumed to generate 3G revenue streams, while the retransmission of existing TV channels (or modified versions thereof) was not projected as a 3G app. It was too mundane to make the list. Yet new media are often used for mundane things – or, as McLuhan put it, their content is the old media.

Deconstructing Mobile TV Adoption

Business discussions of mobile TV tend to focus on three issues:

- How the technology can be made to work better, particularly with respect to signal quality and channel capacity or bit rate
- What kind of content users want – cable channels, P2P, sports or music clips, movies on demand, custom-produced soap operas in mobisode form, or something else. (No one so far has suggested using built-in cameras as video mirrors, which could be checked before sending off personal video mail to a friend or employment recruiter.)
- What the mobile TV business model will be – subscription-based, pay-per-view, ad-supported, transaction-linked, or just fees-for-bits like the postal service and FedEx

In fact, there are many other facets to the question of what form the mobile TV will take as it evolves.

The video quality (frame rate, etc.), screen size and quality (luminescence as well as background light-sensitivity), channel capacity (compression, bandwidth, traffic density, etc.), channel-switching latency, handset design and specifications (including size, weight, and battery life), and digital interface (fingers, not bits, touch screen, 3D, or motion-sensitive) are some of the more obvious elements of what users may – or may not – respond to. What could be more critical, though less obvious (except to those who have studied effective telepresence), are the audio dimensions of the emerging medium.[18]

Good-quality ambient audio can make up for the limitations of a small screen and mitigate poor luminescence, particularly for users familiar with the general format and style of the programming they are watching – or with the person *at the other end* in a P2P context. Clear audio provides a frame of reference and enhances familiarity as well as communication redundancy. Transmitted through a headset, it can also assure privacy in common spaces, whether subway cars, airport lounges, or the back seat of an SUV, allowing the spaces to be shared by mobile TV viewing and other activities.

Across five editions of *Diffusion of Innovations* Everett Rogers developed a framework for understanding innovation adoption that continues to stimulate insights into the complexities of consumer response to new technologies.[19] Rogers identified the attributes of innovations that most affected the rate of adoption as (1) relative advantage, (2) compatibility, (3) complexity, (4) observability, and (5) trial-ability. Each merits some explanation and application to the case of mobile video.

Relative Advantage

Relative advantage encompasses functional and economic as well as status aspects. Mobile TV's advantages can be benchmarked against those of standard television, standard mobile phones, and standard hybrid or combo communications products, including previous versions of portable TV sets. Against standard TV sets, mobile TV offers great portability, especially as TV sets are once again getting larger (with large screen and HDTV specifications) and more immovable.[20] Compared to mobile phones, they offer video screening, whatever the content – in any case a dynamic add-on to the camera phones that were introduced a few years ago and came to outsell traditional cameras, including digitals. Finally, juxtaposed with portable TV sets, mobile phones with TV capability provide not only a more compact and lighter-weight implementation but also the many features of mobile phones – voice calls, photography, ringtones, texting, games, and phone directories, to mention a few.

Similarly, current and prospective mobile video services can be compared to corresponding multichannel TV distribution services (cable-, satellite-, DSL-, or FTTH-delivered), video-on-demand, open-air ad-supported broadcasting, satellite radio, nonvideo P2P, and so on. Generically, mobile video offers greater ubiquity of access when compared with multichannel video services, and more multimedia dimensionality (notably moving images, however stuttering or unstable these images may sometimes be – inside or outside buildings) when compared with the nonvideo media, including telephony, whether mobile or fixed.

At the same time tradeoffs need to be acknowledged in mobile video usage, such as potential service interruptions from lack of coverage, battery failure, poor ambient lighting (outdoor or indoor), more limited channel or content offerings, anxiety about self-broadcasting in a video mode (in a messaging or conferencing context), and complex interfacing, whether the bothersome channel-switching latency that technology providers are working aggressively to minimize or the too-many options and instructions that need to be learned to appreciate the full service offering.

More fundamentally, today's mobile TV product is likely to have a number of even more underlying deficiencies, including poor video, poor audio, a small screen, and no stability other than that provided by a loose hand or an object against which the mobile phone (with video capability) is leaned so that the user can experience an uninterrupted viewing experience, while sitting at a desk, in a bathroom, on a train, or in an airplane seat (in which case the object will itself most likely be propped up by the pull-down tray). Finally, another potential comparative deficiency of the mobile TV device is the interruptions it may be subjected to due to the accompanying mobile phone functions – receiving or making a call, taking a photo, texting a message, and so on.

A large component of the comparative advantage of mobile TV and mobile video is the price. Compared to broadcast TV, the price will invariably be unattractive as long as usage of mobile TV calls for subscribing to a platform data or multimedia service, then a package of mobile TV channels, and possibly additional fees for certain channels or VOD programs. However, this may be less so for short-session users, assuming they avoid standard commercials (which could cut 4-min sessions effectively in half) by paying these tiers of fees. For the 20- or 40-min session viewers, able to be couch potatoes anywhere, the price could be unsupportable, unless such ubiquitous *potato*-ness represents a higher state of being – or nonbeing – for which they are willing to pay the equivalent price of a massage.

On the other hand, compared to data access packages, which also cost about the price of a monthly massage (e.g. $60), mobile TV plans can be seen as relatively attractive, at least for users who gravitate to video inputs rather than text. Such plans are migrating to "all you can eat" in some markets but may revert to volume-based fees as the wireless "open access" movement gains traction (building on the "open access" provisions of the recently auctioned US C-block). Best of all would be ad-supported mobile TV, assuming that the ads were not very obtrusive or intrusive, in which case the main price impediment would be the video-compatible handset and add-ons such as specialty channels or major sports events.[21]

Finally, there is the matter of status. This will depend on how the handset and the programming or other content are perceived by the user's peers. For many members of the below 30 generation, using mobile TV to watch conventional broadcast or cable channels, when these are rarely cited as key sources of news and entertainment, could amount to a status-lowering rather than -raising association.

Conversely, for an addict of sports or news TV, the ability to access the latest key plays or announcements could render him or her an *influential* in the two-step process of information flow and status-determination that still governs many 50-year-olds (and above). In fact, we can expect some ersatz versions of mobile TV handsets to appear for status purposes just as in the early days of black and white TV outdoor antennas were sometimes purchased before the indoor sets. It was more important to be perceived as having TV than actually having it.

Compatability

How will mobile TV match our values, life styles, and behavioral patterns and practices? The overall answer depends on whose values and life styles are being talked about. In the USA most consumers continue to watch television at world-class levels (about a third of waking time), even as a growing minority is starting to watch less TV, switching its orientation for news and entertainment to laptops rather than *the tube* and drawing increasingly upon Web-based sources of content rather than upon the traditional networks and cable channels. Largely under 35, this is the new online generation that parents see navigating a new technological world and that teachers worry are losing all reading and writing abilities, even as most read and write more online than their older counterparts do with respect to newspapers and diaries.[22]

Even more interesting, and ultimately, perhaps, more disturbing, is a growing "in-between" group, for which both laptops and TV sets are familiar media. Outside the office and the performance of certain household functions (communicating with adult children, preparing tax returns, etc.), this group, whose members can be aged from 25 to 75, continues to rely primarily on television for entertainment, even though it is a television supplemented increasingly by NetFlix movie rentals (ordered online), VOD and DVD purchases, and TIVO or DVR activation.

The future of television, including mobile TV, hinges largely on how this group's tastes (regarding both media and messages) will evolve over the next 10 years. Will they switch to the laptop and mobile phone for entertainment and news content or will the tube assisted by the remote control and other accoutrements of TV viewing (NetFlix, TIVO, VOD, and possibly a *quad-play* wireless extension of TV) evolve sufficiently to provide a satisfying hybrid experience?

This in-between group – or *betweeners*, as its members can be called – is important because of its numbers (including many if not most Baby Boomers) and the residual strength of legacy technologies in most innovation diffusion.[23] The high numbers of hits attracted by the most popular YouTube videos (on the order of 100 million per day) should be kept in perspective. Each night the TV networks have a similar reach, just at any given moment. And channel clicking with the remote far surpasses the number of YouTube hits; worldwide, it undoubtedly surpasses the total number of hits of all Web sites, as there are close to twice as many TV sets as online PCs – and on average more users per remote than per mouse.[24]

So the legacy impact of traditional TV viewing, channel tuning, and program formatting remains great. Yet the force of new forms of video accessing behavior, including peer-to-peer forwarding of personal video mail (with assorted attachments of copyrighted work), cannot be denied. Nor can the strong attraction of young users to media and gizmos the use of which can be highly personalized along the lines of the iPod, the iPhone, and the Blackberry. Better still is the ability to put the media to use in the creation and cyber-sustenance of a virtual social community – or ecology of communities – of like-minded individuals.

Complexity

What then does a mobile video technology developer or service programmer to do? This is far from a trivial question, as the architectures and production modes involved in mass, segmented, niche (or "long tail"), and P2P video are so different. This also raises the issue of complexity as a key determinant of – in fact, often the major barrier to – adoption.

For the traditional media user, ease of use and simplification are overriding considerations. Challenged for years by the programming of a VCR to tape a TV show for later viewing, *traditionals* are often overwhelmed by PC behavior and find all but simple call placement befuddling when it comes to using a mobile phone. For such users a mobile TV device should ideally have many fewer functions than most current mobile handsets do and should look as much like a remote control as possible, replicating the same channels as are available on the cable set at home. In fact, signing up and billing for the service should be done through the same distribution channel as the user depends on for at least one other existing service and ideally for all services (voice, TV, mobile, and Internet, if any). The pricing should be simple, either fixed or usage-based and definitely not intricate combinations of the two.

For *betweeners* mobile TV can consist of multiple service choices, as it does largely today – with providers such as MobiTV offering multichannel packages and some pay add-ons, though ideally without having to pay the mobile operator for a platform service in addition to the bucket plan to be eligible to subscribe to the TV option; and other providers or mobile operators offering still other options (mobile VOD, ad-supported mobile TV, etc.). Whether most *betweeners* will be ready for an Internet-based version of mobile TV or for the downloading of a wide range of videos remains to be seen. It will depend in part on how streamlined the pursuit of these options can be made to seem and in part on the evolution of the Internet capabilities of this gradually aging segment of the population. Will the new *old* be able to play with the *new* (IP-based) new media? It is not a trivial question.

Finally, there is the always-online segment itself, made up of, what I call, *umbilicals*. This group is growing, though less quickly in the USA than the *betweeners* because of the demographic bulge of the Baby Boom and the limited IP-orientation of some young populations.[25] It is a group for which even the term *mobile TV* is largely irrelevant and has been replaced by *video* or more functional ones such as news, games, and social network, all with an online and increasingly wireless assumption built-in. Navigating "complex" options and pathways is rarely an inhibitor – and often a stimulus – of adoption. And distribution affinities are somewhere between Google and Facebook, on the one hand, and BitTorrent and YouTube, on the other, with many smaller emerging sites and services, dynamically morphing and evolving, in between.

A recent report from M:Metrics sought to compare the amount of mobile video viewing early adopters of different forms of the medium currently watch. According to their report just 0.6% of US mobile subscribers watched broadcast TV programming on their phones once or more per month last summer. This was partly because only a few phones currently support mobile broadcasts, the report noted. At the same time, the authors suggested that mobile viewers are more interested in bite-sized, YouTube-like clips (which 1% of mobile subscribers watched) as well as in short video messages sent from friends and family (which 2.7% of subscribers watched), not long TV episodes on rigid schedules.[26]

This may or may not represent a full comparison of the three ways of accessing video content over mobile phones, as the 0.6% (over 1 million subscribers, and possibly a major undercount[27]) who subscribe to a rigid-schedule service may watch several hours a week and certainly many hours per month, while their 1% and 2.7% counterparts may not be as routinely tuned to their respective ways of accessing video and may be watching very short clips, though possibly viewing them multiple times. In any case, the different ways (not mutually exclusive) of accessing video content wirelessly while on the go – in the car, on the street, or simply from room to room at home – need to be acknowledged and better understood.

Moreover, the complexity involved in serving each of these major segments is likely to be different, creating in turn immeasurable challenges for the innovation developer and purveyor attempting to serve more than one group with the same product or service. At least initially each of the three groups (or more) should be treated as a separate village in a different remote region of a market about which little is understood. Anthropologists should be sent in to advise the developers on what has a chance of resonating, as they have been sent by companies such as Nokia and Microsoft to India and Africa and elsewhere to determine local mobile and IT needs, requirements, and predispositions.[28] Then product development can begin.

Observability

A rarely examined aspect of innovation adoption is the degree of exposure involved. We know of course that within limits the public promotion of a new gizmo, a new program (or its creator or interpreter), offers a communications shower of hype and cool and buzz – and, in the extreme, frenzy at the nearest site of the product opening, whether iPhone, Indiana Jones 4, or hip-hop megastar Jim Jones. But it is the day to day public exposure – its simple observability – of an innovation that can in a drip-drop fashion enhance its acceptance and appeal more profoundly than the best of all conceivable promotional campaigns.

So mobile TV would seem to come with a built-in advantage – that of widespread public observability. Others, often many others, will be able to watch the watcher of mobile video – in the street, on the train, at the airport, even in an elevator (ear piece, please). Sooner or later our streets could become moving TV dens, desktop small-screens, and sports bar. We could all become peeping toms one or two or three degrees removed, watching the screen, watching someone watching, watching someone watching someone watching, ad infinitum. All of this would be good for the rapid propagation of mobile video around the world, just as the joggers with their Walkmen helped spread this earlier medium of personal and portable communications.

Why after all have the mobile phone as well as the bicycle outpaced the TV set and the wireline phone in worldwide adoption,[29] even though they are more difficult to use? In part it is their public visibility that has propelled what started as innovations into everyday utilitarian tools. In observability terms, the wireline phone, penned up in the house or office, has a much lower profile than the mobile does, even as it is simpler – and in most countries cheaper – to use. On the other hand, if much of the use of mobile TV turns out to be within the home, the observability impact could be much weaker. The heavy home use that has been picked up by surveys in England and Singapore and elsewhere could slow down the technology's diffusion, whether the signal is delivered by satellite, terrestrial waves, micro-DVD capsules, or carrier pigeon. The only person "observing" the mobile TV user would be his spouse (befuddled by why he was not watching the sports event on the large screen in the recreation room) or a teenage child (befuddled why he was not watching it on his laptop over the Web).

This is not the fastest way to propagate mobile video across the world, yet it may be fostered by technology improvements being worked on in the laboratories and being rolled out in the USA and elsewhere – more powerful building/penetration transmission networks, such as MediaFlo or high power S-band satellites. It will also be fostered in areas of high-density urban living where even today's transmission systems can penetrate into apartments and other dwelling units, especially where these are smaller – and therefore have less space further away from external walls – than in the suburban sprawl of the US market. In short, technology, behavior, life style, and adoption rate are more intertwined than the developers and providers of mobile TV may realize.

Trialability

This brings up the final dimension of Everett Rogers' diffusion framework. How easy it is to be able to try an innovation from a simple accessibility standpoint is critical to its diffusion. Without *trialability* a potential user cannot even begin to determine whether the new product or service – whether a new form of birth control in India, hybrid corn seed in Iowa, or multimode cooking slicer on late night TV – can provide value, be useable, and be worth the price. In the early days of black and white TV neighbors would gather at the homes of the first TV household on the block; this was trialability at work. In the mobile phone era, a friend or household member lets you try her phone.

Trialability is also affected by price. Once mobile phones became available on a prepaid basis – first in Mexico,[30] then in Portugal and Italy, and now worldwide— they could be tried by anyone with as little as $30 in their pocket.[31] Prepaid removed the constraint of contract commitments and monthly payments, effectively opening up the market beyond the salaried segment of the work force. In many countries this is the great majority of the population. Correspondingly, advertising-supported mobile TV would narrow the *trialability* margin to the price of a handset with mobile TV capability, which could also come down to $30. In Korea ad-supported mobile TV is being used by 9.7 million mobile subscribers, while pay mobile TV reaches 1.3 million.[32]

For the P2P mobile user there is also the matter of virtual trialability (and virtual observability, for that matter). In social networks operating in wireless cyberspace the trial of mobile TV or mobile video begins when a user sends a sample clip to a peer who may not have been previously exposed to the service. This form of trialability has the potential for exponential, viral testing of an innovation, where the new medium may simply be the handmaiden of a smart mob's interest in particular content, whether Paris Hilton's latest escapade or political misbehavior on the primary trail. In fact, the medium may be the message, as in the case of a "try this out" P2P e-mail with a link to a new social video site or new mobile TV offer.

A Fusion of Hand (Touch) and Eyeball (Vision)

We live in an age of fusion. Hybrid forms of music, fashion, cuisine, religion, even politics have been changing the culture since the withering of the age of the generic sometime in the 1980s. Mobile video is hybrid technology meets hybrid media, a hyphenated experience that may leave few as satisfied as when they first heard Elvis or the Beatles but less unsatisfied than when they can only watch television in predesignated spots or only talk or text on mobile phones and not watch. In McLuhan's lexicon mobile video brings a visual (hot) medium in close contact with a tactile (cool) one. It allows the viewer to have television in the foreground or background wherever he or she is – not only while trying to fall asleep in a bedroom or prepare a meal in the kitchen or iron clothes in the den.

Mobile TV also offers a fusion of indoor and outdoor spaces and what we have traditionally done in them. If mobile phones took an indoor activity – making telephone calls from home – public (in the process privatizing public spaces), how much greater might be the effects of mobile TV? The mobile phone migrated a portion of what generally ranged from 100 to 1,000 min of calling per month, depending on the country, to outside public spaces and other buildings (offices, malls, stores, restaurants, etc.). Now mobile TV could migrate a portion of the 50–150h (or 3,000–9,000 min) of home TV viewing that individuals in different countries engage in to new outdoor places as well as work locations places inside the home that TV has not penetrated to date. The TV viewing that already occurs in airport lounges – for lack of anything better to do – will now spread across the globe.

In this volatile context, designers of mobile video handsets and services will need to learn how to reconcile the requirements placed on mobile video by a wide range of viewing environments. The phrase "Come on over and let's watch some TV," will come to mean a lot of different things, depending on where the *here* is – a public place, an office, a bedroom, almost anywhere but a TV room or den. Similarly, designers need to account for the interaction of senses involved in the mobile TV viewing experience – the respective needs of eyes and ears and hands and fingers, which will themselves vary depending on whether the user is stationary or moving, standing or sitting, and simply viewing or intricately interacting with their mobile video devices.

Ultimately, mobile video may represent a fusion of the relational, even exhibition-istic need of the *extrovert* to carry on many relationships and those of the peeping, passively inclined *introvert*, interested mainly in reception and not expression. The introvert will be drawn to long-session *mobile TV*, while the extrovert will thrive on short-session, interactive *mobile video*. The former, an old-media traditional, will be disoriented without a host of program options to choose from using mobile phone as both clicker and screen, while the latter, a wireless umbilical, will be lost without the social network-maintaining inclusivity of user-generated and -exchanged video clips and messages. Most of us will fall somewhere between these two prototypical personalities of mobile TV. We will be hybrids seeking fusion.

The digital transmission streams underlying mobile technology allow all of these forms of video – and of engagement with video – to coexist on the same network. Digital is the platform of multimedia fusion. At the same time, service designers and providers face difficult issues in the rollout of mobile TV. For *tra-ditionals*, "keep it simple" is the monolithic guideline – simple to activate, simple to use, simple price plans, simple and recognizable programming, simple channel switching, and simple and straightforward customer care (voice-based) when things go complicated for one reason or another. For wireless *umbilicals*, options, features, personalization, video presence, and ability to generate, store, and manipulate con-tent may be as important as FOX, CNN, ESPN, and The Weather Channel.

This leaves the hybrids and *betweeners*, who sometimes want the familiarity of old-media TV, other times want greater control though VOD and TIVO-like control, and occasionally want to prove to themselves and their children or grand-children that they can navigate the new cyber-virtual-video universe. Cool, they say, when they manage to do it – and then revert to *John Adams*, episode 5, segment 22, bookmarked on their mobiles; or to the playback of last night's scoring pass, while shaving in the bathroom, their mobile propped up between the soap dish and the ceramic glass stuffed with extra toothbrushes and backup razors. Mobile TV – who would have guessed?

Notes

1. E. Rogers, *The Diffusion of Innovations*, fifth edition, Free Press: New York, 2003.
2. See the study led by Dr. Robert Hancock, as summarized in 2005 in the *International Journal of Obesity*.
3. Trial results from Oxford, UK, as reported by Dave Campbell, O2 executive, at CTIA Wireless 2006, Las Vegas, April 5–7, 2006; 59% of the use was indoors, mainly at home, but also in the workplace at lunch time. Similar results were reported from an early trial in Milton Keynes, UK.
4. See, for example, C. Sodergard, ed., Mobile television – technology and user experiences (Report on the Mobile-TV project), VTT, 2003, pp. 197–198.
5. A Swedish survey of early users found that two thirds of viewing took place at home, mostly during 7–8 a.m. and 5–10 p.m., with sessions typically lasting 30 min. Respondents also indicated that they preferred a flat monthly pricing approach, with no advertising (at least in content they were paying for). See C. Moore, "Swedes prefer to watch mobile TV at home – study," *DMeurope.com*, December 19, 2006.
6. An Ericsson executive reported that 35% of the viewing sessions lasted 5 min or less at CTIA Wireless 2006.
7. This commuting context, combined with a social prohibition of making and receiving voice calls, is one of the reasons the i-modemobile service has been so successful in Japan and not highly successful in most other countries.
8. With ear pieces for audio reception, mobile TV need not disturb passers-by in public places.
9. PAL is in use in most of Europe, with the major exceptions of France and Russia, where SECAM is the dominant standard. NTSC prevails in the United States, Japan, and Korea, among other countries.
10. For a review of McLuhan's classic *Understanding Media* and its applicability to recent media developments, see K. Kalba, "Understanding McLuhan's Media: 40 Years After," *InterMedia*, Vol. 32, No. 3, 2004.
11. Ofcom, the UK regulator, reported in 2004 that more than 80% of UK households had two or more TV sets, including 8% with five or more. By comparison, the Federal Statistical Office in Germany reported that at the beginning of 2004 about 40% of the households had more than one TV set.
12. Eventually Jane Fonda's exercise video broke onto the charts, calling on the widespread recognition of her name and the repeatability of this first successful how-to video. By this point tens of millions of VCRs had been purchased in the USA.
13. Private communication, executive in Time, Inc.'s Video Division, ca. 1974.
14. For a further explanation of why ageing Eastern Europe has out-adopted youthful Latin America, see K. Kalba, "Why Eastern Europe's Aging Population Has More Mobile Phones Than Latin America's Younger One," *Inter-American Dialogue's Latin America Telecom Advisor*, September 17–21, 2007, p. 1. A broader examination of mobile phone adoption factors is provided in K. Kalba, "The Global Adoption and Diffusion of Mobile Phones – Nearing the Halfway Mark," *Draft*, August 2007, Program on Information Resources Policy, Harvard University. See also K. Kalba, "The Adoption of Mobile Phones in Emerging Markets," *International Journal of Communication*, 2008, forthcoming.
15. K. Kalba, "The Global Adoption and Diffusion of Mobile Phones," op. cit., pp. 33–38.
16. Ibid., p. 59.
17. Ibid., pp. 39 and ff.
18. The author first learned of the critical importance of audio to effective TV conferencing in an early demonstration project connecting Harvard and MIT classrooms in 1973.
19. E. Rogers, *Diffusion of Innovation*, fifth edition, Free Press: New York, 2003; see pp. 219–266.
20. Traditionally, TV set product classes have experienced about a 10–15-year time cycle, often overlapping with other product classes. The product classes that can be easily demarcated include black and white sets, console sets (including combos with radios and record players),

color TV sets, small sets (for use in kitchens or other secondary viewing locations), portable sets, large-screen projectors, sets with built-in VCRs and DVD players, and large-screen TVs.

21. There is also some evidence that ad recall is much higher on mobile TV compared to other forms of TV viewing, though this may be a novelty effect. See "U.S. Mobile video flying," *telecoms.com*, June 27, 2007.

22. Not everyone under 35 falls into this group, as a significant number of young Americans do not know how to use the Internet, have little access to it, or have largely given up using it, according to PEW Research Center and other sources.

23. Even *Wired* has acknowledged this residual strength of the old media in reviewing its forecasts of the last 15 years. See "What We Got Right – and Wrong," *Wired*, June 2008.

24. The number of Internet users worldwide in 2003 was 725 million, compared to 1.15 billion TV households (averaging four members), as cited in G. Sciadas, ed., *From the Digital Divide to Digital Opportunities: Measuring Infostates for Development*, ITU and Orbicom, 2005, p. 19.

25. This includes some poor, rural, and/or immigrant youth with limited access to PCs as well as some who have quit the Internet largely to simplify their lives.

26. See D. Frommer, "As AT&T Bulks Up on Spectrum, Another Mobile TV Plan Fizzles," *Silicon Alley Insider*, October 9, 2007.

27. The two major services that offer such broadcast services over mobile report a subscriber base of 5 million.

28. As described, for example, in S. Corbett, "Can the Cellphone Help End Global Poverty?" *The New York Times Magazine*, April 13, 2008, pp. 35 and ff.

29. There are about 1.8 billion households with TV sets and about 2 billion bicycle owners, whereas mobile phone subscribers are edging up towards 4 billion. Certainly the use of TV sets can be shared by the many members of a large household, but in developing markets this is also the case with mobile phones.

30. Prepaid was first introduced (unsuccessfully) in the Mexican market in 1992. They were re-introduced in 1993 as the peso crisis was unfolding and caught on. From there the concept spread to Europe.

31. The author purchased a phone with minutes of use included for this price both in Europe and in the Caribbean last year; the price may be lower in markets such as India and Bangladesh.

32. "Mobile Broadcast TV Users in Korea Reach 11 Million," *Gamdala Mobile TV Blog*, March 25, 2008.

Chapter 6
Television Via Satellite

Stephen P. Dulac and John P. Godwin[1]

Abstract This chapter provides an overview of satellite direct-to-home (DTH) digital television in the Americas. It covers the history and some technical specifications. Differences between satellite DTH's ATSC (Advanced Television Systems Committee) and terrestrial systems are compared. The paper concludes with notes on key technology evolutions that allowed the introduction of digital DTH satellite service and contribute to its continued growth today.

Introduction

Many consumers worldwide have the option to receive digital television from one or more sources today: terrestrial broadcasts, cable and satellite systems, high-speed Internet connections as well as recorded and prerecorded media like DVDs. However, it was satellite distribution in the United States in 1994 that first provided consumers with widespread opportunity to receive digital television. Addition of IPTV functionality to satellite STBs allows new services to be delivered via customers' broadband connections.[2]

The Development of Digital Satellite Delivery

The History

Although satellite DTH television delivery was the dream of futurists for decades, little technological progress was made before 1980. DTH service in the United States began in 1979 when the FCC declared that receive-only terminal licensing

---

[1] This chapter is based on an earlier paper published in the *Proceedings of the IEEE*, Vol. 94, No. 1, January 2006.

[2] DIRECTV Plus® HD DVR receiver is Media Share compatible with any Intel® Viiv™ processor technology-based PC.

D. Gerbarg (ed.), *Television Goes Digital*,
© Springer Science + Business Media, LLC 2009

was no longer mandatory and individuals started installing dishes, initially with a diameter >4 m, to receive signals intended for distribution to cable head-ends. From roughly 1985 to 1995, millions of 2–3-m dishes were purchased by individuals to receive these analog cable feeds. Although dish installations could cost several thousand dollars, the feeds were initially available without a monthly charge. Reference [1] discusses various DTH business startup attempts in the 1980s that would have used smaller dishes, but planned to charge a monthly fee. None were financially successful. The major challenge for satellite system design was the need to generate, within project cost constraints, sufficient satellite power levels for a practical dish size while meeting reception electronics requirements consistent with consumer electronics price expectation.

The digital DTH satellite era began in 1994 and quickly captured the "big dish" market and other latent market demand. Table 6.1 summarizes satellite DTH growth in the United States over the last 20 years [2–6].

The link geometry for homes in the contiguous 48 states typically affords an elevation angle, which is the line-of-sight angle above the horizon, of at least 30. This geometry means that potential obstacles such as trees or adjacent houses are rarely an actual impediment. The link geometry also means that multipath from hills and buildings are not an issue, especially for microwave frequencies used by DTH systems. Except for the era of big dish DTH, which used a C-band downlink of 4 GHz, all DTH systems in the Americas have operated in the higher frequency Ku-band. For regulatory purposes, the DTH bands are divided into "fixed satellite service" and "broadcasting satellite service" bands. For systems licensed in the Americas for the Broadcasting Satellite Service (BSS) [7,8], the uplink frequencies are in the band 17.3–17.8 GHz and the downlink frequencies are in the band 12.2–12.7 GHz. For Fixed Satellite Service (FSS) systems in the United States, the most common uplink and downlink bands are 14.0–14.5 GHz and 10.7–11.2 GHz, respectively. In either band the primary link environmental impediment is moisture along the line of sight – that is, rain – that causes signal fades. This degradation can be sufficiently estimated to establish margins for practical system designs [9].

DTH systems themselves cause intra-system interference, like that of cross-polarized signals at the same frequency, and intersystem interference, like that from satellites at neighboring orbital locations received via consumer receive dish

Table 6.1 US DTH households

Households with service subscriptions	Year-end figures in millions [2–6]				
	1984	1989	1994	1999	2004
C-band (analog, 2–3 m dish)	~7	~2.7	2.2	1.6	0.27
FSS Ku (digital, .90 m dish)	–	–	0.25	14[a]	–
BSS Ku (digital, 0.45 m dish)	–	–	0.35	10	24
Total Sat DTH	~0.7	~2.7	2.8	13	24
Total TV households	84.9	91.6	94.9	100.8	110.3
Sat DTH penetration	<1%	3%	3%	13%	22%

[a]FSS Ku peaked at about 2.3 M subscribers during 1999

side-lobes. Intersystem interference is illustrated in Figs. 6.2 and 6.3. Careful coordination via ITU, FCC, and other governmental agencies and direct coordination between system operators has kept interference to an acceptable level.

- The advent of Digital occurred round 1990 when a number of key technologies had made sufficient progress to make all-digital satellite DTH economically practical. These developments provided numerous benefits unavailable with analog solutions: Smaller consumer dish size
- Tuning to dozens of channels without the need to re-point the dish
- More standard definition (SD) television channels per unit Radio Frequency (RF) bandwidth
- More consistent quality and potential for improved quality, such as HDTV, and increased number of services without increase in the dish size
- New innovative services using high-quality, high-speed digital path into multiple homes
- Although DTH system designers recognized that they could utilize progress in key areas like video/audio coding and cost reductions in Very Large Scale Integrated (VLSI) circuit technology, several areas were perceived as fundamental technical system interfaces and constraints: Home DTH receiver outputs compatible with home off-air television inputs
- Consumer dish and outdoor electronics power and control via established interfaces
- Set-top boxes consistent with consumer electronics industry practice, such as use of wireless remote controls and adherence to UL safety guidelines
- RF link design, such as RF channel bandwidth and polarization reuse, consistent with existing FSS and BSS frequency plans

The first three constraints, along with a cost target, established many of the high-level requirements for initial DTH home receivers. The last constraint set many fundamental requirements on the design of the RF portion of uplink centers, DTH satellites, and tuner circuitry of home receivers. For the BSS system designs, such as the DirecTV system that went online in 1994, the designers achieved compatibility with ITU BSS Plan for the Americas, [7,8], that based its intersystem interference planning on an analog FM implementation with 1 m receive dishes. Reference [10] provides additional perspective on first-generation digital DTH system designs, including a digital DTH link budget.

The major digital DTH systems in the Americas, as of January 2005, are summarized in Table 6.2.

Service Offerings

The "pay" business model of satellite DTH created a technical role for the DTH service provider that had no counterpart in traditional advertising-supported terrestrial broadcasting. Each satellite DTH provider sets the direction and tempo of

Table 6.2 Major digital DTH systems in the Americas (January 2005)

System	DIRECTV	Dish Network	Bell ExpressVu	Star Choice	Sky Brasil	Sky Mexico	DIRECTV Latin America
Website	http://www.directv.com	http://www.dishnetwork.com	http://www.bell.ca	http://www.starchoice.com	http://www.sky.tv.br	http://www.sky.com.mx	http://www.dirctvla.com
Service area	USA	USA	Canada	Canada	Brazil	Mexico	South and Central America
Subscribers	14 M	11 M	1.5 M	0.8 M	1.1 M	1.1 M	.8 M
Services							
Subscription	X	X	X	X	X	X	X
Per Per View	X	X	X	X	X	X	X
Local channels	X	X	X	X	X	X	X
HDTV	X	X	X	X			
DVR	X	X	X				
Interactive	X	X	X		X	X	X
Satellites							
Number in service	8	6	1	2	1	1	2
>1 orbit slots	Yes	Yes	No	Yes	No	No	No
Bands used (Ku = 10–17 GHz) (Ka > 18 GHz)	BSS Ku, FSS Ku, FSS Ka	BSS Ku, FSS Ku	FSS Ku	FSS Ku	FSS Ku	FSS Ku	FSS Ku
Transmission							
Transport	System B	System A	System A	System C	System A	System A	System B
Program Guide (EPG)	Proprietary	System A with proprietary extensions	System A with proprietary extensions	Proprietary	System A with proprietary extensions	System A with proprietary extensions	Proprietary
CA Provider	NDS	Nagra	Nagra	Motorola	NDS	NDS	NDS
Middleware Provider	NDS	OpenTV	OpenTV		OpenTV	OpenTV	OpenTV
Reception							
Dish size (typical)	45 cm	45 cm	45 cm	60 cm	60 cm	60 cm	60 cm
Number of dishes	1 or 2	1 or 2	1	1	1	1	1

evolution of its delivery system. It may or may not tend to use open standards, but service must be compelling, cost effective, and secure. Each new technology evolution can require a substantial investment in customer education, customer premises equipment provisioning and installation, and back-office systems, such as billing. For the US providers, nurturing customer relationship has been one of their great successes. One satellite DTH company has been selected as having the highest customer satisfaction rating among all multi-channel programming providers for seven out of the last nine years [11].

DTH system service offerings include the following:

- Subscription TV
- Pay per view (PPV)
- *Local channel rebroadcasts.* To provide a seamless, high-quality experience, satellite DTH services offer subscription packages of local NTSC "off-air" stations. In the United States, by law [see sidebar on "US Local Channels Regulatory Evolution"], these stations may only be rebroadcast into the same "local market" where they are broadcast terrestrially. By year-end 2004, Dish Network had announced that it was re-broadcasting local channels into 152 markets representing 93% of the US population, while DirecTV's totals were 130 markets and 92% respectively.
- *High-definition television (HDTV).* Since the enjoyment of HDTV necessitates purchase of- relatively expensive HD monitor, HDTV viewer-ship has grown slowly in the United States since ATSC terrestrial broadcasts were initiated in 1998 [12].
- *Digital video recorders (DVRs).* DVRs have proven to beexcellent ancillary application for satellite services. Aggressive marketing of new receiver types to "early adopters" gave US satellite service providers majority of all DVR households at the end of 2004. DVR application benefits from two basic satellite DTH service attributes, availability of electronic program guide (EPG) information and all-digital broadcasts. For a given program, as indicated in the EPG, digital content can be directly recorded to a hard disk drive without the need to perform A/D conversion.
- *Interactive television.* The simplest interactive television services are not associated with any particular video services: for example, an electronic program guide, or screens displaying personalized and localized information, including weather, news, financial information, lottery results, and so on [13]. More complex interactive services are integrated with program video which requires more complex implementations. Due to great complexity and need for careful management of receiver resources, technologies deployed to date by satellite DTH operators have used proprietary middleware implementations (Table 6.2). Considerable work has been done to create standards for interactive services, and the ATSC "ACAP" standard [14] and the OpenCable "OCAP" standard [15] are noteworthy examples.
- *Home networking.* DTH providers' newest services feature satellite receivers with integrated home networking features, including support for connecting to a terrestrial broad-band path such as DSL. Networked receivers enable digital television to be recorded on one receiver and played on another. The linkage to

the Internet permits remote DVR scheduling over the Internet and applications such as transfer of electronic photos from cell phones to the family's home network [16].

- *Special markets.* Although satellite DTH may be symbolized by small roof-mounted antenna on a single-family home, services provide programming for various special markets including multiple dwelling units' hospitality market of hotels, bars, and restaurants, mobile vehicles [17]; and commercial aircraft [18].

DTH System Architecture

Figure 6.1 provides a simplified diagram of an all-digital multi-channel satellite DTH system.

Broadcasting Facility

Most DTH subscription channels are delivered to the DTH broadcasting or uplink facility via existing "backhaul" satellites or fiber. These backhaul signals are often the same feeds used to deliver programming to other satellite and cable distributors. Some programs, such as theatrical films for PPV, arrive at the facility as prerecorded

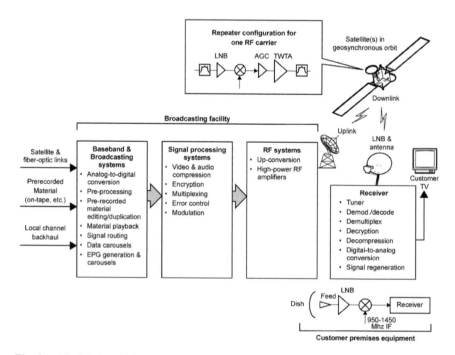

Fig. 6.1 All-digital multichannel satellite DTH system

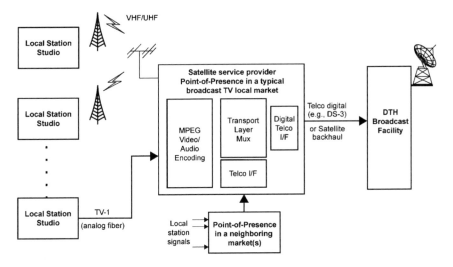

Fig. 6.2 In-market local television backhaul solution

digital tapes. Satellite delivery of local television channels has necessitated use of in-market digital facilities to preprocess and backhaul, signals to a DTH broadcasting facility via leased terrestrial transmission facilities. Figure 6.2 summarizes the components of a typical in-market backhaul solution. The broadcasting facility provides a number of functions common to any broadcasting facility, such as incoming signal monitoring, adjustment, and resynchronization, signal routing within the facility, and for prerecorded content, quality control, cloning, and playback. Program content for most channels is unchanged by the facility. Certain channels, by agreement with the originator, may have commercials or promotional spots inserted at points identified, by in-band tones for example, by the originator. Prerecorded material is copied from digital tape masters to video file- servers. Video servers use redundant arrays of independent disk (RAID) technology and play back the content on a digital satellite channel at a time established by the daily broadcast schedule. The "pay" business model of DTH systems also requires that the broadcast site provide conditional access equipment in addition to service information/electronic program guide (SI/EPG) equipment, compression encoders, and multiplexing, error control, and modulation equipment. The conditional access system, which includes equipment within the home, permits customer access to programming services only when certain conditions are met – for example, the customer's account is in good standing and he is located in a geographic area where that particular programming is available per agreement with the content owner, e.g., is not subject to sports blackout. The SI/EPG equipment creates data streams that are used by in-home electronics to display information about the programming channels and individual programs.

The EPG data typically include program title, start and end times, synopsis, program rating for parental control, alternate languages, and so on. The signal processing equipment performs redundancy reduction processing (compression) on both television video and audio. Digital video/audio is typically routed within the broadcasting facility in the serial digital component format [19] at 270 Mb/s, but is reduced to the range of 1–10 Mb/s prior to transmission via compression encoding. This signal processing dramatically reduces the transmission path investment – in satellites, for example – and conversely also increases the entertainment channels available for a given amount of transmission bandwidth and investment. Most operational digital DTH systems in the Americas use Motion Picture Experts Group (MPEG)-2 encoding standard or a proprietary system with nearly identical signal processing characteristics. The compressed video/audio streams from multiple programming channels are typically multiplexed into a single high-speed stream. Each of the constituent streams may have a fixed data rate or individual channel rates can vary dynamically depending on their instantaneous "image complexity." The latter approach is called statistical multiplexing. With either method, the resultant stream is processed by forward error control (FEC) logic. The FEC method, often concatenating convolutional block codes, provides excellent delivered quality at signal-to-noise thresholds below those available with previous analog methods. For systems deployed in the 1990s, quadrature phase shift keying (QPSK) modulation was used in virtually every instance in the Americas. This modulation is more bandwidth-efficient than binary PSK' is a constant envelope modulation and therefore appropriate for satellite transmission systems with repeater output stages driven into the limiting region.

Broadcasting Satellites

Each uplink signal from the broadcasting facility or facilities is received and rebroadcast by an RF "transponder" of a frequency-translating repeater on board a geosynchronous communications satellite. For BSS band operation, the satellite receives signals in the range 17.3–17.8 GHz [8], down converts each signal by 5.1 GHz, and retransmits it in the range 12.2–12.7 GHz [7]. The satellites used in DTH systems are very similar in architecture to geosynchronous communications satellites that have been deployed for international and domestic telecommunications since the mid-sixties. For DTH systems, the satellites' greatly increased physical size and weight permit relatively high levels of received solar energy- and hence dc power – and relatively large onboard antennas enabling downlink beam shaping. Figure 6.3a illustrates a typical DTH satellite as deployed in the 1990s [10,20–22]. The configuration is dominated by sun-oriented solar panels for dc power generation and parabolic reflectors to create downlink beams.

Each satellite's communications "payload" is a microwave frequency-translating repeater. A broad-band front-end receiver, one per polarization, down-converts to the downlink frequency and drives multiple RF chains, one per carrier, with each RF chain or "transponder" having a high-power Traveling Wave Tube (TWT) transmitter [10]. Typically, each TWT amplifier has a saturated-power rating of 240 W [20]. The primary repeater functional elements are shown within Fig. 6.1.

In the United States,, a single system operator often uses multiple satellites at a given orbital location and, additionally, multiple satellites at adjacent orbital

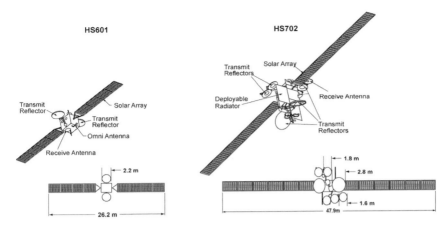

Fig. 6.3 Progress in satellite platforms provides more delivered bandwidth per spacecraft and bandwidth reuse via spot-beam technology, (**a**) D1 (HS601). (**b**) D11 (HS702)

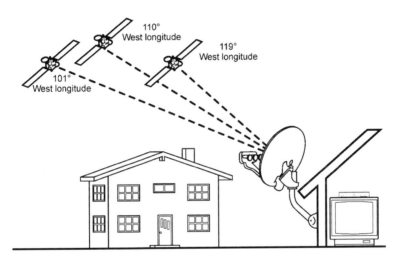

Fig. 6.4 Use of adjacent orbital locations permits spectrum reuse

locations to increase the total available capacity. Multiple satellites at a single orbital location – separated in longitude by at least 0.1° – permits full use of the available spectrum by effectively pooling the capabilities of several satellites. This implements futuristic visions from past decades for massive "earth-facing communications relay platforms" without the necessity for a single physical vehicle. Use of adjacent orbital locations permits spectrum reuse by a single system operator. This is illustrated in Fig. 6.4.

A single orbital location – separated in longitude by at least 0.1 – gives full use of the available spectrum by effectively pooling capabilities of several satellites. This implements futuristic visions from past decades for massive "earth-facing communications relay platforms" without the necessity for a single physical vehicle. Use of adjacent orbital locations permits spectrum reuse by a single system operator.

Customer Electronics

As illustrated in Fig. 6.5, the DTH customer electronics consists of a small aperture antenna and low-noise block down-converter, an integrated receiver/decoder (IRD) unit (or simply "receiver") and a handheld remote control. The antenna is typically an off-set parabolic reflector in the range of 45–60 cm in diameter. The RF signal collected by the horn at the focus is coupled with a low-noise amplifier and then block down-converted to an L-band IF of 950–1,450 MHz, or as wide as 250–2,150 MHz for recent models. The "outdoor" electronics, shown diagrammatically in Fig. 6.1, receives low-voltage dc power via the same coaxial cable used to deliver the down-converted signal into the customer's home and, specifically, to the receiver. The receiver provides the many functions listed on the extreme right in Fig. 7.1. The unit's circuitry includes an IF tuner, a QPSK demodulator, FEC decoder, stream de-multiplexer (to capture a single programming channel), decryptor under conditional access control, an MPEG video/audio decoder, and TV signal regenerator. In the Western Hemisphere, most DTH receivers also utilize a replaceable "smart card" with an embedded secure microprocessor used to generate cryptographic keys for decryption of individual services. In the event that security is compromised, the system operator may only need to replace the smart card to allow economic upgrade of a portion of the conditional access logic instead of far more costly replacement of entire receivers. The receiver outputs signal to various home entertainment devices such as standard definition, HD televisions and audio amplifier systems. The receiver may have front panel controls but it is routinely controlled via signals from a handheld remote control using IR, and in many cases – RF transmission.

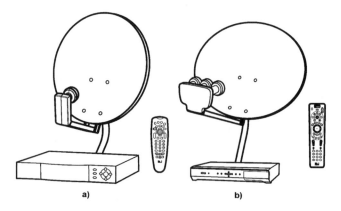

Fig. 6.5 DTH customer electronics. (**a**) ~1995. (**b**) ~2005

ITU Recommendation ITU-R BO.1516 [23], published in 2001, presents a generic reference model for a digital DTH receiver. This model presents the common functions required in a satellite IRD. The reference model is arranged in layers, with the physical layer located at the lowest level of abstraction, and services layer located at the highest level.

Terrestrial DTV receivers share these reference model functional elements, with notable differences that reflect both business and technical differences in these services.

- The physical and link layers of the terrestrial receiver are designed to support antennas and modulations required for off-air (terrestrial) signal reception.
- The conditional access layer of the terrestrial receiver is optional, whereas in satellite systems all services, even local channel rebroadcasts, tend to be encrypted. While there are "digital-cable-ready DTVs" having decrypt capabilities, there are no "satellite-ready DTVs."
- The EPG and interactive service capabilities tend to be highly customized in a satellite receiver, to meet the competitive needs of the service operator.

Common Functional Elements of Digital DTH Systems in the Americas

Beginning in 1994 and driven by business imperatives, the first digital DTH satellite systems were launched prior to the creation of industry standards for either modulation and coding, or transport and multiplexing, or video and audio source encoding. Nevertheless, standards for digital DTH application did follow, and there are four of note for the Americas: ITU System A/DVB (used by Dish Network, Sky Brasil, Sky Mexico, and Bell ExpressVu), ITU System B (used by DirecTV and DirecTV Latin America), ITU System C (used by Star Choice), and the more recent ATSC A/81 standard (adopted in 2003, but not yet in use).

A high-level description of the first three standards is presented in "Digital multi-program television systems for use by satellites operating in the 11/12 GHz frequency range," International Telecommunication Union, Recommendation ITU-R BO.1516, 2001 [23]; Table 6.3 excerpts some summary characteristics from Table 6.1 of that document, which correctly concludes that common receiver designs supporting all of these systems are possible. It is to be noted that as service offerings evolve, architectures of service providers in the Americas may diverge from these standards.

Analog to Digital Evolution

The first decade of evolution- culminating in 1994 with the introduction of all-digital DTH- is marked by maturation of four key technologies (Table 6.4). These technologies combined to dramatically increase the number of standard-definition (SD)

Table 6.3 Summary of ITU DTH formats as of 2001

	System A	System B	System C
Modulation scheme	QPSK	QPSK	QPSK
Symbol rate	Not specified	Fixed 20 Mbaud	Variable 19.5 and 29.3 Mbaud
Necessary bandwidth (−3 dB)	Not specified	24 MHz	19.5 and 29.3 MHz
Roll-off rate	0.35 (raised cosine)	0.2 (raised cosine)	0.55 and 0.33 (4th order Butterworth filter)
Reed–Solomon outer code	(204, 188, $T = 8$)	(146, 130, $T = 8$)	(204, 188, $T = 8$)
Interleaving	Convolutional, $I = 12$, $M = 17$ (Forney)	Convolutional, $N1 = 13$, $N2 = 146$ (Ramsey II)	Convolutional, $I = 12$, $M = 19$ (Forney)
Inner coding	Convolutional	Convolutional	Convolutional
Constraint length	$K = 7$	$K = 7$	$K = 7$
Basic code	1/2	1/2	1/3
Generator polynomial	171, 133 (octal)	171, 133 (octal)	117, 135,161 (octal)
Inner coding rate	1/2, 2/3, 3/4, 5/6, 7/8	1/2, 2/3, 6/7	1/2, 2/3, 3/4, 3/5, 4/5, 5/6, 5/11, 7/8
Net data rate	23.754–41.570 Mbits/s given symbol rate of 27.776 Mbaud	17.69–30.32 Mbits/s at fixed 20 Mbaud symbol rate	16.4–31.5 Mbits/s given symbol rate of 19.5 Mbaud
Packet size	188 B	130 B	188 B
Transport layer	MPEG-2	Non-MPEG	MPEG-2
Commonality with other media (i.e. terrestrial, cable, etc)	MPEG transport stream basis	MPEG elementary stream basis	MPEG transport stream basis
Video source coding	MPEG-2 at least main level/main profile	MPEG-2 at least main level/main profile	MPEG-2 at least main level/main profile
Aspect ratios	4:3 16:9 (2.12:1 optionally)	4:3 16:9	4:3 16:9
Image supported formats	Not restricted, recommended: 720 × 576, 704 × 576 544 × 576, 480 × 576 352 × 576, 352 × 288	720 × 480, 704 × 480 544 × 480, 480 × 480 352 × 480, 352 × 240 720 × 1,280, 1280 × 1,024 1920 × 1,080	720(704) × 576 720(704) × 480 528 × 480, 528 × 576 352 × 480, 352 × 576 352 × 288, 352 × 240
Frame rates at monitor (per second)	25	29.97	25 or 29.97
Audio source decoding	MPEG-2, Layers I and II	MPEG-I, Layer II; ATSC N53 (AC3)	ATSC A/53 or MPEG-2 Layers I and II

(continued)

Table 6.3 (continued)

	System A	System B	System C
Service information	ETS 300 468	System B	ATSC A/56 SCTE DVS/0 II
EPG	ETS 300 707	System B	User selectable
Teletext	Supported	Not specified	Not specified
Subtitling	Supported	Supported	Supported
Closed caption	Not specified	Yes	Yes

(Excerpts From Table 6.1 of [23]. Reproduced With the Kind Permission of the ITU)

Table 6.4 Evolution of US DTH systems

	1984–1986	1994–1996	2004–2006
General			
Primary system application	Delivery to cable head-ends	Direct-to-Home	Direct-to-Home
Dish size	2–3 m	0.45–0.90 m	0.45–0.65 m
Receivers per home (typical)	1	1	2–4
Cost of home electronics	>$ 1,000	<$700	<$100 per receiver (service provider cost)
Viewable TV channels per home (typical)	24 (plus additional channels given antenna re-pointing)	>200	>200 plus >10 HD
Total TV channels	Dozens	>200	1,000s
Transmission			
Downlink frequency	~4 GHz	>10 GHz	>10 GHz
Downlink beam shape	Single 48-states beam plus some AK/HI coverage	Single 48-states beam plus some AK/HI coverage	48-states beam plus AK/HI coverage plus spots for local markets
Number of orbit locations per system	>10	1	>3
Total satellites per system	N/A	Up to 3	More than 10
Video/audio encoding	None	MPEG 2 with statmux	MPEG 2 plus MPEG 4 for certain new services
Modulation & FEC	Analog FM	Reed–Solomon and convolutional codes, QPSK	Prior solution plus 8-PSK for certain new services
Service offerings			
Subscription TV	X	X	X
Pay Per View TV	–	X	X
High Def TV	–	–	X
Interactive	–	–	X
Local channels	–	–	X
Digital video recorders	–	–	X
Home networking	–	–	X

television channels offered, while simultaneously reducing the receive antenna to easily manageable dimensions and allowing less expensive consumer equipment.

1. *Video/audio encoding.* Beginning in the late 1980s, experts from many organizations developed the MPEG-1 and MPEG-2 standards for video and audio "source coding," with the latter standard approved in 1995 [24]. This international effort meant that a tool kit capable of providing substantial compression gains could be reduced to commercial silicon with the confidence that the chips would be used in mass-produced consumer electronics. Use of MPEG by most DTH systems in the Western Hemisphere contributed substantially to its early adoption.

2. *Modulation and error control.* Although concatenated coding for Forward Error Control was first recognized in the late 1960s [25], the earliest concatenated coding applications on a mass-market basis were digital DTH satellite systems [23].

3. *Consumer electronics.* The 1.2 m microelectronics feature size available in the early 1990s permitted low-cost implementation of required MPEG and FEC processing. With "Moore'sLaw" improvements in digital memory and other circuits, retail prices for DTH home electronics, including outdoor equipment, was below $700 by 1994.

4. *Satellite platforms.* The early 1990s saw a new generation of satellite platforms specially designed for DTH application. These satellites deployed sun-oriented solar panels developing 4 kW of dc power [21]. Also, in the early 1990s, satellite TWT amplifier designs began routinely using phase-combined conduction-cooled TWT pairs to generate the desired >200-W RF power levels.[20]

Evolution Since 1994

In the second decade of evolution, various US systems have substantially expanded their capacity and service offerings. In general, this evolution has not required major technology breakthroughs but rather the identification, customization, and deployment of available technology most appropriate for the desired application.

1. *Video/audio encoding.* With a market demand for more HDTV channels, DTH systems are deploying MPEG-4 advanced video compression (AVC) [26] and audio compression [27] to reduce required capacity per HD and SD channel by one-half. Existing MPEG-2 broadcasting and customer facilities for SD DTH signals are expected to continue to be used for some time because of the cost involved in replacing tens of millions of fielded MPEG-2 receivers. One consequence of using MPEG-4 for retransmission of ATSC broadcasts via satellite is that the satellite DTH operator has no choice but to decode the MPEG-2 and re-encode in MPEG-4, introducing an additional distortion source into the distribution chain. It is anticipated that, as the use of MPEG-4 technology increases, efficient transcoding schemes will be developed to mitigate this effect.

2. *Modulation and error control.* Again driven by an increased demand for HDTV, DTH providers spearheaded the development of a new modulation and coding technique, DVB-S2 [28], that was approved and put into use from 2005 (Fig. 6.6).

The standard's FEC uses a Bose–Chaudhuri–Hocquenghem (BCH) code concatenated with a low-density parity check (LDPC) inner code yielding performance within 0.7 dB of the Shannon limit. Figure 6.7 shows the 30% bandwidth efficiency of DVB-S2 compared to prior satellite solutions.

3. *Outdoor equipment.* It is expected that the simplicity, low cost, and high performance of the offset fed parabolic dish will continue its prominence as the receive antenna technology for systems in the Americas. An alternative- the dual-circularly-polarized phased array antenna- remains more costly and is used only in very specialized applications such as truly mobile services – i.e., operation while in motion – for motor vehicles [17].

As illustrated in Fig. 6.5, outdoor equipment has increased in complexity, using conventional technology, by adding multiple feed/low noise amplifier/block down

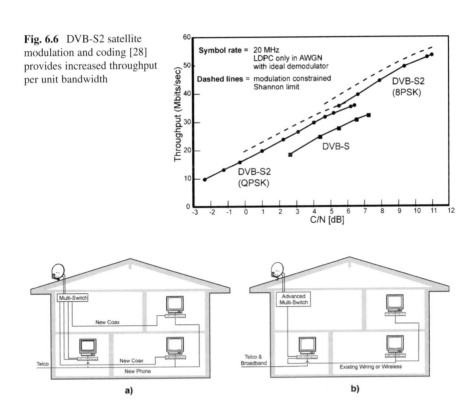

Fig. 6.6 DVB-S2 satellite modulation and coding [28] provides increased throughput per unit bandwidth

Fig. 6.7 (a) Traditional installations require new wiring from outdoor equipment to each TV served. (b) Home networking between DTH receivers require new wiring only from outdoor equipment to home gateway

converter assemblies near the dish focal point. These additional assemblies give access to signals from additional orbital locations. Outdoor equipment giving the customer access to signals at three orbital locations, 101°, 110°, and 119° West longitude, was deployed in the United States in 1999 (Fig. 6.5b presents an example of equipment that has been in use since 2002). Reference [29] presents key outdoor equipment electrical performance specifications.

4. *Consumer electronics.* DTH systems continue to benefit from general cost/ performance improvements in digital electronics and other specific progress in consumer and personal computer electronics.

The introduction of new technologies such as MPEG-4 and DVS-S2 increases the chip count and receiver cost; however, the same integration trend will soon apply to this new class of receiver.

It is common practice for the receiver to support secure software upgrades delivered as data files via the satellite. This allows significant flexibility to a digital DTH operator to add (within the constraints of the receiver's hardware, of course) new functionality, and to correct software bugs. For example, a software download may occur as a result of additional satellites or transponders becoming available to a satellite operator. Confidence in the reliability of satellite-delivered receiver software delivery has increased to a point where a receiver may conceivably ship from a manufacturer with only simple "bootstrap loader" software. This software guides the installer through the setup of the receiver and ODU and then authenticates and loads into memory, additional software downloaded via satellite on a continuously available data service.

By the end of the year 2000 with hard drive capacity improvements allowing cost-efficient storage of dozens of hours of standard-definition video, integrated digital video recording became an important DTH application at the turn of the century. DVRs for satellite-delivered HDTV became available in 2004 with total capacity of 250 MB allowing 25–30 h of MPEG-2 encoded HD programming.

Typically, DTH programming flows from the customer's dish to one or more indoor receivers, e.g., one in the family room, the den, and the master bedroom. As illustrated in Fig. 9, home receiver networking, introduced in 2005, permits DTH programming to flow between receivers [16]. With home networking, a program recorded on the DVR in the family room can now be watched in either the den or bedroom, for example. Using industry standard home networking protocols as a basis, these home media networks feature automatic device discovery, QoS bandwidth management, and advanced content security.

5. *Satellite platforms.* Satellite platforms continue to progress by providing substantially more bandwidth per satellite, but without proportionally greater costs for the satellite and its delivery to orbit. Figure 6.3 illustrates progress in satellite platforms over a ten-year period. The platform on the right provides 16 kW end-of-life total dc power vs. 4 kW for the satellite type on the left, first used for DTH in 1994 [20,30]. The newer platform also permits substantial increases in "shelf space" allowing more than twice as many active transponders [31].

The newer platforms achieve greater dc power levels by increasing the total solar panel area and by using more advanced solar cells. The triple-junction – that is, triple-layer – gallium arsenide (GaAs) solar cells of 2005 provide more than double the dc power per unit area than single-junction silicon cells of a decade earlier [32]. Satellite platform weight has been controlled by addition of electric ion propulsion for satellite orbital position station-keeping. Ion propulsion is ten times more efficient, allowing for a reduction in propellant mass of up to 90% when compared with traditional chemical propulsion [33]. This reduction can be used to reduce launch cost, add payload functionality, and increase satellite in-orbit lifetime.

The DTH satellites, currently in the planning stage as shown in Fig. 6.3b have six offset parabolic antennas for downlink communications as against two such antennas in the satellites of a decade earlier [30]. Although there is little change in basic technology of these antenna systems, the design has been customized through careful placement near the dish focal point of sometimes dozens of feed horns, to synthesize both national beams and local spots. The spot beams permit frequency reuse between some noncontiguous local beams and hence improve overall spectrum efficiency. The spot beams are used for local channel delivery back into the originating markets [30].

6. *Satellite fleets and backhaul networks.* The largest DTH operators in the US, DirecTV and Dish Network, have increased their total delivery capacity by using satellites at multiple orbit locations, with each new location providing a full "reuse" of the spectrum. Operators create high downlink power levels over their licensed spectrum and provide backup capability by deploying multiple satellites at many of their assigned orbital locations. Figure 6.8 shows the planned 2007 satellite fleet for DirecTV. Figure 6.8 also illustrates the extensive fiber

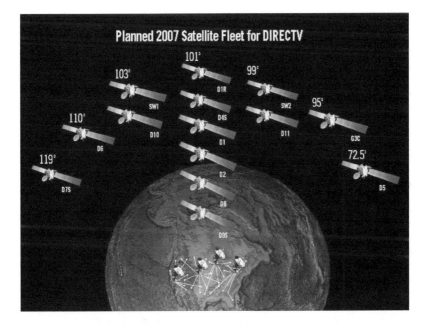

Fig. 6.8 Shows the planned 2007 satellite fleet for DirecTV

networks used, along with satellite links (not depicted), for backhaul of local channels. As more and more local HDTV is rebroadcast by satellite services, these networks are expected to expand significantly.

Finally, since the original IEEE paper in 2006, new services have been added. A notable advancement since then, for example, is the addition of IPTV functionality to satellite STBs to allow video on demand services delivered via customers' broadband connections.

References

1. W.L. Pritchard and M. Ogata, "Satellite direct broadcast", Proc. IEEE, vol. 78, no. 7, pp. 1116–1140, July 1990
2. Satellite Broadcast and Communications Association (SBCA), Satellite Industry Key Dates [Online]. Available: www.sbca.com/ key_dates.html
3. "Annual reports of DirecTV and Dish Network," [Online]. Available: http://www.directv.com; http://www.dishnetwork.com
4. Media Trends 2002 Monterey, CA, Kagan Research LLC
5. Media Trends 2003 Monterey, CA, Kagan Research LLC
6. Media Trends 2004 Monterey, CA, Kagan Research LLC
7. International Telecommunication Union (ITU), Radio Regulations 1982 ed., rev. 1985, 1986, 1988, vol. 2, appendix 30. BSS (Broadcasting-Satellite Service)
8. International Telecommunication Union (ITU), Radio Regulations 1982 ed., rev. 1985, 1986, 1988, vol. 2, appendix 30A
9. L.J. Ippolito, Jr., Radiowave Propagation in Satellite Communications. New York: Van Nostrand-Reinhold, 1986
10. J.P. Godwin, "Direct satellite television broadcasting", in Wiley Encyclopedia of Electrical and Electronics Engineering, J.G. Webster, Ed. New York: Wiley, 1999, pp. 590–602
11. J.D. Power and Associates, "Residential cable/satellite tv customer satisfaction studies," [Online]. Available: http://www.jdpower.com
12. Advanced Television Systems Committee, "History of the ATSC," [Online]. Available: http://www.atsc.org/history.html
13. DirecTV Inc., "DirecTV launches new advanced TV services," Jan. 6, 2004 [Online]. Available: http://www.directv.com/DTVAPP/aboutus/Headlines.dsp
14. ATSC Standard: Advanced Common Applications Platform (ACAP), A/101, Advanced Television Systems Committee, Washington, DC, 2005 [Online]. Available: http://www.atsc.org
15. Cable Television Laboratories, Inc., "OpenCable Application Platform (OCAP) specification," [Online]. Available: http://www.opencable.com/specifications/
16. DirecTV, Inc., "DirecTV debuts home media center at CES trade show," Jan. 6, 2004 [Online]. Available: http://www.directv.com/ DTVAPP/aboutus/Headlines.dsp
17. KVH Industries, Inc, "Mobile satellite TV," [Online]. Available: http://www.kvh.com/ tracvision_kvh/
18. JetBlue Airways, "DirecTV inflight service," [Online]. Available: http://www.jetblue.com/ havefun/directv/directv.html
19. Society of Motion Picture and Television Engineers, SMPTE 259 M Television – 10-Bit 4:2:2 Component and 4fsc Composite Digital Signals – Serial Digital Interface (1997) [Online]. Available: http:// www.smpte.org
20. Boeing Company, "Satellites to deliver TV direct to home viewers," [Online]. Available: http://www.boeing.com/defense-space/space/ bss/factsheets/601/dbs/dbs.html
21. Boeing Company, "Boeing 601 fleet: High-power spacecraft for the 21st century," [Online]. Available: http://www.boeing. com/defense-space/space/bss/factsheets/601/601fleet.html

22. DirecTV, Application to FCC for authorization to launch and operate DBS-1 (call sign DBS8402) File No. SAT-LOA-1984011200024
23. "Digital multiprogramme television systems for use by satellites operating in the 11/12 GHz frequency range," International Telecommunication Union, Recommendation ITU-R BO.1516, 2001
24. L. Chiariglione, "The development of an integrated audiovisual coding standard: MPEG," Proc. IEEE, vol. 83, no. 2, pp. 151–157, February 1995
25. G.D. Forney, Jr., Concatenated Coding. Cambridge, MA: MIT, 1966
26. Information technology – Coding of audio-visual objects – Part 10: Advanced video coding, [MPEG-4 AVC] ISO/IEC 14 496–10
27. Information technology – Coding of audio-visual objects – Part 3: Audio, [MPEG-4 AAC] ISO/IEC 14 496–3
28. Draft ETSI EN 302 307 v1.1.1 (2004–06), Digital video broadcasting (DVB), second generation framing structure, channel coding and modulation systems for broadcasting, interactive services, news gathering and other broad-band satellite applications, Standard DVB-S2 (draft) [Online]. Available: http://www.dvb.org
29. DBS Antenna Products. California Amplifier [Online]. Available: http://www.calamp.com
30. DirecTV, Application to FCC for authorization to launch and operate DirecTV D11 (call sign S2640) File No. SAT-LOA20040909-00168
31. Boeing Company, "Boeing 702 Fleet," [Online]. Available: http://www.boeing.com/defense-space/space/bss/factsheets/702/ 702fleet.html
32. Company Information. Spectrolab, Inc. [Online]. Available: http:// www.spectrolab.com/com/ com.htm
33. Boeing Company, "Xenon ion propulsion," [Online]. Available: http://www.boeing.com/ defense-space/space/bss/factsheets/ xips/xips.html

Chapter 7
Creation and Distribution of 4 K Content

Laurin Herr

Abstract Until recently, electronics-based video (whether analog or digital) could not achieve the same high-quality motion pictures at comparable cost, as could a 35 mm analog film. But rapid advances in key digital technologies over the past decade have brought digital cinema to effective parity with film-based cinema in terms of image quality. The advent of 4 K digital motion pictures, high-end format of new digital cinema distribution specifications, offers four times the resolution of 2 K digital cinema or broadcast HDTV. But 4 K poses unique technical challenges related to specialized imaging devices like cinema-grade digital cameras and displays capable of this high resolution. Creation and distribution of 4 K in a productive manner also requires access to advanced cyber-infrastructure such as high-speed digital networks, high performance digital storage and powerful computing resources. Creative techniques of cinematography and sound recording, design of performance spaces, and psycho-perceptual optimization of audience viewing/listening environments are also impacted. This also has an effect on the whole notion of what can be done with media remotely via network as opposed to what can only be done locally, in person. These are issues not only for the entertainment industry, but also for scientists, educators, medical researchers and government agencies who are adopting digital media and digital networking for their own demanding applications. There is thus a growing need for professionals with interdisciplinary experience covering media arts/technology, computing/storage systems and digital networking. The members of CineGrid, a non-profit international research consortium, are building advanced media-capable nodes connected by high-speed networks to create a global-scale test bed that can be used by an international community of collaborators working on a variety of projects exploring the future of content creation and distribution in bandwidth-abundant environments while "learning by doing" to train next generation media professionals through hands-on experiments.

D. Gerbarg (ed.), *Television Goes Digital*,
© Springer Science + Business Media, LLC 2009

Introduction

Modern society is becoming increasingly media-dense and communications intensive. The future promises both higher quality media experiences and a noisy proliferation of digital media formats, large and small. Content will be created in many places, often by distributed teams linked by high-speed networks capable of transporting professional digital media assets fast enough to satisfy creative workflow. Digital media at very high quality will be distributed ubiquitously and securely, with high-speed networks playing a critical role.

For the past 40 years, numerous forms of media have been undergoing a historic conversion from analog to digital technology. This process started with text and grey-scale graphics, advanced to monochrome and color still photography, then audio, which extended further to digital video – first at standard, and later at high-definition. The adoption of digital technology in both media and communications has spurred a proliferation of media sources, channels and consumption platforms.

Digital imaging technology has got so much better, faster and cheaper in recent years that many imaging applications that traditionally relied on film cameras are converting to electronic cameras. Broadcast television production, which once shot everything on film, converted to video cameras and video tape recorders starting late 1970s – initially using analog electronics – then upgrading to digital electronics in the 1990s. As we approach 2010, almost everything seen on broadcast television is shot using digital video technology.

Until quite recently, electronics-based video (whether analog or digital) could not achieve the same high-quality results at comparable cost as 35 mm analog film. But rapid advances in key digital technologies over the past decade have brought digital cinema to effective parity with film-based cinema in terms of image quality, while at the same time enabling more creative control and offering some commercial advantages over film. This is not to say that film and video will not continue to have differences, including subtle variations in the "look" of the image.

Where once there existed a clear dividing line between film-based motion pictures and electronics-based video imagery, there is now a continuum of creative, technical and budgeting choices that can result in both approaches being used in the same piece of media. It used to be that film was reserved for higher quality, higher budget content with full post-production scheduling, such as cinema, premium television programming and broadcast advertising commercials. Electronics-based video imagery was used primarily for lower quality, lower budget content with little – or in the case of live programming – no post-production, such as television news, sports, reality shows, documentaries, or industrial/educational programs.

Movies, in particular top-quality Hollywood movies, are still shot predominantly using 35 mm film cameras for original live-action photography. But even in the movie business, digital cinema cameras are gaining in popularity.

Modern media is created to be delivered to consumers. With deployment of digital terrestrial television, digital satellite broadcast, digital cable television, digital radio and the Internet, most consumers receive most of their media via digital distribution of some form or another today. Exception has been movies until quite recently.

Historically, films were simply of too high a quality to be handled digitally. In particular, the critical obstacle to digital distribution of cinema was the lack of electronic projectors capable of throwing up a bright enough images on a large enough screen with sufficient dynamic range, rich color, strong contrast and high spatial resolution to satisfy an audience accustomed to seeing 35 mm film projection in a movie theatre.

These sorts of technical limitations have largely been overcome with the development of high-performance digital cinema projectors featuring 2 K resolution (2,048 pixels[1] horizontal × 1,080 pixels vertical) from manufacturers Christie, NEC and Barco, all using the Texas Instruments DLP technology; and digital cinema projectors featuring 4 K resolution (4,096 pixels horizontal × 2,160 pixels vertical)[2] from Sony using its own SXRD technology. (JVC has also introduced a commercial 4 K projector using their own D-ILA technology, but this device features lower light output and is not designed for installation in large cinema theatres.)

In the last few years, movie theatres in North America and elsewhere have begun converting large numbers of screens to digital infrastructure. This has entailed installing digital cinema playback servers and digital projectors designed to handle interoperable digital cinema packages (DCP) containing compressed and encrypted movie in the industry-standard 2 K and/or 4 K image formats.[3] The roll out of digital cinema is allowing cinema distribution without film for the first time in history. But most movie theatres around the world still use film physically threaded through a mechanical projector.

Today, both the "front-end" (motion picture photography) and "back end" (motion picture projection in the theatre) of cinema workflow are moving through a transitional phase wherein both older and newer digital technologies co-exist. But the "middle" of the cinema workflow – creative post-production – started going digital more than 30 years ago and has today almost entirely converted over from film-based editing and optical special effects to digital technology.

---

[1] "Pixels" is a term of art for "picture elements," used when describing computer graphics or digital visual imagery.

[2] The convention in denoting HDTV has been to indicate the vertical dimensions of the image first, whereas projected formats such as 4 K and 8 K (7,680 × 4,320) state the picture height second.

[3] 4 K is a digital format (using dots or pixels across a single line), whereas standard definition television is analog (using scan lines). By way of comparison, HDTV is currently broadcast in the U.S., Japan and Korea at 1080i/30, or 1,080 vertical pixels interlaced/30 frames per second, whereas standard definition NTSC analog TV has 525 scan lines. Panasonic also has created a version of HDTV that's broadcast (by the ABC network in the USA, among others) at 720 pixels, progressively scanned at 60 frames per second. (Traditional television uses a technology to interlace lines to create an image, whereas computers and digital TV uses progressively scanned lines, repeating from left to right.)

In Europe, standard definition PAL uses 25 frames per second with fewer scan lines than used in the US. If HDTV ever takes off in Europe (slowed by the difficulty of frame rate conversion), it will be broadcast at 1080i/25 frames per second. In general we can state that HDTV has six times more pixels than standard definition TV, and 4 K has four times more pixels, or 24 times the real state of "standard def."

Faced with a mixed analog/digital "front-end," an all-digital "middle" and a mixed "back-end," the cinema industry has pioneered a hybrid approach to content creation and distribution commonly called the "digital intermediate" (DI). In a DI workflow, 35 mm negative film shot in the traditional manner is run through a high-resolution digital scanner that converts chemically recorded image into a digital image composed of bits of data organized as pixels. Once film frames are converted to digital, all post-production can occur digitally, using file-based workflows and computer-based creative tools for color-grading, editing, visual effects, compositing, etc.

After all creative post-production work is completed in the DI process, the producer/ distributor can choose to output the finished movie, the so-called "digital source master" (DSM), to film via a digital film printer. Digitally controlled lasers are used to precisely "burn," or expose, an analog film negative from which traditional film release prints can be manufactured. Alternatively, they can choose to create a digital cinema package (DCP) for digital cinema distribution. Today, and for the foreseeable future, movies will be distributed using both film release prints and digital cinema DCP in parallel, as the worldwide cinema theaters goes through a multi-year infrastructure upgrade.

The same DSM can be used to generate derivative formats with lesser resolution and/or higher compression to reach non-theatrical markets such as DVD, hotel pay-per-view, conditional-access cable or satellite television, airplane viewing, and eventually, broadcast television. DSM can also be used to generate archival assets for long-term preservation.

Historical Context

In every period of civilization, the state-of-the-art in visual media has been driven primarily by requirements and funding of three important sectors of society:

- The science/medicine/research/education nexus
- What can be considered cultural interests – entertainment/publishing/art/ advertising
- "The state" – military/intelligence/police/emergency response.

When these different sectors used analog media technology optimized for their particular purposes, there was little need for inter-domain communication regarding media applications. But, this is changing. Even at the highest image quality levels, new digital media technology is becoming acceptable – even desirable – which means that in all three sectors, even the toughest imaging applications formerly only possible with film, can now "go digital."

These different sectors of society are increasingly adopting similar digital platforms, and often buying the same devices. They face similar challenges related to cameras and microphones, recorders and players, speakers and projectors/ displays, data storage, computation and networking, system integration, digital asset management, distribution and preservation, etc.

Photo courtesy of Dr. Takashi
Fujio, NHK Laboratories

Convergence of cinema and television is considered by many to have started in 1981 when NHK Laboratories in Japan brought the first generation of analog HDTV devices – cameras, recorders, and monitors – to the SMPTE Engineering Conference in Los Angeles. There, Dr. Takashi Fujio, leader of the team at NHK Labs that developed the first HDTV systems showed them to Hollywood cinema director, Francis Ford Coppola. According to people who were present at the time, Coppola took a long look at this early HDTV gear and encouraged its continued development in order to create a new way of making movies, which he called "electronic cinema." Coppola's vision inspired further development of HDTV for non-broadcast applications. It took almost 20 years to achieve Coppola's and Fujio's shared dream for an "electronic cinema." But eventually, top video equipment manufacturers and traditional motion picture film camera makers introduced HD video cameras that satisfied particular requirements of professional cinematographers.Today, not only cameras, but all computer-based tools and digital devices required to make "electronic cinema" at HD resolutions have become available, at various prices and levels of quality for people from Hollywood professionals to home amateurs.

Meanwhile, other aspects of digital technology were advancing rapidly. By 2001, Nippon Telegraph and Telephone (NTT)'s Network Innovation Laboratory was able to develop the world's first 4 K experimental digital cinema system capable of displaying four times the spatial resolution of HDTV and sending it compressed over digital IP networks.

NTT and the Digital Cinema Consortium of Japan demonstrated this prototype 4 K digital cinema system at the SIGGRAPH 2001 Conference on Computer Graphics and Interactive Techniques in Los Angeles. The demonstration was viewed by thousands of attendees, including representatives of major Hollywood studios and leading post-production houses, most of whom were seeing 4 K motion pictures with their own eyes for the first time.

Since the industry – producers, distributors and exhibitors, and vendors that support them – would have to live for quite a long time with whatever digital cinema standards were adopted, some felt the future of cinema should be limited to resolution of commercial digital projectors available in the year 2001, which was just 1,280 × 1,024 pixels (1.3 K) with 8-bit dynamic range. Others, however, believed that 1.3 K was "good enough" and that waiting for higher quality would unnecessarily delay deployment of digital cinema.

In 2002, the Digital Cinema Initiatives, LLC (DCI) was created as a joint venture of Disney, Fox, Paramount, Sony Pictures, Universal and Warner Bros. Studios. The DCI's primary purpose was articulated as, "establishing and documenting voluntary specifications relevant to an open architecture for digital cinema, thereby ensuring a uniform and high level of technical performance, reliability and quality control."

There were numerous demonstrations, tests and comparative evaluations of digital cinema using various formats running on various technologies in Los Angeles, Rome, London, Tokyo and elsewhere. After considerable technical debate, commercial competition and international wrangling that is beyond the scope of this account, in late 2003 the DCI published its unanimous recommendation for digital cinema. It specified 2 K (2,048 × 1,080) and 4 K (4,096 × 2,160) image formats, both compressed using JPEG2000 and extractable from a common file. The DCI also made recommendations regarding many other specifics dealing with color, sound, packaging, encryption and key delivery security architectures for digital cinema.

Meanwhile, those using very high-quality digital images outside of the "cultural context"—the scientific, educational, military and intelligence communities – welcomed commoditization of HD-quality media and potential access to higher resolution cinema-grade 4 K cameras and projectors. However, these communities did not want to be constrained by existing television formatsor installed movie business infrastructure.

To exemplify the point, scientific visualization pioneers at the University of California San Diego and University of Illinois at Chicago involved in the NSF-funded OptIPuter project were prepared to think in terms of frame buffers with 100–200 megapixels, or more. Their users needed to be able to step back from the display and take in at a glance the largest possible context, and then step closer to study the image at the greatest possible detail. The OptIPuter team understood that no one monolithic display or image format was likely to work for all applications. They developed hardware and software to control tiled displays as an extended frame buffer featuring on-screen windowing, drag-and-drop, and point-and-click graphical user interfaces that had been popularized on personal computers. By 2004, the OptIPuter research vision of the future was gigapixel wallpaper with streaming video at various resolutions mixed with still graphics of arbitrary size and number, augmented by virtual reality implemented without special glasses or tethered glove. All this visualization capability was to be integrated with general purpose computing and storage resources, connected seamlessly by high-speed networks to similar facilities at distant locations.

What Is 4 K?

Generally speaking, the term "4 K" is broadly used to describe any new format for motion pictures with eight or more mega-pixels per frame, which works out to roughly 4,000 pixels horizontal × 2,000 pixels vertical for a widescreen with an aspect ratio of 2.0.

Some content referred to as "4 K" can be more accurately described as Quad HDTV[4] or Super High-Definition (SHD) with a resolution of 3,840 × 2,160 pixels per frame, exactly twice the horizontal and twice the vertical resolution of HDTV (1,920 × 1,080). Quad HDTV frame rates are typically 24, 25/30 and/or 60 fps, with a 1.77 aspect ration (16:9). Quad HDTV is called so because it is comprised of four quadrants each HDTV resolution and often interfaced using four HD-SDI signals encoded as either 4:2:2 YPbPr with 10-bit dynamic range in the Rec. 709 color space, or as 4:4:4 10-bit RGB. A variety of compression techniques can be used and there is no upper or lower limit to the compressed bit-rate for Quad HDTV (*a.k.a.* SHD).

Strictly speaking, however, "4 K" is one of two new motion picture image formats for digital cinema theatrical distribution, as recommended by the DCI in 2003 and subsequently standardized by the Society of Motion Picture and Television Engineers (SMPTE) in 2007–2008. According to the digital cinema standard, "2 K" is defined at 2,048 × 1,080 image container while "4 K" is defined as an image container with 4,096 × 2,160 pixels per frame. Within the 4 K image container, cinema directors can fit images in either of the two aspect ratios most commonly used in cinema: 2.39 (4,096 × 1,716) or 1.85 (3,996 × 2,160). The frame rate of 4 K is fixed at 24 frames per second. Color encoding is always 4:4:4 (equal sampling of the primary colors) with 12-bit dynamic range in the SMPTE XYZ color space for extended color gamut, with progressive scanning and square pixels. Only JPEG 2000 is used for compression in digital cinema, and there is an upper limit of 250 Mbps on the compressed bit-rate for DCI-compliant digital cinema distribution.

Why Is More Resolution[5] Important?

Generally speaking, increasing the spatial resolution of motion pictures allows the audience to sit closer to a larger image display without any degradation in the perceived sharpness of the picture or awareness of the underlying technical structure of the picture. Sitting closer increases the viewing angle. A number of researchers around the

---

[4] Among the many compression/decompression schemes HDTV, or Quad HDTV uses are MPEG2, MPEG4, HVC (also know as H274), JPEG2000, and numerous proprietary codecs. Some of the latter include VC1 from Microsoft, as well as lossless codecs, low latency, and very fine-detailed codes.

[5] With reference to resolution, visual acuity is assumed to be 20/20.

world have confirmed that an increased viewing angle produces a stronger emotional response in the viewer. So, increasing resolution enables presentation of visual media in larger formats that can elicit a stronger emotional connection with viewers.

For example, a standard definition television format like NTSC used in the USA and Japan (486 active pixels vertical × 720 pixels horizontal) is best viewed at a distance of seven times the picture height, producing a 15-° viewing angle. HDTV with a wider aspect ratio and six times the spatial resolution compared to standard definition TV (1,080 pixels vertical × 1,920 pixels horizontal) is ideally viewed at three times the picture height, producing a 30-° viewing angle. The numbers for 2 K digital cinema format are comparable. Doubling horizontal and vertical resolutions of HDTV brings us effectively to "4 K," which allows for an optimum viewing distance of 1.5 picture heights, yielding a viewing angle of 60°s that significantly increases the sense of visual presence and emotional involvement, especially when accompanied by multi-channel spatialized audio.

Since the early 2000s Japanese national broadcaster, NHK, has been developing a next-generation format in its Tokyo laboratories with "8 K" resolution (7,680 × 4,320), effectively doubling both horizontal and vertical resolution compared to "4 K." Put another way, 8 K is equivalent to 16 frames of HDTV. With an "8 K" format, the viewer will be able to sit just 0.75 of a picture height away from the display, which gives a viewing angle of 100°. Combined with 22.2 digital surround sounds, the 8 K system creates an extraordinary immersive, digital IMAX-like experience.

High-Quality Media, Fast Networking and the Next-Generation Professionals

The ways in which humans use pictures and sounds will evolve to take advantage of communicability and malleability of digital media even at very high quality levels.

To explore this new convergence of high quality media and high speed networking, a non-profit organization, CineGrid, was formed in 2006 with the mission to build an international interdisciplinary community focused on research, development, and demonstration of networked collaborative tools in order to enable production, use and exchange of very high-quality digital media over photonic networks. CineGrid members are organizing themselves to create a prototype infrastructure that can be used as a test-bed for member-driven explorations of new approaches to remote collaboration and distributed project management that can take advantage of the new capability to move very high quality picture and sound at high speed over great distances using advanced photonic networks.

CineGrid is not only about technology challenges. Media education is also at a historical cusp. As today's analog experts and hybrid analog/digital veterans retire over the coming years, and all-digital media come to dominate, there will be increasing demand for inter-disciplinary professionals who understand the whole of networked digital media at high quality. This will require people who can master specific requirements of their particular application areas, as well as the larger legal and economic contexts. They will need to comprehend practical issues of media production, and be able to navigate (or design and administer) complex storage, computation and software architectures. They will have to have had enough experience working with high-speed networking infrastructure to be able to tie all components together into an integrated system that might be distributed around the world. Universities and art schools, research laboratories and movie studios, and government agencies will all need talented, well-trained people with this extremely broad skill set to exploit the full potential of digital media beyond HDTV and DTV.

Characteristics of CineGrid

The essential idea of CineGrid is that its members will build media-capable nodes that are connected by high-speed networks. The aim is to create a global-scale test bed that can be used by an international community of collaborators working on a variety of projects exploring the future of content creation and distribution in bandwidth-abundant environments while "learning by doing" to train next generation media professionals through hands-on experiments.

The networks used by CineGrid are generally part of what's called the Global Lambda Integrated Facility (GLIF), a "virtual" consortium of national research and educational network operators (Fig. 7.1). These operators have agreed to peer their networks at Global Open Lambda Exchanges (GOLEs) under flexible acceptable use policies that allow for various types of experimentation. GLIF members are particularly interested in pioneering what are called Lambda Grids. Lambda refers to light waves used to carry data over fiber optic cables. Lambda Grids is an approach to establish a grid of point-to-point links connecting known and trusted users using light waves over photonic networks. Historically, the GLIF was designed primarily to support scientific applications like high-energy physics, radio astronomy and remote-control electron microscopy, as well as conduct networking research and systems design experiments.

The CineGrid membership is a new kind of self-organizing GLIF user community drawn together by common interest in the convergence of high-quality digital media and photonic networks, with access to next generation networking resources that allow members to be linked to each other at 1 Gbps and 10 Gbps speeds on a global scale.

It is important to clarify that CineGrid projects do not run over the commercial Internet nor even commercially operated private networks. CineGrid uses excess capacity of research and educational networks donated on an *ad hoc* basis by CineGrid's own Network/Exchange members around the world. In many cases, these members operate national networks, such as SURFnet in the Netherlands, or CANARIE in Canada. In other cases, the networks are operated by consortiums of universities, such as the National Lambda Rail and Internet2, both based in the USA. CineGrid members also include regional network operators like the State of California's CENIC.

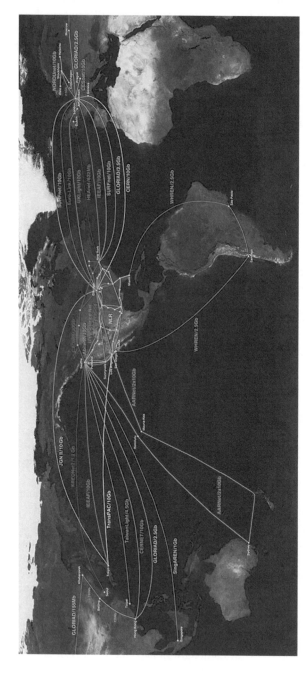

Fig. 7.1 GLIF map 2008 (Courtesy of Bob Patterson, NCSA). The Global Lambda Integrated Facility (GLIF) Map 2008 visualization was created by Robert Patterson of the Advanced Visualization Laboratory (AVL) at the National Center for Supercomputing Applications (NCSA) at the University of Illinois at Urbana-Champaign (UIUC), using an Earth image provided by NASA. Data was compiled by Maxine D. Brown of the Electronic Visualization Laboratory (EVL) at the University of Illinois at Chicago (UIC). Funding was provided by GLIF and US National Science Foundation grants # SCI-04-38712 to NCSA/ UIUC and # OCI-0441094 to EVL/UIC. For more information on GLIF, and to download the world map and several close-ups, in a variety of formats and resolutions, see http://www.glif.is/

Fig. 7.2 © Laurin Herr, 2005

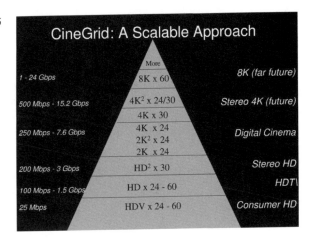

CineGrid manifests as CineGrid networks/exchanges and CineGrid nodes. The first nodes were established in 2005 at Keio University in Tokyo and at the University of California San Diego's California Institute for Telecommunications and Information Technology (Calit2). Keio's Digital Media Research Center installed Sony 4 K projectors, Olympus 4 K cameras, an IMAGICA 4 K film scanner, and NTT JPEG2000 4 K streaming codecs (compression/decompression), all connected via 10 Gb Ethernet to the Japan Gigabit Network (JGN2). At UCSD/ Calit2, a newly constructed 200-seat auditorium was outfitted with an 8.2 Meyer Sound system, a Sony SXRD 4 K projector, a SGI Prism with 21 TB of fast storage, a NTT JPEG2000 4 K streaming codec, all connected via 10 Gb Ethernet to CENIC and NLR. In subsequent years, more CineGrid members have built-up their own CineGrid nodes around the world.

Architecturally and philosophically, CineGrid has a digitally oriented perspective on image formats: There are many media formats in life, with different parameters, quality levels and price/performance trade-offs. From the vantage point of a networked community, bit rates required for a given format relative to available bandwidth and last-mile connectivity are usually decisive constraints on CineGrid projects. As an organization, CineGrid is vendor neutral and format-agnostic. Anticipating future availability of faster networks and more advanced image sensors/displays, CineGrid will take a scalable approach to accommodate higher quality formats with greater frame sizes, variable frame rates, and stereoscopic capabilities that are expected to emerge in coming years.

The pyramid depicted above (Fig. 7.2) represents a basic assumption of CineGrid: The number of users decline as the quality of the format increases, because quality requires more bandwidth (and therefore, is expense) at every step up the pyramid. This refers not just to network bandwidth requirements, but also the performance needed in every device in every system that uses that format.

The CineGrid scalable hierarchy of formats starts at the bottom with consumer HDTV quality recorded heavily compressed on popular HDV digital videotape. The chart goes up through broadcast HDTV to digital cinema in 2 K, 2 K stereoscopic, 4 K and 4 K stereoscopic – and even beyond to 8 K and higher resolutions implemented with tiled displays and camera arrays. On the left of the pyramid, bandwidth is expressed as bit rate (or, if there are two numbers, as compressed/uncompressed rates). In the center of the pyramid is the name of the format and its frame rate(s). The far right of the chart identifies the format in terms of image quality and R&D horizons.

CineGrid Projects

CineGrid members are encouraged to collaborate on CineGrid projects that will "push the envelope" in terms of networking and media technology, while exploring new methods of production, post-production, distribution and presentation. Members choose their favorite formats to accomplish their project goals.

For example, some CineGrid members have long been interested in how 4 K digital camerawork differs when shooting live performance art, as compared to that for standard definition or even high-definition television. Also, they wonder whether these changes in camerawork will affect audio recording techniques or viewing/listening environments.

In 2006, CineGrid members in Tokyo recorded a string ensemble playing Mozart in 8-channel audio using a single 4 K camera placed in the audience with a fixed view of the stage filling the frame. The long-distance audience experience of the recorded performance was uniquely realistic, with enough resolution that enabled the viewer's eyes to naturally flit from place to place on the screen, just as if they were in the audience watching the live performance in person, the high-quality audio filling the auditorium.

Other CineGrid members are more interested in the potential of networked post-production. For example, is it feasible to perform the final mix of sound-to-picture over networks at digital cinema quality when the sound is coming from one location while the picture is coming from a different one, all combined and synchronized in a third location? This was the essence of the CineGrid demonstration at the Audio Engineering Society (AES) 2006 conference in San Francisco. The sound mixer said that he had no sense that the video server and the audio server were thousands of miles from one another, and from him. "I don't feel it," he said. "I am not inhibited in my creative effort." This experiment confirmed a basic premise of CineGrid, that it is possible to use networks to reduce the sense of distance between distributed teams working on digital media at the highest quality.

In June 2007, CineGrid transmitted a 75-min live opera performance in 4 K with 5.1 surround audio from the annual Holland Festival to the 200-seat auditorium at UCSD/Calit2 in southern California, nearly 10,000 km away. There were 700 paying guests in Amsterdam listening to the female singer and seven-piece Baroque ensemble in an all-acoustic hall, so the CineGrid production team was not allowed to turn up the lights nor make any sound that might disturb the performance. CineGrid recorded 24-channels of uncompressed sound that was mixed-down to 5.1 on-the-fly and sent to San Diego synchronized with live 4K motion pictures at 30 frames per second. The sound and picture were JPEG 2000 compressed to 500 Mb a second for network transmission, twice the maximum bit rate of the DCI specification for digital cinema distribution.

The San Diego audience enjoyed the opera projected in 4K life-size on a large screen with surround sound just a few seconds after the audience in Amsterdam enjoyed the same performance. Many people commented that they felt as if they were sitting in the actual concert hall listening to the live concert in person. The director of the Holland Festival joked that the audience reaction from San Diego was so positive that perhaps he should put a box office in San Diego the next time.

CineGrid members were even more technically ambitious when conceiving two experiments at the GLIF International Workshop in the Czech Republic in 2007. The first experiment was to use networks for international delivery of 4K digital "dailies," the results from each day's shooting that is typically sent back to studio headquarters for preliminary processing and review. After recording with a 4K DALSA digital cinema camera in Prague, the CineGrid team sent the selected RAW-format camera shots over the network to San Diego where "de-mosaic" pre-processing was done using a UCSD/Calit2 computer cluster under remote control. Then, Prague commanded San Diego's server to send the uncompressed RGB frames via network back to Prague for post-production.

For the second GLIF experiment, CineGrid members demonstrated remote color grading of 4K digital cinema content over a 7,500 km local area network (LAN). The colorist, located in Toronto at the Rogers Communications Centre of Ryerson University, was operating the "control surface" of a Baselight 4 system whose main storage and computation hardware were located at the CinePost's facility in Prague's Barrandov Studio. The Baselight4 system in Prague held the uncompressed full-resolution RGB 4K digital cinema sequences that had been pre-processed the night before in San Diego.

The color grading took place under real-time interactive creative direction of a cinematographer sitting in the Prague screening room experiencing everything the colorist in Toronto was seeing and hearing. The CineGrid team used 10 Gb VLANs to carry multiple parallel payloads between Prague and Toronto: an uncompressed HD "proxy" sent from Prague to Toronto; bi-directional HD over IP video confer-encing; and the control signals between the Baselight4 "control surface" in Toronto and the main system in Prague. This ground-breaking test demonstrated how 10 Gb networking infrastructure can be used to create a shared visual workspace rich enough to accomplish real-time interactive collaboration on color grading, which is one of the most expensive and specialized steps in the 4K digital intermediate cinema workflow.

Several CineGrid members have been particularly interested in 4K applica-tions because 4K technology is such a new and challenging format to work with.

Experimentation, prototyping and "learning by doing" within CineGrid are helpful to understanding the real potential of 4 K in various applications. However, that does not mean that CineGrid is focused exclusively on 4 K. Some members are very interested in working with uncompressed low-latency HD, some with stereoscopics, and others with much higher resolutions. Practically, during those years, 4 K represented the newest, highest quality motion picture format for which it was possible to purchase (or rent) devices like cameras, projectors, displays, recorders and playback servers, compression encoders/decoders, etc.

From an engineering perspective also 4 K (and its associated audio channels) generates digital media files of enormous size that can be used to stress test networks, storage and computational infrastructure in useful ways. CineGrid members have had to also learn how to store, transport and exchange their own Terabytes of 4 K digital camera originals, JPEG 2000 encoded versions of selected 4 K clips, and various multi-channel uncompressed audio originals and mixes.

Since 2007, CineGrid members have been actively creating the CineGrid Exchange, a distributed data storage scheme to hold 4 K, 2 K, HD, SD, monoscopic and stereoscopic, digital still and motion picture or digital audio content. The goal is to make CineGrid Exchange assets accessible to CineGrid nodes via secure high-speed networks. CineGrid members contribute networked storage capacity linked by secure fast networks to support member-driven test-beds for research into networked digital media asset management, digital distribution and digital archiving.

Conclusion

These are exciting times for media and networking. The long-term challenge of 4 K content creation and distribution is the coordination of:

- The integration of media devices with computation platforms connected to networks to form distributed systems.
- Workflows that take advantage of the talent and resources connected to the network organizational structures that are aligned with distributed workflows.
- Human resources to staff the organizations that run the workflows which are taking advantage of the networks.

Part III
Content

Chapter 8
Is TV Dead? Consumer Behavior in the Digital TV Environment and Beyond

Gali Einav and John Carey

Abstract On April 8, 1966, *Time Magazine* startled readers with a provocative cover that asked in large type, "Is God Dead?" After reading many newspaper, trade and journal articles, we might ask a similar, if less profound, question – Is TV Dead? The headlines have been screaming about the demise of television: "Let's Just Declare TV Dead and Move On...The End of TV as We Know It...The Internet Is About To Kill TV."

The atmosphere of doom and gloom, fueled by fundamentalist Netizens (those who believe in the Web with near-religious fervor), is reminiscent of the story of Chicken Little who, after being hit on the head with an acorn, declared to the world that "The sky is falling." Looking at the changes in the TV viewing environment through the prism of a researcher's eye, we will argue that not only is the sky not falling, but we are actually at a very low risk of bidding goodbye to television business. Further, rather than looking at the rise of new digital platforms and technologies as a threat, we believe the TV industry is on the verge of a Golden Age of Media – a time when vast new opportunities are opening up for content creators and distributors, and, most importantly, for the consumer.

A Point of Change in TV Viewing

We are at an important point of change in television viewing. There are many new ways of accessing and watching television. We have to re-examine many of our assumptions about television, for example: all TV viewing follows a schedule; with a few exceptions like sports or movies, programs are 30 or 60 min in length; we watch TV programs only on a TV set; most people use print guides to find out about TV shows; and TV gets to us in one of three ways – over-the-air broadcast, cable or satellite. Significant changes in television viewing environment have occurred before. The first major change, which industry veterans will remember, was when TV viewing moved into the home. In the late 1940s, when TV sets were very expensive, most TV viewing was in bars or department stores. Media historian and

D. Gerbarg (ed.), *Television Goes Digital*,
© Springer Science + Business Media, LLC 2009

scholar Leo Bogart called this the era of "Tavern Television" (Bogart, 1972). In the early 1950s, as the price of TV sets dropped, millions of people purchased TVs and began to enjoy television in their homes. Other substantial changes in TV viewing patterns occurred with the adoption of remote controls (more channel changing and a greater sense of control over TV viewing), the purchase of a second or third TV set for a bedroom or kitchen (more personalized viewing), the construction of large cable systems in cities (more niche channels) and the introduction of the VCR (time shift viewing of recorded programs). Each time, some industry analysts saw these changes as a threat to existing television business, when, in fact, they created opportunities for those who did not have their heads in the sand.

The new Millennium brought with it an accelerated pace of change – more changes in the first decade of the new century than in the previous five decades. The internet, digital cable and satellite, broadband, laptops, videogame consoles, wireless networks, portable TV devices, HDTVs and DVRs have created a world in which content is available to consumers whenever and wherever they want it. TV programs are available simultaneously on display devices that are larger and smaller than in the past and there are more ways to transmit programs to consumers. Further, the presence of laptops, with broadband and wireless networks in homes has created a powerful new video portal that can make Web television available anywhere in a household, often in combination with regular TV viewing. While none of these technologies is in as many homes as TV sets, many of them are becoming mainstream – adopted by very large numbers of consumers. Technologies such as HDTV enabled sets, broadband and video games have been transformed from niche media to mainstream media. Other technologies such as DVRs and video capable cell phones are also growing and with them alternative options for TV viewing.

In this chapter, we review several patterns associated with digital television: where it has been and where it is heading, especially as they relate to consumer behavior. These patterns include technology convergence, the impact of digital technology on traditional TV, large screen high resolution TV, small screen TV, interactive television and the narrowing of the digital divide.

Convergence Reconsidered

Convergence is the merging of media, for example, merging of newspapers, radio and television on the Web or merging of electronic program guides, video-on-demand, Web content and interactive services on television. The term has been around for a long time, moving in and out of favor. Though perhaps overused in the past, convergence captures a process that is clearly underway in digital media environment. There are many dimensions to convergence, including technology integration, functional melding of content services, audience fragmentation and geographic convergence. It is a response to rapid changes in technology and shifting behaviors of consumers. What concerns us most here is technology convergence, changes in media behavior and the impact on content production and distribution.

Technological integration of media, for example a cell phone that provides text messaging, music, access to the Web and videos as well as voice communication, is a cornerstone of convergence. Technological integration is made possible by the digitization of media transmission and storage into zeroes and ones of computer code. In a digital world, text, audio and video are all the same – a string of numbers. This makes it easier for one device to provide many different forms of content. At one time, it was thought that certain technologies, the computer for example, would eliminate the need for other devices such as a television set but this did not happen. The reality is that most of the media we use have taken on additional features: computers can play videos as well as display text and graphics; digital TV sets have many computer-like features such as interactivity and are capable of displaying Web content.

There is a seeming contradiction between the convergence process (the coming together of media) and proliferation of media devices. If one device can perform the functions of other devices, why do we need all of them? The reality is that both are happening. We have more media devices than in the past, but technologies we use also have more features and services. One consequence of the proliferation of media devices is fragmentation of audiences. Most people in a town do not read the same morning newspaper and choose among three broadcast networks in the evening, as millions did decades ago. Our consumption is spread across a broad range of media services. Convergence, in the sense of distributing content on multiple platforms, is one way of dealing with audience fragmentation.

Convergence involves the functional merger of services, for example, text, photos and video in news (Kolodzy, 2006). This is most notable on the Web, where a news site may have stories in multiple formats, along with reader forums, blogs, polling, interactive maps and direct links to sites with more information. Similar patterns of merged services are apparent on television and MP-3 players.

Convergence is also notable in news production. Many news organizations have, under different names, a News Center where stories for multiple platforms originate. Frequently, reporters in these News Centers are not distinguished by the medium for which they create a story but by their beat. So, a crime reporter in such a News Center may create stories for the organization's newspaper, Web site and TV news programs (Quin, 2006). A good example of convergence in the newsroom is NBC's Ann Curry's reporting on brutal rapes of women and girls in the Congo. Ms. Curry and her producers created stories for the *Today* show, NBC *Nightly News*, and MSNBC cable. Working in close collaboration with the Msnbc. com Web teams, they also created extra content for the *Today* show and *Nightly News* Web sites, which included additional interview materials and a Web only Q & A link through which viewers could ask Ann questions directly. Selected questions were answered in video on location in the Congo and posted by producers on the *Nightly News* Web site. Further, segments were promoted across media, posting the video on the Web and teased on the broadcast.

The news producer in such a center must think through how to cover a story, for what media, by whom and the context in which a viewer will experience the story. The consumer of news is also more active in the converged media environment.

They comment about stories and sometimes provide news in the form of photos they submit or news tips they provide.

Are there limits to convergence? Consumers have widely adopted cell phones but do they want to shop, watch a football game and prepare a spreadsheet on a cell phone? There may be generational differences, where younger people will readily accept the cell phone as a multi-application device and older people will just want to use a cell phone to make telephone calls and receive a limited set of additional features. Further, we may learn from other countries such as Japan and Korea, which have more advanced cell phone networks, what advantaged features consumers want.

Noteworthy for our premise of expanded opportunities, convergence has created a voracious appetite for content. This provides an opportunity for content producers and distributors. There is demand for new content, advanced platforms that support new and creative forms of content, and ways to distribute content that did not exist before.

New Video Media Are Not Replacing Established Media

One might think that mainstreaming of some technologies is achieved at the expense of others, with new video media replacing established technologies, but this is not the case. It is true that online streaming experienced phenomenal growth in the middle of the decade and went from rare to occasional to mainstream in a very short period of time. According to Comscore, within a period of 18 months, from early 2006 to mid 2007, the number of unique streamers doubled from approximately 65 million to 130 million. The number of total streams grew from approximately 3.5 billion to 9 billion. By the third quarter of the decade nearly three in four internet users streamed video content in any given month. Interestingly, television viewing has not been affected by this growth. According to Nielsen Media Research, persons using television (PUT) ratings among people 18–49 grew from 16.9 to 18.8 over the same period. PUT growth is also strong among teens. Further, online video viewing helps extend the reach of TV shows. The most popular television shows tend to be the most viewed online as well (Stelter, 2008).

How is this possible? The buzz word of the media industry is multitasking. According to the Ball State University Middletown media studies (Papper et al., 2005), we manage to consume more than 12 h of media in 9 h on an average day, through multitasking (for example, a person who listens to an iPod for 10 min while simultaneously watching TV would be classified as consuming 20 min of media). By comparison, we experience seven hours of sleep and nine hours of work on an average weekday. As a result, we are experiencing more media use than ever before. This is one reason for our argument that we are entering a Golden Age of Media (Fig. 8.1) in which there are many more opportunities to reach new and existing audiences over a plethora of platforms. We are experiencing a move from viewing habits to new choices, framed by availability of new technologies.

Television viewing is breaking out of the conventional box that marked our expectations of how people utilize TV. New viewing platforms and behaviors

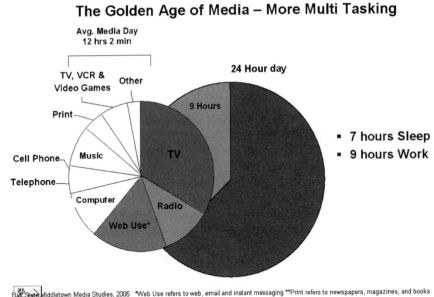

Fig. 8.1 Golden age of media

such as time shifting with the help of a DVR, streaming online via broadband and watching TV over bigger and smaller screens are all legitimate forms of viewing television content. Does choice have a negative effect on television viewing? A number of studies have shown that DVR owners watch more television, especially prime time shows, since they have control over when to watch them. Further, they like TV more since they are watching shows that they can choose from the entire 24-h lineup. In addition, specific prime time shows garner viewers who may have been lost if not for the option of time shifted viewing. Nielsen has begun to capture this viewing in new ratings data that include live plus the next seven days of time shifted viewing. By way of example, *The Office* during the week of October 1–7, 2007, showed an exponential growth of more than 40% once time shifted viewers were included. Online streaming adds even more viewers and the distributor can control whether or not people can fast forward through commercials while watching online.

DVRs and the 'Death of TV'

Concern that the DVR will be the death of television advertising are reminiscent of Mark Twain's comment, upon reading an obituary of himself in the newspaper – "reports of my death are greatly exaggerated." There are no indicators that television advertising will go away. Questions about television advertising in the DVR environment have led to interesting developments in an attempt to shed light on how fast forwarded ads are actually viewed by consumers. For Example, NBC, with research partner Innerscope, conducted a groundbreaking biometric DVR study that tracked measures such as eye movements and heart rate to test ad retention and recall (Kang, 2008). The study found that, consistent with Nielsen data, some DVR viewers actually stop to watch commercials. It also found that those who do fast-forward through commercials are in a state of "hyper-alert" which enables them to process ads at a pre-conscious level. These viewers actively scan the content, follow the action and see brand logos and text. As a result they recall ads they fast forward through, even at six times the normal speed. The analysis showed that most recalled commercials were those that concentrated action and the brand's logo in the middle of the screen. Successful commercials (those most likely to be remembered) also had minimum scene changes, did not rely on audio to tell the story, (since it becomes irrelevant in a fast forward viewing mode) and often used familiar characters. Viewers were more likely to remember an ad in fast-forward mode if they had seen it once before in live viewing mode.

These fascinating results may have interesting implications for advertisers by potentially influencing decisions on media placements, i.e. choosing to advertise on live shows, learning how to copy test (both live and FF modes) as well as incorporating findings in the creative process. For example, in a commercial that was not part of the study Visa used a visual tag, "Life Takes Visa," in blue lettering on a white screen and kept it on a few extra seconds, making it more prominent and visible for a person fast forwarding through the commercial on a DVR. The study also mirrors a substantial change which is taking place in the media industry: the collaboration between networks and advertisers/agencies, to better understand consumer behavior. Formerly on opposing sides of the table, agencies now reach out to networks for assistance in obtaining insights on consumer behavior and they work together to plan strategies that will benefit both.

Online Video Viewing Patterns

Looking more closely at online video, new viewing patterns are beginning to emerge. In addition to "video snacking" on short clips – the main form of online video available in the middle of the decade – there has been an incredible growth in full episode viewing. Although they are a small share of TV viewing overall, TV episodes have been a significant driver of streaming video growth – according to Harris Interactive – rising from a very small percentage of all online video streaming in the spring of 2006 to nearly 20% in the spring of 2007.

"I just wanted to catch up on shows I missed"

– Respondent in an NBC Research Study, 2007

NBC's study of its Rewind video player, showcasing prime time shows on nbc.com, uncovered another interesting pattern of viewing. While there has been some video "snacking" of (mainly) short form video content during the day, majority of NBC Rewind viewing has taken place at home and at night, a behavior similar to TV viewing. This is not to say that online viewing is replacing traditional television viewing. The study showed that online viewing is creating an incremental audience, with majority of people falling into a "catch up viewer" category, stating that they have used Rewind to watch an episode that they missed on TV. In addition, a majority of respondents in the study were new viewers, who were exposed to a show for the first time online. Many of these viewers remained loyal to the show and kept viewing both online and TV. A second pattern of online video use is to re-watch favorite shows a person has seen before, sometimes in their entirety and sometimes favorite scenes. A third use of online video is to watch shows that friends recommend after the show has aired. In this way, online video has an advantage over DVRs. With DVRs, one has to anticipate what one wants to watch and set the DVR to record it; with online TV programs one can go back and watch a program that was on TV the day before even though one did not record it. It is worth noting that content providers are now developing online video download models that will imitate online DVR recording capabilities, mainly pre recording a full season of programming, thus providing consumers even more opportunities for consuming content online. This suggests that, at this point, the online video experience is not cannibalizing viewers but building loyalty to favorite shows and exposing people to new shows they have missed. At a basic level, the number of ways people can receive and watch television programs has expanded from over-the-air broadcast, cable, satellite and purchased or rented DVDs to all of those plus DVRs, telephone company video systems, online video and portable video devices such as iPods. It is an expansion of choice, with consumers having more control over the viewing experience.

Big Screen, High Resolution TV

Beginning in 2008, nearly all TV sets sold in the US were digital; most were high definition and many were large screen TVs (30 in. or more). Larger screen size and higher resolution of these digital sets have led to a number of effects on viewing behavior. We have been studying households that acquire large screen, high definition digital TVs for a number of years and can offer some observations about their viewing behavior and attitudes.

Why do people get HDTV? Upto the mid 2000s, most of those buying HDTVs were classic early adopters who were willing to pay a high price in order to be the first in their neighborhood to have the new technology. As price came down and more people learned about HDTV, the mix of adopters was more varied. Some specifically wanted to get HDTV, but many got it because an existing set went on the fritz and HDTVs dominated the showrooms at electronics' stores – it seemed the natural thing to buy. It was more of a mainstream purchase rather than a 'high tech' purchase.

In a similar pattern, a few years ago nearly all the households we studied who had HDTV said it was a "wow" technology. It made television much more enjoyable, they watched more TV, and they invited neighbors over to show off their dazzling new technology. More recently, most households have told us that HDTV was a big plus in their lives but not a wow. If the wow factor has diminished somewhat, it has been replaced by a commitment to HDTV (no one would give it up) and the expectation that all programming and all TVs will eventually be in HD.

When asked if they planned to replace other sets with HDTV, some people told us they were planning to get a second HDTV in the next year; nearly all said they would eventually replace other TVs with HD. This was couched in terms of an expectation that HDTVs would continue to drop in price over time. Further, since most of the other TVs in their households were smaller "secondary" TVs, they expected that by the time they replaced them, the price would not be much more than a similar size analog TV.

People we studied said that there was moderately more group viewing of HDTV. Teens who normally locked themselves in their rooms with their personal TVs would sometimes venture out to watch favorite shows on HDTV, even if they had to tolerate their parents. A number of people described 'lingering in the HDTV room' when in the past they would leave. For example, in the past if a show they didn't like came on, they would leave and watch another program in a different room. Now, if a show came on, there was a more complex decision: if a favorite program can be watched in another room, leave; if one really dislikes the show that a spouse wants to watch, leave; but if the show is tolerable, probably stay because it is in HD.

We also investigated the issue of multi-tasking, which many have reported as a common accompaniment to TV viewing. A going-in hypothesis was that the strong engagement of the HD image might reduce multi-tasking. People reported (and we observed) a lot of multi-tasking – about the same amount as before- most said. There appeared to be two countervailing forces which in the end, led to the same amount of multi-tasking. First, the picture was very engaging and many seemed riveted to what they were watching (so, less multi-tasking). However, in most households, the HDTV was very large, allowing people to watch it from a distance – where they were engaged in other activities. For example, one woman showed us how she watched the living room TV from the kitchen, where she prepared meals, paid bills, etc. In addition, we observed many laptops in the same room as the HDTV and the use of laptops while watching HDTV. Much of this activity was related to what they were watching (e.g., checking TV listings on an online TV guide, looking up sports statistics, going to a blog about an actor in a TV show, going to a Web site for a program and voting, etc.) but more of it was general Web activity such as checking email, shopping, paying bills, etc. A few years earlier, when the PC was in a different room from the main household TV, there was less synergy between TV programs and Web usage since people would have to remember the linkage after they finished watching TV and went to the room with the PC.

The location of the HDTV and its impact on 'social definition' of the space it occupies is very important. Most of the HDTVs we have observed have been located in a living room or other main room of the home such as a den or family room. Since the HDTVs are generally large, they often dominate these rooms – they define the space as a 'TV environment.' Males are generally ok with this but some females are not. They do not want to give up the esthetics of the living room to technology. Flat screen sets that hang on a wall and smaller HDTV sets are less of a concern than large HDTVs that occupy considerable space within the room. The growth in sales of flat screen HDTV is both a reflection of and a solution to this concern. Flat screen TVs can be integrated into the room design without taking it over.

Small HDTVs are often chosen for environments like a kitchen or bedroom. Here too, the issue is that the TV should not dominate the room or, in the case of kitchens, get in the way of other functional tasks. Technology is evolving to fit comfortably in a range of social spaces

Large screen HDTVs have led to some changes in viewing behavior. When asked where they go when they first turn on the HDTV, many of the people we interviewed said they go first to the HD tier of channels. In some cases, they go to a favorite HD channel or a specific program in HD. Others simply go to the HD tier of channels and see if they can find something enjoyable to watch. Only if they cannot find anything to watch on the HD tier do they go to other sections of their TV service.

A related issue is the sheer size of TV services with HD – they have many (often hundreds) channels. Regardless of the HD channels, it is more difficult to surf very large channel services. Many HD owners say they do less channel surfing than in the past. Further, some sections of the channel lineup can become isolated neighborhoods that few visit. It is also more difficult to know what is on so many channels. Printed TV guides are fading away; electronic program guides (EPGs) are replacing them.

HDTV is not without flaws and obstacles to further growth. Many people are confused by the multiple menus and settings on HDTVs and associated set-top boxes that feed the HD signal to the TV. One problem is simply to figure out which remote to pick up to change a setting (the TV remote or the one for the set-top box). Aspect ratios (i.e., the ration of width to height of the TV screen: 4 to 3 for earlier analog programs; 16 to 9 for HDTV; and customized settings such as 'panoramic') confuse many. Some do not understand them at all; others do not like it when the picture does not fill the entire screen. There is also confusion over multiple inputs and modes. If one is watching a DVD, how does one get back to TV? Nearly all can do it but many said it is confusing. When asked about settings on older TV sets, many told us that they never changed a setting on their old TVs other than to choose a channel and adjust the volume.

Our research suggests that the future for large screen HDTVs is bright. HDTV is moving from the realm of high tech early adopters to average TV households. If some of the superlatives and luster of HDTV have diminished, it is also becoming mainstream – the expected norm, as with color television several years after it was introduced. The households we have studied would not give up their HDTV and they plan to eventually replace all household TVs with HDTVs. They want and expect all channels and all content to eventually be provided in HD. It is also clear that channels on the HD tier have a distinct advantage over those not on the HD tier since many people go to the HD tier first. If there is a change needed for HDTV to become ubiquitous, it is for greater simplicity in the design of HDTVs and more attention to ease of use in menus. The consumer electronics industry has been reacting to these trends by producing cheaper, thinner and higher resolution HDTV's, including OLED screens with a million to one resolution ratio. Other devices such as wireless HD and HD storage capabilities on flash drives will all push forward the HDTV consumer experience.

Small Screen TV

What is the effect of smaller, portable screens on media consumption? Although there is a proliferation of small screens such as video iPods and cell phones, the majority of Americans still prefer to watch television content on a bigger television screen. According to a Harris Study, two thirds of people would always prefer to watch video on their TV versus a computer or portable video device (Harris Interactive, May 2007) However, laptops and portable video devices are useful secondary TVs when a big set is not available or to watch a second program along with the TV show on a large set. The same study revealed that only 6% have ever connected a computer to a TV to watch internet video. So, while TV programs are being viewed on the Web, growth has been modest for Web videos that are viewed on TV sets. This could change. Scenarios that might lead to more Web video viewing on TVs include placing those videos on the servers of cable operators and making them available through video-on-demand, introduction of a new generation of devices that make it easier and cheaper to move Web videos from a computer to a TV set, such as the Sling Box and building the ability to access the Web into cable, satellite and telephone company video boxes.

Most Americans do not use their cell phones and video MP-3 players for video at all. However, those who do use an MP-3 player for watching TV programs, report that it is a positive experience (early experiences with cell phone video were not as positive). How could watching a TV program on a small MP-3 player screen be positive? It is important to remember that people sit much closer to an MP-3 player screen when they are watching TV programs compared to regular TV sets. Viewing a TV program on an MP-3 player that is 18 in. away is like watching a 30 in. TV set from six feet away. People also have developed many ways of positioning an MP-3 player so that it is not tiring, for example they set it against a pillow, rest the hand holding the MP-3 on a lap or use one of the stands that are made for the devices. It may come as a surprise to some that most viewing of TV programs on MP-3 players and other portable video devices is in the home. Some people watch TV programs on a portable device while in bed, before they go to sleep. They report that ear buds are very useful since they do not disturb a spouse but if they laugh too loudly at a comedy show, it may lead to a poke in the side. Others use portable video devices to stay in a room even when they do not like the show playing on the main TV. People have told us that when they are watching TV with a spouse and a favorite show of one person comes on (which the other doesn't like) it was common in the past for one to leave the room and watch a different show on a TV set in another room. One person called this the "TV divorce." Now, they stay together and while one watches the main TV, the other watches a recorded show on the portable player, using ear buds to not disturb their spouse.

There is an important distinction to be made between television content and its distribution screen. Good television content is still and will always be in demand. There is a strong preference for professionally produced content online, now that video quality has improved. A few years ago, in a dial-up narrowband internet world, streaming video was the size of a postage stamp and frequently out of sync with the audio. In that environment, professional and amateur content all looked bad. In the new broadband environment, high quality video looks very good, if not quite as good as regular television, and viewers can see a difference between amateur and professional content. Though many like short, off-beat amateur content, professional content dominates long form viewing.

Interactive TV

Interactive television trials in the US have spanned more than five decades, initiated by the first video phone call between Washington and NYC made in 1927 by then Secretary of Commerce, Herbert Hoover (Einav, 2004). In following decades, various interactive platforms have been experimented with, ranging from phone, cable and the Internet. Most initial trials had failed due to lack of consumer adoption, poor user experience and pitfalls deriving from nascent technology. However, this has changed.

Three recent changes in consumer media use have helped revive interactive television trials.

1. The advent of broadband, which by the middle of the decade was available to 50% of US households, created a substantial increase of online use. Internet use has become main-stream across gender and generations. As a result, consumers have become more accustomed to and comfortable with the concept and use of interactive applications. The increased use of EPGs (electronic program guides) which according to Forrester research is used an average of 4.7 times per day by more than a third of users, has been a substantial catalyst of interactivity (McQuivey, 2007)

2. The number of computers located in the same room as television sets has reached approximately 50% of the US population (HTM, 2007). Although consumers are not necessarily surfing the Web for television related content, proximity of the devices helps create a ripe environment for interactivity. A third change is

the growth in cell phone ownership, which has reached more than 80% of US households. This has made the cell phone and SMS a mass medium platform for interactivity.

3. As of the second half of the decade, there has been an increase in real time participation with television shows, mostly reality and game shows. Some of this followed the lead set by European broadcasters during the early 2000s. US television networks have been offering a growing number of real time, program related participation opportunities. For example, NBC's game show "Deal or no Deal", offers a "Live TV Challenge" that allows viewers to play along live with the game show. The multiplayer game allows for live predictions, mini games tied to which cases get opened, and opinion polls, in which viewers can compete for points and prizes with other fans of the show. Voting and participation was also available via SMS and one screen interactivity through the television remote control. Millions of votes have been attributed to each show.

The Digital Divide Narrows As Mainstreaming Takes Over

In the mid 1990s, a widely read government report, *Falling Through The Net* (NTIA, 1996), proclaimed that there was a wide digital divide between those who had access to new information technologies and those who did not, based on age, ethnicity and geographic location. Communications research scholar Horst Stipp has analyzed a range of data on technology adoption and demonstrated that the digital divide has narrowed considerably. Focusing on age, young people are more likely to use a device like a video MP-3 player, but there is considerable adoption across age groups for DVRs, HDTVs, broadband and laptops. Another study, by Katz and Rice (2009) found that the gender gap identified in the 1990s has all but disappeared and predictions that media, like the Web would foster social isolation have not materialized. These and other studies support the concept of mainstreaming which we introduced earlier. While not all of these technologies are available in a majority of US households, they have moved past the early adopter stage and have found wide acceptance across a broad range of households.

The Future

It is difficult to predict what the television landscape will look like ten years from now. What we do know is that old habits are slow to change. Traditional media habits still apply, with television viewing growing and big screen preferences still the norm. On the other hand, consumers are exploring new choices such as time shifted viewing, online viewing and video over portable media and their growing expectation of control over content consumption is not likely to recede any time soon. What has not changed are the core functions of television – to relax, to escape, to be entertained (Mendelsohn, 1966) but people might choose to do so over less traditional platforms than the television set depending when and where they are at the time.

If prediction is risky, it is possible to point out some implications or changes that may follow from the digital media environment. The first set of implications relates to content and production. Who will create content? Most content that people actually watch will be created by professionals but amateurs will have a role and they will post a great deal of content, most of which will be viewed by only a few people. Beyond amateurs with cell phone cameras who record pratfalls or the offbeat, and professionals who work for large media organizations, there is a third group: serious programmers who aspire to create professional content. A number of such groups have emerged and some of these have developed a commercial relationship with or been absorbed into mainstream media organizations. This should lead to a lot of experimentation which will be good for consumers and mainstream media industries in the long run. There will also be more mash-ups or content that is made available on the Web and then, legally or illegally, edited or supplemented by Web users.

Producing content for large and small screens will be both a challenge and an opportunity. How do you cover a sporting event or produce a drama program that will be viewed by some on a 60-in. screen and by others on a 2-in. screen? Production units in a converged media organization may choose to optimize for one environment with the most viewers, edit a program differently for large and small screen, or develop new technology that will automatically re-size some content so that it is optimized for the medium on which it appears.

Will high definition digital television lead to new types of actors, announcers and politicians who come across better in this new medium? It happened in the transition from silent films to talkies, stadium orators to radio politicians, and radio stars to TV stars. Marshall McLuhan famously declared that John Kennedy was well suited to the cool medium of TV and Richard Nixon was not (McLuhan, 1964). Will digital JFKs emerge?

There are many implications for advertising. One implication which we touched on earlier may be a need to learn how to produce commercials for a DVR environment. Advertising, like sports coverage and drama, must also be adapted for large and small screens. Commercials can become more interactive, either by using two-screen TV (Web content that complements a TV commercial) or allowing viewers to interact with the commercial over two-way cable systems. As digital TV systems advance and we know more about individual viewers, it will be possible to dynamically insert commercials based on interests of each viewer. In other words, a movie fan may see a commercial for a recently released movie and a car enthusiast for a new sports car while both are watching the same TV program. Viral marketing will take on new meaning in an environment where advertisers can release video components of a commercial and invite viewers to create mash-ups using the video.

From time to time a side effect of a new technology has as much impact as the core reason why people acquired it. For example, most people got broadband for faster delivery of Web content but one side effect of broadband has been that people keep their broadband service on all the time or whenever they are at home. 'Always on' has, in turn, led to many new behaviors such as very short Web sessions (e.g., to check the weather) and going into the Web dozens of times a day. The dial-up Internet "session" has all but disappeared for broadband users. Side effects are sure to happen in the new digital TV environment. One candidate side effect is the reduction in importance of a TV schedule in an environment where we can easily DVR content and watch later or catch up on missed programs through video streaming. In the television industry, the term 'watercooler TV' has been used for decades to describe the phenomenon of people talking about TV shows at work after watching them the previous evening. All producers want their shows to be 'watercooler TV.' In an environment of DVRs and streaming media, it becomes more difficult to produce watercooler TV. The model of TV viewing is changing. While not a perfect analogy, TV viewing is becoming more like reading magazines – people consume TV, like magazine articles, at different times and in different places. Further, we are entering an age of replay TV where it is very easy to watch programming a second time or simply after the time when it was originally aired.

As the number of distribution points for digital television programming expands, we are likely to revisit the debate about whether content or distribution is king. The television industry has shifted back and forth on this issue over many decades. More recently, the shift is moving back to content. When there were relatively few distribution points, it was better to be a distributor and leave the expense of creating content to others. With an abundance of distribution points, the pendulum swings back to owning content and licensing it to multiple distributors.

It is important to remember that not everything is successful. In fact, most new technologies, new TV programs, and new consumer services fail. The burst of the Web bubble in the early 2000s taught all of us a painful lesson. Moving forward, it will be necessary to scrutinize new ventures for consumer appeal and business viability. It is also important to ask where we are in the technology development, behavioral change and content development cycle. That is, new television technologies often lead to new forms of viewing behavior which, in turn, lead to new content. Think of the remote control which led to more channel changing which in turn supported niche content. In the digital television age, we appear to be early in the process. Some new technologies have emerged, but many more are likely enter the marketplace over the next decade. This suggests that we should be actively monitoring changes in behavior and thinking about creative new content that will serve the digital viewer.

To return to our original question, is TV dead? The answer is clearly, no, but TV viewing environment is changing in ways as profound as the shift from Tavern TV to Home TV in the early 1950s. We need to be aware of change and continue to monitor it. Let's lean back, or forward, and enjoy one of the most exciting times television business has experienced since the introduction of the television set those many years ago.

References

L. Bogart, *The Age of Television (3rd Edition)*. New York: Frederick Unger Publishing, 1972

G. Einav, *I Want My iTV: Content, Demand and Social Implications of Interactive Television*. Ph.D. Dissertation, Columbia University, 2004

S. Kang, "Why DVR Viewers Recall Some TV Spots", *The New York Times*, February 26, 2008, p. B-5

J. Katz and R. Rice, "Falling into the Net: Main Street America Playing Games and Making Friends Online", *Communications of the ACM*, 2009

J. Kolodzy, *Converging Journalism: Writing and Reporting Across The News Media*. New York: Rowman and Littlefield Publishers, 2006

M. McLuhan, *Understanding Media: The Extensions of Man*. New York: McGraw Hill, 1964

J. McQuivey, *Interactive TV's Renaissance*, Forrester research, August 14th, 2007

H. Mendelsohn, *Mass Entertainment*. New Haven: College and University Press, 1966

National Telecommunications and Information Administration, *Falling Through The Net: A Survey of the "Have Nots" in Rural and Urban America*. Washington, DC: US Department of Commerce, 1996

Knowledge Networks, *HTM Ownership and Use Report*, 2007

R.A. Papper, M.E. Holmes, M.N. Popovich, and M. Bloxham, *Middletown Media Studies II: The media day. Muncie*, In: Ball State University Center for Media Design, 2005 (available online www.bsu.edu/cmd/insightresearch)

S. Quin (editor), *Conversations on Convergence: Insiders' Views on News Production in the 21st Century*. New York: Peter Lang Publishing, 2006

B. Stelter, "Serving Up Television Without the TV Set", *The New York Times*, March 10, 2008

Chapter 9
Video on the Internet: The Content Question

Jeffrey A. Hart

Abstract What is the effect of Internet distribution of digital video on content? Is there evidence that content will be different from what is available through other conduits or will it just be more of the same? Who will be producing it and who will be consuming it? How important will user-generated video content be? These are some of the questions addressed in this essay.

Introduction

The video content produced for transmission via the Internet and other digital television conduits is likely to be different from that produced for analog television. One key difference is that less than 50% of US households currently have access to digital TV services of some kind while almost all households have access to analog TV broadcasts. An even smaller percentage has a connection to the Internet that is fast enough for the delivery of broadcast-quality digital TV. Thus, audience for digital content is currently smaller and possibly more elite than for analog content. As a result, digital content tends to be a bit "edgier" than analog content. This difference will decline over time and especially with continued rollout of high-speed broadband services and transition to digital broadcasting. As more and more households get access to high-quality digital video, at least some of the newer, edgier content will survive only in market niches. Yet, it is likely that range and variety of content will be greater than it was before.

Why is this an important topic? We would like to know if new information and communications technologies are contributing positively to free speech and creative activity, because the latter is crucial to democracy. There has been much discussion of the role that analog television has played in enhancing or detracting from democracy. Some social scientists argue, for example, that analog television has had a negative impact because of the dependence of voters on TV news for coverage of election campaigns and because that coverage (especially of local elections) is not as good as it was when voters got their information primarily from print media like newspapers.[1] In addition some argue, that concentration of ownership of broadcast networks and limited competition in local TV markets reduces the

D. Gerbarg (ed.), *Television Goes Digital*,
© Springer Science + Business Media, LLC 2009

number of political viewpoints that voters can access.[2] New digital media has the potential to permit more voices in society to be heard. But are they realizing that potential?

Recent debates over digital transition revealed that less than 20% of US households now get TV signals delivered via terrestrial broadcasts. That means that more than 80% of households get TV via cable or satellite.[3] Cable and satellite are already competing with digital TV delivered by phone companies (see below for details).

Increased competition between telephone and cable companies for telephone, television, and high-speed Internet customers is a consequence of policies adopted during the 1990s by Congress, particularly the Telecommunications Act of 1996, and the Federal Communications Commission. Although the rollout of broadband Internet services in the United States has been slower than in at least a dozen other countries,[4] once it gathers momentum growing numbers of people are likely to be able to access digital TV content via conduits other than terrestrial broadcasts, cable, and satellite. These new digital TV audiences already seem to have developed habits different from those of analog TV viewers, and analysts are trying to guess which of those habits will persist. So the task at hand is to examine carefully what video content is currently available to audiences via the Internet and use that information to make informed guesses about near-term and mid-term future of digital TV content.

Frameworks for Analysis

Key to analysis is identifying the most important factors behind content strategies of content producers. One crucial factor is the potential size of the audience. Analog TV is aimed generally at large audiences, while much of pioneering digital TV content is aimed at small, specialized audiences. Some digital content, however, is for mass consumption; while some analog content is for niche markets, especially after the rise of multi-channel services like cable and satellite. Large audience video content can be supported by sponsorship or advertising; while small audience content may be distributed without charge with customized advertising or provided on a download-to-own or pay-per-view basis. Although one might generally think of large audience video as having higher production values than small audience video, occasionally content off the diagonal (see Fig. 9.1, below) is successful.

An example of large audience content with low production values would be a highly successful YouTube clip produced by a single individual with a Web cam (see, for example, Chris Crocker's videos emotionally defending Britney Spears[5]). LonelyGirl15 is a hybrid with a full production crew producing video episodes for a series that is only distributed via the Internet.[6] An example of small audience content with high production values would be a high-definition digital video program introduced via the Internet as a means of finding a more conventional outlet (e.g., Sanctuary).[7] From the producer's perspective, mass audiences with low production

Fig. 9.1 Production values
and potential audience size

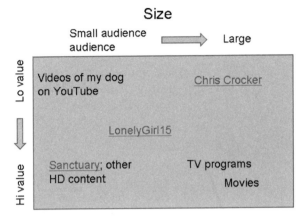

Table 9.1 The MeTV hypothesis (Eli Noam)

Stages	Delivery	Audience size	Regulation	Business model
Limited	Terrestrial	Large	Regulated	Ad-Supported
Multi-channel	Cable, satellite	Smaller	Lightly regulated	Subscription
MeTV	Internet and other digital	Niches	Lightly regulated?	Download to own, pay per view

costs are valued highly because of potential for large profits. Nevertheless, the movie industry, which sets standards for all full-motion imagery, generally opts for high-cost productions combined with heavy advertising to assure large audiences.[8]

Another way to look at this issue is the MeTV hypothesis of Eli Noam.[9] Noam argues that the first phase of TV was what he called "limited TV": broadcasting-based, large audiences, regulated, and ad-supported. The second phase of TV was "multi-channel TV": delivered by cable or satellite, small to medium-sized audiences, lightly regulated, and subscription-based. The third phase will be "MeTV": delivered by various digital media, stored on TiVo like boxes, largely unregulated, and paid for on a file-by-file basis. A distinctive feature of the third phase would be user programming of content instead of network or channel programming (see Table 9.1).

Vint Cerf predicted the "end of TV as we know it" generalizing from success of iPod/iTunes in audio content.[10] The user downloads audio and video clips from the Internet to a computer and then transfers them to and plays them on a convenient device. Whereas audio clips are mostly played on iPods or MP3 portable devices, it is likely that video content will be downloaded also to set-top boxes to be played on televisions. Nevertheless, the same business model of downloading content via the Internet will apply to both types of content, according to this theory.

Part of the Noam/Cerf theorizing is premised on the importance of time-shifting for consumers, and hence of storage of programs for later viewing. This coincides nicely with relative strengths and weaknesses of digital delivery media, where

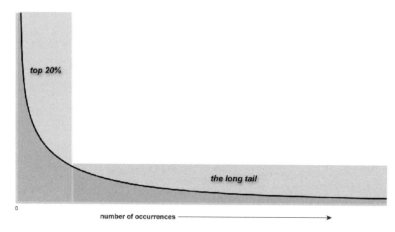

Fig. 9.2 The long tail (Pareto distribution).
Source: http://blogs.idc.com/ie/wp-content/LongTail_01.jpg

greater efficiencies are realized by taking advantage of lower cost of transmitting information when traffic is low. The capacity of the Internet may be challenged by too much real-time usage for transmission of real-time programming, which is one of the reasons why telephone and cable companies want to reserve bandwidth for their own IPTV services. But another response by market players is to offer services that involve downloading of large files via the Internet to DVRs and set-top boxes for later viewing.

A third perspective that can be used for analysis is the long-tail hypothesis. Popularized in a best-seller by Chris Anderson,[11] the long tail is simply an expected distribution curve called a Pareto Distribution (or power law) where the highest ranked services in terms of audience dominate the total but where, as the ranking declines there are still many services commanding smaller and smaller audiences (see Fig. 9.2). If the distribution has a "fat tail" – i.e. if a large percentage of service providers are in the right-hand half of the tail – then that is a sign of market diversity even if a small number of large providers dominate the market. Degree of inequality in a distribution can be measured using a variety of indices, including the Gini and Hirschman/Herfindahl indices. Another way of restating the long tail hypothesis would be to say that introduction of digital delivery via the Internet will decrease the Gini index for video content providers (measured in terms of audience share).

Mass-Audience TV Migrates to IPTV

Until recently, delivery of digital video broadcast content by television channels and networks was limited mainly to short clips or lower-resolution streamed video on Web sites. All broadcasting networks are offering both clips and whole programs

Table 9.2 Web sites of the four television broadcasting networks

Network	URL	Comments
ABC	http://www.abc.go.com	4:3, Free
CBS	http://www.cbs.com	4:3, Free
Fox	http://www.fox.com	4:3, Free
NBC universal	http://www.nbc.com	16:9, Ad-supported

using Flash for playback; so far only NBC is offering ad-supported 16:9 video (see Table 9.2). A combination of advertising and fees for downloading or streaming will eventually be used to obtain revenues for these services, but for the moment they are primarily used to advertise broadcasts themselves and/or to allow fans of particular programs or series to watch entire programs at their convenience.

Business strategies of telephone and cable companies now include delivery of digital video content via their networks, mainly through what is called IPTV or Internet Protocol Television.[12] Such services will typically be bundled with Web access and Voice over Internet Protocol (VoIP) telephone services. The bundling of cable TV, Web access, and VoIP services for a slighter reduced fee in the United States is called "triple play." In the future, mobile services may be added to constitute a "quadruple play." Addition of quadruple play may mean high-quality mobile video services will become widely available. Some mobile video is currently offered by cellular carriers but at relatively low quality and high prices. An example of this is Verizon's V CAST Video service.

In 2006, AT&T launched its U-Verse IPTV service offering over 300 channels in 11 cities with more to be added in subsequent years. U-Verse provides high-speed Internet access at a speed of around 6 Mbit/s via a fiber to the node (FTTN) architecture. The fiber goes to a DSLAM box in the neighborhood; copper cable goes from there into the subscriber's home. The service was launched in San Antonio, Texas. Thirty of the 300 channels offered in the most expensive U-Verse package included high-definition television (HDTV) content.[13] At the end of 2006, there were only 3,000 U-Verse customers; by September 2007, there were 100,000. AT&T expected the U-Verse service would be available to 8 million homes by the end of 2007; and more than double that by the end of 2008.

Verizon launched its pilot FiOS service in Keller, Texas in September 2005. FiOS is a high-speed broadband service offering (eventually) 100 megabit per second (mps) downloads via fiber to home (FTTH) architecture. Actual FiOS services started at 10 mps which was raised to 20 mps in 2007. By the end of March 2007, Verizon had passed 6.8 million homes. Verizon hoped to add 3 million homes per year by the end of 2010. The total investment in the FiOS network through 2010 was projected to be $18 billion.To the end of September 2007, Verizon had over 500,000 FiOS subscribers. The video service part of FiOS was expected to have over 200,000 subscribers by the end of 2007.

Table 9.3 summarizes similarities and differences between AT&T and Verizon services. The purpose of TV services of U-Verse and FiOS is to permit the two telephone companies to compete with cable companies for cable TV customers by

Table 9.3 Verizon FiOS vs. AT&T
U-Verse

	FiOS	U-Verse
Architecture	FTTH	FTTN
Video Customers, end 2007	1,000,000	231,000
Download speeds	10 mps	6 mps

using broadband infrastructure. The channel lineups and pricing of the two services are clearly pointed in that direction and early reports show that they are taking
customers away from local cable competitors.

While rollout of U-Verse and FiOS is important for building of broadband
infrastructure in the United States, so far the implications for TV content are fairly
minimal. The same content that is being provided by terrestrial broadcasters, cable
operators, and satellite services will be available on U-Verse and FiOS with only a
few exceptions. The same can be said for certain Internet video aggregators like Joost,
hulu.com, and others. More important is that customers of these services will have
high-speed Internet access if they did not have it already, and edgier Internet Television
content will also be available to them via the Web if they choose to access it.

Internet TV Viewers and Their Habits

Whereas IPTV is basically a set of technologies and market strategies that allow
telephone companies to compete with cable companies for current mass-audience
TV viewers, Internet TV is a broader phenomenon involving use of the Internet to
distribute digital video images of all sorts. To capture on paper the enormous variety of types of video on the Internet is impossible, and much time will be wasted by
scholars in vain attempts to bring order to chaos. Nevertheless, some patterns can
be identified and some order can be imposed artificially for the sake of inquiry.

A report released by Veronis Suhler Stevenson (VSS) in August 2007 reported
that total time spent on various media declined for the first time since 1997,
although the hourly average usage was still 3.53 h per day. In 2006, consumers
spent most of their media time viewing TV and listening to radio (70%); next came
recorded music (5.3%), newspapers (5%) and accessing the Internet (5%). Increase
in Internet usage was mainly at the expense of newspapers and recorded music.[14]

A random-sample survey entitled the "State of Media Democracy" conducted
by Deloitte & Touche at the end of October 2007 found that 38% of respondents
were watching TV shows on-line, 36% were using their cell phones as entertainment devices, and 45% were creating online content such as Web sites, blogs,
music and videos. About half the respondents were using social networking Web
sites. A major increase had occurred in all of these activities when compared with
a survey taken eight months earlier.[15]

In December 2007, the Pew Internet Project reported that 48% of respondents
who were Internet users said they had visited a video-sharing Web site, up from
33% a year earlier. The same survey showed that visitors to video-sharing sites
tended to be male, young, well-educated, and from relatively wealthy households.

The gaps in usage between males and females, young and old, well-educated and less educated, wealthy and poor had declined somewhat over a one-year period.[16]

Roughly 24% of households had a digital video recorder (DVR) by the end of 2007 and 48% used video on demand (VOD) services from their cable operator. More people reported watching TV via replay rather than during scheduled broadcast times.[17] DVR penetration was projected to rise to 35% by 2012.[18] Programs recorded on DVRs were viewed mostly within a week of being recorded.[19] DVR manufacturers like TiVo and set-top box manufacturers like LG were beginning to offer movie downloading services using the Internet.

As a result of growing penetration of DVRs and growing use of the Internet for entertainment, companies like Nielsen are beginning to change their techniques for measuring the size of audiences. Nielsen has already replaced their old system of relying on informants to record time spent on particular TV programs with a set-top box that automatically records information. Similar devices were being created to attach to DVRs, computers, video game consoles, and cellular telephones. Accurate statistics on these alternative media access points will soon be available for a fee. A major potential use for such statistics will be to permit advertisers to make more informed decisions about where to advertise.

Downloading Vs. Streaming

The two main methods of delivering Internet Television are downloading and streaming. Downloading involves transfer of a digital file to the consumer, usually via some variant of the file transfer protocol (FTP). Whereas to view the content by downloading, the user must wait for the entire file to download and must then view it through media player software that is compatible with the video file's format. In streaming, the viewing starts prior to completion of the download and the user does not get access to the entire file after viewing it. Whereas downloading is based on FTP, streaming works on protocols built on top of the User Datagram Protocol (UDP) such as the Real-time Streaming Protocol (RTSP), Real-time Transport Protocol (RTP), and Real-time Transport Control Protocol (RTCP).

Content producers hoping to maintain control over content consistent with their interpretation of "digital rights management" (DRM) tend to prefer streaming to downloading; but all producers are concerned about illegal uploading and downloading of their content, especially in the light of rapid growth of file-sharing systems. Users may prefer streaming to downloading because less local memory is required for viewing video files. If the user wants to port the file to another playback device, such as a portable or handheld video player without wireless Internet access, then downloading is the only practical choice.

There were four main competing systems for streaming video: Apple's QuickTime, Microsoft's Windows Media Player, RealNetwork's RealVideo, and Adobe's Flash. All these systems required that the users have the appropriate software installed on their computers. By the end of 2007, most video-sharing Web sites were using Flash (see Table 9.4). Flash players had been downloaded

Table 9.4 Non-pornographic video-sharing Web sites

Web site	Software download required	Production values	Features
http://www.atomfilms.com	Yes for HD, no for other content	High	See text below
http://www.babelgum.com	Yes	Medium	Original content
http://www.blip.tv	No	Flash	User-generated, Creative Commons License
http://www.bloggingheads.tv	No	Medium	Split screen dialogues
http://www.break.com	No	Flash	Combat clips from Iraq
http://www.broadcaster.com	No	Low	Humor mostly
http://www.channelflip.com	No	Medium	Game reviews, how to videos (unwired.tv), film reviews (Discus)
http://www.currenttv.com	No	Medium	Social news site
http://www.dailymotion.com	No	Flash	Combines licensed and user-generated
http://www.GoFish.com	No	Low	Humor mostly
http://video.google.com	No	Flash	Wide variety
http://www.imeem.com	No	Flash	Rock videos, soccer matches
http://www.jalipo.com	No	Flash	Real-time TV from overseas
http://www.jaman.com	No	Flash	Movie trailers, Bollywood
http://www.joost.com	Yes	High	TV with social networking
http://www.jumptv.com	No	Medium	TV from other countries
http://www.justin.tv	No	Low	Webcam videos
http://www.metacafe.com	No	Medium	User-generated, contributors paid
http://vids.myspace.com	No	Flash	Music videos, celebrities
http://www.outloud.tv	No	Flash	User-generated
http://www.revision3.com	No	Flash	Techno-geek shows
http://www.sevenload.com	No	Flash	German site: photos and videos
http://www.spiketv.com	No	Medium	Man Show, Ultimate Fighters, iFilm shorts
http://www.tudou.com	No	Flash	Chinese video site
http://www.twango.com	No	Low	Includes videos, audio clips, and photos
http://www.veoh.com	Optional	Medium	Anime, Manga, mulitple channels
http://www.vimeo.com	No	Medium	User-generated
http://www.yahoovideo.com	No	Flash	Wide variety
http://www.youtube.com	No	Flash	Wide variety
http://www.zattoo.com	Yes	n.a.	Foreign TV channels, not yet available in the US

to over 98% of personal computers with Internet connections; the corresponding percentage for Windows Media Player was 83%, QuickTime 68%. Many users preferred Flash because of shorter time required for playback after clicking on a thumbnail version of the video. Many content producers preferred Flash because of the ease with which videos in various formats could be converted to compact files for streaming.[20]

Pornography

Any treatment of Internet television would be remiss if there was no mention of the enormous and pioneering role of the pornography industry.[21] All examples below of non-pornographic types of Internet video services have their counterparts (and, in some cases, predecessors) in the pornosphere. Revenues for the global pornography industry in 2006 were just short of $100 billion, up from $57 billion in 2003. China was the number one revenue earner with $27.4 billion; the US was fourth with $13.3 billion. US Internet pornography revenues were $2.84 billion in 2006. A high proportion of Internet pornography revenues come from rental or sale of online digital video content.

Twenty-eight thousand Internet users per second are viewing pornography on an average and 372 are entering adult content search terms into search engines. Porn viewers tend to be higher income individuals, 35% of who earn $75,000 or more annually. US firms lead the world in producing pornographic video content and US nodes host the most pornographic Web pages: 244 million of them.[22]

Because pornography does not contribute in any significant way to the number of voices in society that can be heard, it does not help to build or sustain democratic systems, I will focus on non-pornographic video-sharing Web sites in the rest of this chapter. Before leaving this topic, however, I wanted to call the readers' attention to a humorous YouTube video – "The Internet is for Porn"[23] – which is not too far off the mark and which has been viewed over four million times since its upload to YouTube.

Internet Video Advertising

There are two main business models for Internet television: free downloads in exchange for viewing advertisements and paid downloads to own. Some Internet videos are distributed for free without advertising under the banner of "viral marketing" in the hope that down-loaders will be so grateful that they will purchase related products and services. There is some movement in the direction of downloading to rent, where there is a time limit on the use of a downloaded file. AppleTV and iTunes have started an on-line movie rental service, as also Amazon and Netflix.[24]

Wal-Mart partnered with HP, broadcasters, and major movie studios to offer TV shows and movies. Wal-Mart downloads required devices with Windows that supported Windows Media Player software. The videos will not play on iPods or Microsoft Zunes. The cost of most films was about $15. When HP decided to drop out of the deal, Wal-Mart shuttered the project.

A slight variation on the two basic models involves video streaming. Streamed video content does not reside on the user's computer like downloaded content but rather on the content provider's network. The primary advantage for the vendor is that the user cannot use the content for anything other than viewing; this is a disadvantage from the perspective of the user, who might want to transfer the content to local storage devices and/or edit or sample the content for creative purposes. Streamed video, like downloaded video, can be distributed for free, with or without advertising.

User-Generated Video

One of the key differences between video for TV broadcast, cable, satellite and IPTV delivery and the rest of the Internet TV universe is *user-generated video*. While most videos uploaded to user-generated video sites are donated, some sites pay users to submit videos. Why do people upload short videos for sharing on Web sites, and why do the Web sites solicit donations? The shortest and simplest answer is that these videos generate traffic and traffic sells advertisements. User-generated video is the essence of what enabled YouTube to acquire sufficient market value to be purchased by Google for $1.65 billion in October 2006. It is also part of what makes a multi-million-dollar investment in FaceBook attractive to Microsoft. Advertising revenues from user-generated video sites are expected to reach $900 million by 2011.[25] Microsoft's hostile takeover bid of Yahoo! in February 2008 was partly an attempt to make up for Microsoft's failure to make MSN a true competitor to either Google or Yahoo as a search engine or Web-based email service.

Social Networking and Internet Video

A number of Internet video services offer social networking along with sharing of videos. The largest social networking services, like MySpace and FaceBook, allow users to upload videos and share them with their friends. But so do smaller and newer services like Joost, Broadcaster, Twango, and Vimeo. YouTube allows you to share a video with a friend via email, and to comment on videos with videos. Combining social networking with Internet video allows users to employ video files along with text, photographs, and audio files to build and maintain a network of friends and relations.

Characteristics of a Sample of Video-Sharing Web Sites

Examples of video-sharing Web sites listed can be found in Table 9.4, below. This is not a comprehensive list but it does include many of the most popular non-pornographic video Web sites.

The remaining portion of this chapter will be devoted to describing some of the Web sites in Table 9.4 and examining their potential to add to the diversity of viewpoints.

YouTube, Google Video, Yahoo Video, and AOL Video

Video-sharing services of the three major Web portals, Google, Yahoo, and AOL, are the most popular services on the Internet because the combination of video-sharing and search makes it easier for users to find what they want. In addition, these sites provide access to very large numbers of videos, many of which are located on smaller Web-sharing sites.

The most popular of them all is YouTube, according to Alexa Rankings (see Table 9.5 below). YouTube was founded in 2005 by three former employees of PayPal. As on August 2006, YouTube was hosting 6.1 million Flash videos which required 45 TB of storage.[26] Besides being the fastest growing Web site in the history of the Internet, YouTube streamed an average of 100 million videos per day. Over 50% of all Internet videos are watched on YouTube. Between 30 and 40% of the content on YouTube is copyrighted, and the combination of licensed and user-generated content constitutes one of YouTube's competitive advantages over other sites.[27]

YouTube contains an enormous variety of videos. As in February 2008, a YouTube search for "*" returned about 69 million videos. The very large subset of videos that express political views covers wide ranges of topics and perspectives. One important political use of YouTube was CNN's solicitation of YouTube videos to use as questions for televised debates of both Democratic (July 23, 2007) and Republican (November 28, 2007) presidential candidates.[28] Another example of

Table 9.5 Alexa ranking of internet video Web sites

Site	June 2006	February 2008
YouTube	23	3
Zippyvideos	1,544	11,807
Dailymotion	2,171	31
Vidilife	2,245	9,680
Veoh	6,934	77
Vimeo	7,400	6,224
GoFish	8,645	2,208
Imeem	–	150
Metacafe	–	179

Source: http://www.alexa.com/site/ds/top_500

this potential for political expression occurred during the national debate over net neutrality in the summer of 2006 when both proponents and opponents uploaded videos to YouTube as part of their efforts to mobilize support.[29]

Even though YouTube is now owned by Google, it continues to operate independently from Google's video-sharing service. Google's video search engine returns video thumbnails from all video-sharing Web sites on the Internet that are free or ad-supported. As in all other Google searches, Google obtains revenues by selling advertisements on the top and right side of the search results pages.

AOL and Yahoo also provide some original video content, user-generated videos, and links to videos of other aggregators, but they are dwarfed in size by YouTube and Google Video. There is a real advantage to content producers to have their content listed on one of the major search engine portals, and a small percentage of producers are paid to license their content.

Searching for Talent: AtomFilms, Current, Revision3, and Spike TV

This group of Web sites commission original Web videos from independent producers that involve, on the average, considerably higher production values than those found on the video-sharing Web sites of search engine portals. In order to pay for the right to share these higher quality videos, the managers of these sites must either give the producers a share of online advertising revenues or find sponsors for their productions. The earliest and most successful example of this is AtomFilms.

Launched in 1998, AtomFilms created a Web site for independent film producers that survived the dot.com bust. Its comedy series includes such memorable and popular offerings as Possum Death Spree and Ninja Babes from Space; the animation series include Angry Kid and Joe Cartoon. All content on AtomFilms is edgy, and much of it could not be shown on broadcast television.

AtomFilms merged with Shockwave in early 2001 to form Atom Entertainment, Inc. In September 2006, MTV Networks purchased AtomFilms for $200 million. In October 2006, the CEO of AtomFilms, Mika Salmi, was named CEO of MTV. MTV Networks is a subsidiary of Viacom. After the MTV purchase, AtomFilms introduced a high-definition version of the site optimized for broadband connections. It also added a new channel based on programming from the Comedy Channel. AtomFilms shares ad revenues with film makers in order to attract high-quality content to the site. Some AtomFilms directors, like Jason Reitman, have gone on to direct full length Hollywood feature films.

iFilm was one of the pioneers of Internet video when its Web site launched in May 2000. iFilm specialized in licensing short videos that appealed to males in the 18–34 age group. MTV purchased iFilm in October 2005. The acquisition of iFilm signaled that at least one major cable television group was taking Internet TV seriously. In March 2007, iFilm merged with Spike TV which was part of the Entertainment Group of MTV Networks. While Spike had created programs for its cable channels like World's Most Amazing Videos and Ultimate Fighters, which also appealed to the young adult male demographic, until the merger Spike had not had much of a Web presence.

Current TV is an Emmy Award winning independent media company led by former US Vice President Albert Gore. Current's cable TV network went on air on August 1, 2005. On September 20, 2006, Current TV started a short-lived partnership with Yahoo to supply topic-specific channels to the Yahoo video Web site. The first four of these became very popular on the site and additional channels were planned. However, on December 6, 2006, the relationship ended but Current TV continued to broadcast its Internet content on its own Web site. Besides channels focusing on politics and culture, Current TV invites young film makers to submit original material. The best material is featured on the site's home page.

Revision3 is a relatively younger video-sharing Web service based in San Francisco that is specializing in original productions. These productions are organized as "shows" with multiple episodes such as Diggnation, GigaOM, Mysteries of Science, NotMTV, PixelPerfect, Tekzilla, and Web Drifter. PixelPerfect, for example, is a how-to-do-it show about how to manipulate images with Adobe's Photoshop software. Diggnation provides reviews of items posted recently to Digg. Tekzilla features reviews of new electronic gadgets. The intended audience, clearly, is Geeky/Nerdy.

This group of Web sites serves as a paving ground for new talent. One of the reasons why young content producers are willing to work with these services is the prospect of being discovered by better-paying employers. Not all of the talent here will go on to produce content for large audiences, but increasingly they do not have to do so to earn a decent living. Production costs have gone down to the point where it is possible to raise production values sufficiently to win large enough audiences to provide steady flow of advertising revenues. Consumer dissatisfaction with content provided by broadcast TV, including on cable and satellite, will continue to fuel demand for this sort of content.

Conclusions

The importance of video-sharing Web sites is that they represent the potential for Internet TV to create opportunities for new voices to be heard by large audiences. We want our media to underpin democracy by allowing a broad spectrum of political voices to be heard. Until the rise of what Eli Noam calls multi-channel television (see Table 9.1 above), there was insufficient competition among television networks and their associated content producers to allow much diversity of viewpoints to be heard on TV. With the advent of cable and satellite television, and the rise of new specialized channels and networks, there was some increase in the variety of content, but also a division of the audience into smaller niches. News coverage increased a bit in variety with the addition of mainly right-wing news channels. Cable access and left-wing channels like Democracy Now had the effect of widening the spectrum of views also. Cable channels like C-Span and gavel-to-gavel coverage of state legislatures, city councils and school boards helped to increase the transparency of government for citizens who subscribed. To put it in the language of the long tail, the long tail got a bit fatter. The competition from cable and satellite gave the broadcast networks an incentive to improve the quality of their prime-time offerings in order to maintain their audience shares (which continue to decline slowly). Now the competition from Internet TV appears to be continuing these processes pretty much in the same direction.

While a change from mass-audience dominated television to a television with many more voices, more variation in production values, and more niche and/or specialized markets/audiences appears to be occurring, that transition has both positive and negative aspects. On the plus side, the long tails are getting fatter and more voices are being heard. Precise measurement of this awaits the availability of audience measurement techniques that are still being developed. On the minus side, there is the potential for people to organize their lives, a la the MeTV hypothesis (see Table 9.1 above), so that they never encounter a discordant idea that might help them to understand or respect the views of others. There was always some tendency in the past for people to do this simply by avoiding exposure to the media (including the print media). Now it will be possible to do it while immersed in a highly evasive and fluid media environment that reinforces all pre-existing attitudes and beliefs. In my view, most individuals in a free society will not do this, especially if the average level of education/schooling continues to rise, so the net effect of the rise of Internet TV is likely to be positive for democracy.

Notes

1. See, for example, Robert D. Putnam, *Bowling Alone: The Collapse and Revival of American Community* (New York: Touchstone, 2000), p. 36.
2. Robert McChesney, "The New Global Media: It's a Small World of Big Conglomerates," *The Nation*, November 29, 1999; for a contrary view, see Eli Noam, "Media Consolidation," Testimony before the Senate Commerce Committee, July 17, 2001.
3. Media Bureau, Federal Communications Commission, *2007 Annual Report* (Washington, DC: FCC, January 17, 2008).
4. OECD Directorate for Science, Technology, and Industry, Broadband Portal, "Broadband Statistics to June 2007," http://www.oecd.org/document/60/0,3343,en_2649_201185_39574076_1_1_1_1,00.html.
5. http://www.youtube.com/watch?v=kHmvkRoEowc.
6. http://www.lg15.com.
7. http://www.sanctuaryforall.com.
8. David Waterman, "Business Models and Program Content," in Eli Noam, Jo Groebel, and Darcy Gerbarg, eds., *Internet Television* (Mahwah, N.J.: Lawrence Erlbaum Associates, 2004).
9. Eli M. Noam, "The Stages of Television: From Multi-Channel Television to Me-TV," CITI Working Paper Series, 1995.
10. Bobbie Johnson, "Vint Cerf, aka the Godfather of the Net, Predicts the End of TV as we Know it," *The Guardian*, August 27, 2007, http://www.guardian.co.uk/technology/2007/aug/27/news.google.

11. Chris Anderson, *The Long Tail: Why the Future of Business is Selling Less of More* (New York: Hyperion, 2006). See also Anderson's web site and blog at http://www.thelongtail.com.

12. Judith Estrin and Bill Carrico coined the term IPTV when they founded Precept Software in 1995. Cisco acquired the firm in 1998. A definition of IPTV is "a system where a digital television service is delivered using Internet Protocol over network infrastructure…" http://en.wikipedia.org/wiki/IPTV. Experts in the field are beginning to distinguish between IPTV and what they call "Internet Television." Whereas IPTV can be delivered over either public or private IP networks, Internet Television is only delivered over the public Internet. See also, Working Party on Communication Infrastructures and Services Policy, *IPTV: Market Development and Regulatory Treatment* (Paris: OECD, December 19, 2007).

13. http://www.att.com/gen/sites/iptv?pid=8695.

14. Peter Thomasch, "More Time Spent on Web than Newspapers: Study," *Reuters*, August 7, 2007, http://www.reuters.com/article/internetNews/idUSN0721570920070807?feedType=RSS&rpc=22&sp=true.

15. Gail Schiller, "Americans More Wired: Survey," *Reuters*, December 28, 2007, http://www.reuters.com/article/domesticNews/idUSN2844258220071228.

16. "Video Sharing Websites," Pew Internet Project Data Memo, January 9, 2008.

17. IBM Media and Entertainment Consumer Household Survey Fact Sheet, undated but released in Fall 2007, http://www-03.ibm.com/industries/media/doc/content/bin/media_consumer_entertainment_survey_fact_sheet.pdf.

18. Ned Randolph, "DVR Penetration to Double in Five Years," *Video Business*, January 3, 2008, http://www.videobusiness.com/article/CA6516769.html.

19. "Nielsen: 10% of Broadcast Primetime Viewing via DVR Playback," http://www.marketing-charts.com/television/nielsen-10-of-broadcast-primetime-viewing-via-dvr-playback-536/.

20. Email correspondence with Regic Gaughan and Bryan Paul on LinkedIn, February 4, 2008.

21. For an excellent scholarly treatment, see Blaise Cronin, "Eros Unbound: Pornography and the Internet," in William Aspray and P. Cerruzzi, eds., *The Internet and American Business: An Historical Investigation* (New York: Cambridge University Press, Mar 31, 2008).

22. "Worldwide Pornography Market at Least $97 Billion," *Contacto Magazine*, March 2007, http://www.contactomagazine.com/computers/pornrevenues0307.htm: TopTenREVIEWS, Inc. statistics at http://internet-filter-review.toptenreviews.com/internet-pornography-statistics.html#anchor2.

23. http://www.youtube.com/watch?v=eWEjvCRPrCo.

24. Brad Stone, "In Deal with LG to Stream Movies Directly to TV, Netflix Shifts its Digital Strategy," *New York Times*, January 3, 2008, p. C3; http://www.apple.com/appletv/.

25. "$1.5 Billion to Be Spent on Online Video Advertising by 2011," *Wireless World Forum*, March 1, 2007, http://www.prlog.org/10009422-do-these-statistics-mean-anything-to-you.pdf.

26. Lee Gomes, "Will All of Us Get Our 15 Minutes On a YouTube Video?," *The Wall Street Journal Online*, August 30, 2006.

27. http://www.startup-review.com/blog/youtube-case-study-widget-marketing-comes-of-age.php.

28. http://www.youtube.com/profile_videos?user=YTdebates&p=r.

29. For example, Public Knowledge's video in favor of net neutrality is at http://www.youtube.com/watch?v=l9jHOn0EW8U; the National Cable and Telecommunications Association's clip is at http://www.youtube.com/watch?v=oPIYxtjLFeI&feature=related.

Chapter 10
YouTube Changes Everything:
The Online Video Revolution

Liz Gannes

Abstract A group of Web startups is fundamentally altering how people, especially younger people, consume video content. The underlying cause is not just DVRs, time-shifting, and commercial-skipping. In just three years, because of the Internet, the nature of television consumption has changed dramatically.

This younger group is not comprised of passive consumers. They are multi-taskers, forum-chatters, mashup creators, and video stars themselves. Along with making the content personal, they are creating opportunities and challenges, while covering the costs of their entertainment with advertising.

While the transition to this next generation of television watching is inevitable, it is not clear exactly how and when the new industry developments will mature. This paper examines the developments in the last three years to understand how this has come about.

YouTube, the most popular video site, with 35% share of streams, dominates the US market today.[1] The site's rise came on the back of its technology. YouTube's early premise was simple and groundbreaking: give users the ability to upload large video files and then send a link to their friends that would allow the videos to play directly in the friend's browser. This does not sound so crazy now, but getting this to work needed a huge effort.

The compelling nature of video content... silly clips just asking to be forwarded... like Saturday Night Live's Lazy Sunday and a home video depicting the "Evolution of Dance," drove more and more people to the site. YouTube's creators also did some very smart things: widgetizing their tools, making their video players embeddable on other Web pages, and tying into the popularity of personal expression sites like MySpace and blogs (Fig. 10.1).

From late 2005 to 2006 was a wild time in the world of Web video. Users uploaded anything and everything to YouTube, creating a sort of Library of Alexandria for all the world's movie and television content. YouTube was expected to flame out much like Napster, becoming yet another casualty in the arduous process of digitizing media. But then Google, the maverick, wealthy search company, stepped in and paid $1.6 billion for YouTube. This occurred despite the fact

D. Gerbarg (ed.), *Television Goes Digital*,
© Springer Science + Business Media, LLC 2009

Fig. 10.1 YouTube traffic (US uniques visitors per month, according to comScore)

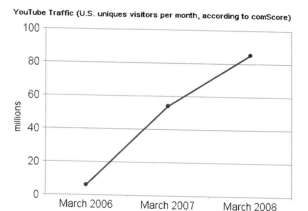

that Google Video was one of YouTube's top three competitors, based on traffic. Google's purchase of YouTube resulted in three developments:

1. It put an end to the uninhibited era of Web video
2. It instantly attracted lawsuits and payoffs to avoid lawsuits
3. It ensured that YouTube was going to be around for a long time

Google, which was not exactly big media's best friend, tried to pave the way for its newly purchased company by partnering with media companies. They had some success with major labels, which enabled them to post music videos and license the use of songs in member videos. But that came at a price. Due to deals for equity in YouTube, Warner Music Group, Universal Music Group and Sony BMG received as much at $50 million from Google, soon after the sale.[2]

NBC and CBS, along with thousands of smaller partners, started posting promotional clips to the site. Viacom sued for $1 billion, claiming that the "DMCA safe harbor provision," which YouTube and other sites used to protect themselves from copyright infringement liability arising from members uploading unauthorized content, was not valid.[3]

In a press release accompanying the lawsuit, Viacom asserted:

"YouTube is a significant, for-profit organization that has built a lucrative business out of exploiting the devotion of fans to others' creative works in order to enrich itself and its corporate parent Google. Their business model, which is based on building traffic and selling advertising off of unlicensed content, is clearly illegal and is in obvious conflict with copyright laws. In fact, YouTube's strategy has been to avoid taking proactive steps to curtail the infringement on its site, thus generating significant traffic and revenues for itself while shifting the entire burden – and high cost – of monitoring YouTube onto the victims of its infringement."[4]

YouTube has maintained that it is not legally required to screen uploaded videos before they are available on the site and furthermore that it would be a significant hindrance to the site's performance to do so. However, in the meantime, it has introduced tools to screen for copyrighted video, albeit only the video that copyright holders have provided to YouTube for the purposes of such tests.[5]

In a recent filing, Google argued that Viacom's seeking to hold carriers and hosting providers liable for online communications "threatens the way hundreds of millions of people legitimately exchange information, news, entertainment and political and artistic expression."[6]

That case is yet to reach trial, though a judge has ruled that Viacom cannot seek punitive damages.[7]

It is unclear to what extent YouTube was built on big media's back. Some argue copyright holders' concerns are overblown. In April 2007 an independent research firm found that only 5.93% of the site's 6,725 most-viewed videos over the previous three months were removed at copyright holders' request. The methodology was not perfect, but a proper study would have been impossible without the cooperation of YouTube.[8]

Once rationality came to the world of YouTube, the site realized its core resource was its community. An early set of lonely and creative souls had bonded together and made stars of each other, claiming a significant part of the huge audiences pouring into YouTube. Two years later, users like "Smosh"[9] and "LisaNova"[10] could easily claim one million views for every video they posted.

Another big portion of YouTube video is home videos, some of which will never find an audience and some of which hits a nerve or receives some fortuitous promotion, quickly climbing to the top of the charts. Yes, these are the oft-cited cats playing the piano and dogs riding skateboards. YouTube did offer a private option from early on, but public videos have always defined the site.

Sometimes user participation does not even involve turning on a camera. Video is an amazing tool of cultural commentary, and users used video editing to create mashups – for example, "Brokeback to the Future,"[11] with George Bush and Tony Blair spliced together to sing "Endless Love.[12]"

Users were also able to quickly post raw footage of events they had witnessed simply because they were in the right place at the right time. Two young men being tasered by security officers for disorderly conduct at two different events, in a college library[13] and at a political event,[14] touched off widespread debate about the use of force. American soldiers in Iraq posted videos of themselves at work and at play. When Zinedine Zidane headbutted Marco Materazzi in the 2006 World Cup finals, barely anyone in the stadium noticed it except the referee, who gave him a red card, ejecting him from the final game of his storied career. But viewers who logged in online were quickly treated to replay after replay of the incident.[15] Mashups became a part of this cycle too; "Don't Tase Me Bro" remixes[16] and Zidane headbutt games and parodies[17] flew across the Web. There are also some bizarre tendencies to overshare, such as when criminals post recordings of themselves committing crimes.

Though all these examples involve violence, they are not the whole story. Users have also made use of their personal broadcasting platform to advocate for causes they believe in and add to the public dialogue. An international politics student named James Kotecki at Georgetown even scored interviews conducted in his dorm room with the 2008 presidential nominee hopefuls Ron Paul and Mike Gravel, and video responses from the other candidates Dennis Kucinich, Mitt Romney, and Tom Tancredo.[18] In addition, politicians are increasingly held to a much higher standard, as their flip-flops and misspeaks can be juxtaposed and widely disseminated. YouTube is apolitical in its ability to spread such incidents far and wide. Some key examples from the recent primaries include Hillary Clinton being exposed for lying about the dangerousness of a visit in Bosnia[19] and John McCain giving conflicting statements on all sorts of things.[20]

On the flip side, good things come to those who embrace real-time politics. When Barack Obama gave an unusually long and cerebral speech on the issue of race, he posted the entire thing to YouTube (getting special permission to exceed the usual 10-min limit) and as of mid-June had received more than 4.5 million views.[21]

So far, while YouTube has democratized production and consumption in all sorts of interesting and increasingly impactful ways, it has missed the boat on professional content. Early on, big media companies felt threatened and challenged by the site's harboring copyright infringement and the feeling continues because YouTube is outsizing their online presences. Along the way, however, they realized that reaching their viewers online was not such a bad idea.

For instance, "Lazy Sunday," a short created by a team of three young writers who had actually been recruited to NBC's Saturday Night Live at least in part because of their online video resume, was an instant hit after being shown in the December 17, 2005 SNL episode. The two-and-a-half-minute video depicts Andy Samberg, one of the three writers, and fellow SNL cast member Chris Parnell rapping about going to see the movie "The Chronicles of Narnia." With geeky and irreverent exchanges like the one below, "Lazy Sunday" was a perfect fit for the Web:

Parnell:	"Let's hit up Yahoo Maps to find the dopest route."
Samberg:	"I prefer Mapquest."
Parnell:	"That's a good one too."
Samberg:	"Google Maps is the best."
Parnell:	"True that."
Together:	"Double true!"

The clip, taped by fans from their TV sets and posted to the Web, gained a far larger and broader audience on YouTube than it saw in its initial airing, a fact that can in part be attributed to a huge growth spurt on YouTube around the turn of 2006. Though "Lazy Sunday" was posted on multiple video sites, YouTube's version became the most popular one, drawing millions of views and holding the top search spot for "Lazy Sunday" on Google.

NBC was not quite sure what to do. The network eventually posted a version of "Lazy Sunday" on its own site, which barely had a video section at the time, and which did not work as reliably as YouTube. Then 2 months after the video had been initially aired, the network contacted YouTube to have unauthorized versions taken down. For a while fans fought back, reposting versions. But eventually, if you fight your fans long enough, they stop caring so much.

From June 2006 to October 2007, NBC got into the action with a YouTube channel of its own for posting short, promotional clips.[22] But in late 2007 the network pulled all its content from the site again as it prepared to compete with YouTube by launching Hulu, a video aggregator of its own (http://newteevee.com/2007/10/22/nbc-confirms-pulling-youtube-content-for-hulu/).

Today, at least within the United States, "Lazy Sunday" is easy to find and watch on Hulu, a joint venture of FOX and NBC. The site is a direct descendant of YouTube, but with its parental support it has access to massive libraries of premium content. However, to simplify the licensing process, the content is geo-blocked against international users.

Good, established content is a sure way to lure viewers. Hulu used, and expanded upon, the principles of simple, accessible, shareable Web video and added content, initially from its parents, FOX and NBC and eventually from other partners. According to Nielsen, Hulu broke into the top ten US video sites in its second month of public availability (http://newteevee.com/2008/05/20/hulu-leads-network-sites-adds-partners/).

Perhaps the biggest surprise of this latest post-YouTube era was how quickly viewers were willing to change their habits. Give them access to TV programmes where and when they want it and they will come running. In October 2007, *before* the launch of Hulu, TNS and a Conference Board survey found that 16% of American Internet households watch TV broadcasts online (Fig. 10.2).[23]

There is no way around it: the past few years have witnessed the birth of a new mode of content consumption. This introduces significant questions about changing economics – after all, US broadcast television advertising alone was worth $45 billion in 2007,[24] while online video advertising was worth $471 million according to one estimate.[25]

But we will get to advertising in a minute. Meanwhile, the amount of traffic other video sites have is a testament to how game-changing this phenomenon is. It is almost correct to tell this as the story of YouTube, but there are still many other sites attracting communities of their own and pushing boundaries in ways such

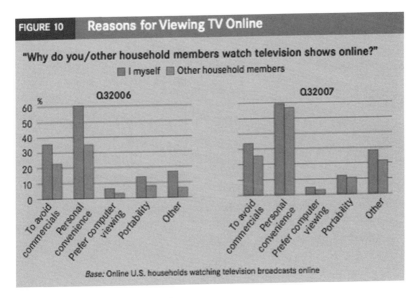

Fig. 10.2 Reasons for viewing TV online

ONLINE VIDEO PORTAL STARTUPS

Startup	Funding	Investors	Traffic	Exit
YouTube	$11.5 million	Sequoia Capital	66 million*	Sold to Google for $1.65 billion in October 2006
Metacafe	$45 million	Highland Capital Partners, DAG Ventures, Accel Partners and Benchmark Capital	5.9 million	
Dailymotion	$43.5 million	Advent Venture Partners, AGF Private Equity, Atlas Venture and Partech International	5.7 million	
Veoh	$69.5 million	Intel Capital, Adobe Systems Inc., Gordon Crawford, Shelter Capital, Spark Capital, Goldman Sachs, Michael Eisner's Tornante Company, Time Warner Investments and Jonathan Dolgen	4.3 million	
Heavy.com	$28 million	Polaris Venture Partners, Jacobson Investments	4.2 million	
Grouper/Crackle	$5.25 million	Deutche Telecom's T-Online	2.5 million	Sold for $65 million to Sony Pictures Entertainment in August 2006
Break.com	$21 million	Lionsgate	1.9 million	
Atom Films	unknown	Sequoia Capital	1.9 million	Bought by Viacom's MTV Networks for $200 million in August 2006
Hulu	$100 million	Providence Equity Partners	1.8 million	
Revver	$12.7 million	Comcast Interactive Capital, Turner, Draper Fisher Jurvetson, Bessemer Venture Partners, Draper Richards and William Randolph Hearst III	.76 million	Sold for under $5 million to LiveUniverse in February 2008
Vuze	$34 million	New Enterprise Associates, BV Capital, Greycroft Partners and Redpoint Ventures	.42 million**	
Joost	$45 million	Sequoia Capital, Index Ventures, Viacom, CBS, Li Ka-shing, Janus Friis and Niklas Zennström	.18 million**	
Babelgum	$13.2 million plus potentially $130 million more	Silvio Scaglia	.17 million**	
TidalTV	$15 million	New Enterprise Associates, Valhalla Partners	too small to measure	
IFILM	at least $10 million	Axiom Ventures, Eastman Kodak Company, Sony Pictures Entertainment, Vulcan Ventures, Baroda Ventures, Falcon Cable Founder, Marc Nathanson, Leo Hindery and Yahoo!	now redirected to Spike.com	Bought by Viacom's MTV Networks for $49 million in October 2005

*This is smaller than other numbers quoted because comScore now breaks out video viewers as well as unique visitors, so many people watch YouTube (and other sites) through embedded video around the web

**These sites mainly interact with their users through downloaded software, so it makes sense that they'd have less web traffic

Fig. 10.3 Online video portal startups

as paying their users, scoring original Web content, and seeking out rewarding verticals. Of course, a lack of profits will necessarily catch up with many of these venture-backed sites (Fig. 10.3).

Among the many other consumer-facing areas of online video innovation, such as video search and social video discovery, the backend technologies are actually getting the most attention, and they deserve it. Transmitting video is no easy feat, and it is getting expensive.

For instance, Move Networks, which powers video distribution for FOX, ABC, and ESPN, has got wide distribution despite its requiring end users to download a piece of software that is an alternative to the widely adopted Adobe Flash. Move says it expects to have it installed by 65 million of its software clients by the end of this year, and it is seeing average viewer sessions of 50 min an hour. By using techniques like caching and finding the best prices it can get from various content delivery networks, Move has brought the cost of transmitting a gig to less than $0.10. The company has raised $67.3 million from Cisco, Comcast Interactive Media, Televisa, Steamboat Ventures, and Hummer Winblad Venture Partners. And it has many competitors, including Maven Networks (acquired by Yahoo), the Platform (acquired by Comcast), Brightcove, Delve Networks, Vusion, and GridNetworks.

What is next for online video? Certainly the continuing expansion of trends like online television watching, real-time politics, and viral video phenomena is to be expected. Around the corner, a new group of companies are working to professionalize the creation of Internet content. By using their knowledge of how the Web works, finding niches, and fostering interactive communities, companies like Next New Networks, EQAL, JibJab and Revision3 are showing that new media can actually be quite different from old media. With this new body of knowledge, they may well scoot ahead of video portals as next in line to be acquired by old media dogs looking to learn new tricks. EQAL, for instance, which created the innovative "lonelygirl15" series, already has a "first look" and consulting deal with CBS.[26]

These new content companies embed their content within the online and offline contexts fans already inhabit – for instance, turning fiction into a game that meshes with reality by having viewers help characters solve a puzzle, giving watchers tools to place their own faces on the dancing figures in a silly video, enlisting stars to appear in extra online bonus footage, or incorporating fan submissions into an episode's script. These new avenues for viewer engagement are endemic online, but they have no problem fitting into traditional television as well: for example, in situations such as "American Idol" text message voting, "The Office" blogs and Webisodes, and TV news reporters collaborating with viewers to gather details and videos about a local event.

New media, however, still faces a major revenue gap, especially considering its viewers are the most savvy and perhaps least willing to sit through commercials. Unfortunately, while low-budget productions have their converts, creativity and efficiency mix about as well as oil and water.

Among the potential revenue options are new ad units, often called overlays or in-video ads, which occur within a video player. These depend on a user clicking to activate them. Often they are priced on a performance basis – meaning advertisers only pay if users take an action. The assumption is that people who choose to view the unit are far more engaged with it. Just about every vendor offers such ad units, and they have been approved by the Interactive Advertising Bureau.[27]

Another area of exploration is ad targeting – utilizing information about the nature of a piece of content, or a viewer's location, stated demographics or behavior to show more relevant ads. YouTube even has a program that allows advertisers to target content as it is taking off among its viewership, allowing them to be associated with whatever is going viral on the site at that moment.[28] In addition, advertisers and content makers are experimenting with combining their efforts through product placement and integration, user-generated advertising contests, and brand community portals. Some representative video advertising startups include Broadband Enterprises, YuMe, and BrightRoll (video ad networks); Adap.tv (video ad optimization); ScanScout and Digitalsmiths (video ad targeting), Vitrue and Reality Digital (brand-centric communities), and Jivox (small business video ad creation and distribution).

For the moment, the most lucrative approach remains brand advertising – bringing the names everyone has heard a million times to this new mass medium. This is especially problematic for user-generated content, of which major advertisers remain wary. But in an online video world that is continually dominated by the meme of the moment, which, often as not, comes from a new source, this leaves out a huge portion of the viewership. User-generated content is not always a tour of a kitchen remodel suitable for an audience of one, or a bootleg copy of Comedy Central's "The Daily Show with John Stewart." It may just be the new, previously completely unknown, touch point for a million water cooler discussions.

Meanwhile, it is not as if traditional media has tremendous security in its own revenue streams. The process of evolving to best serve and monetize viewers will inevitably be a learning process across all platforms.

Lastly, the next big frontier is bringing Internet content to wherever people want to view it. That includes mobile devices, but is primarily about those big-screen TVs so many people have installed as a focal point in their homes. Improving upon the expensive and complicated setups of the past, a new group of devices and software seek to get content that is transmitted over the Web in front of the comfortable sofa. It may be that such devices will be less important for future generations, who happily watch their laptop screens, but for now they are an important part of bringing online video mainstream. Look for new solutions such as Internet-connected set-top boxes and televisions, wireless transmitters, and next-generation routers. Some names on this list: the Apple TV, Netflix and its consumer electronics partners, the Sony Bravia Internet Video Link, the HP MediaSmart, Panasonic VieraSmart, Verismo, Vudu, Xbox, ZeeVee, and of course TiVo.

It is hard to believe that YouTube was founded in February 2005, just a little over three years before the writing of this chapter. The average US online video watcher now streams 235 min of video per month![29] But as there is so much left to figure out, the next three years will not be boring either.

Notes

1. http://www.comscore.com/press/release.asp?press=2268
2. http://www.nytimes.com/2006/10/19/technology/19net.html?ex=1318910400&en=
   fb18406e3a1e91dd&ei=5088&partner=rssnyt&emc=rss
3. http://wsj.com/public/resources/documents/ViacomYouTubeComplaint3-12-07.pdf
4. http://www.prnewswire.com/cgi-bin/stories.pl?ACCT=104&STORY=/www/story/
   03-13-2007/0004545033&EDATE=
5. http://newteevee.com/2007/10/15/youtube-finally-launches-video-id-tool/
6. http://news.yahoo.com/s/ap/20080526/ap_on_hi_te/youtube_lawsuit;_ylt=AuZ6K9BjHrnLo
   D17idGCjK4jtBAF
7. http://docs.justia.com/cases/federal/district-courts/new-york/nysdce/1:2007cv02103/
   302164/95/
8. http://www.vidmeter.com/i/vidmeter_copyright_report.pdf
9. http://www.youtube.com/user/smosh
10. http://www.youtube.com/user/LisaNova
11. http://www.youtube.com/watch?v=zfODSPIYwpQ
12. http://www.youtube.com/watch?v=nupdcGwIG-g
13. http://www.youtube.com/watch?v=AyvrqcxNIFs
14. http://www.youtube.com/watch?v=6bVa6jn4rpE
15. http://www.youtube.com/watch?v=vF4iWIE77Ts
16. http://www.youtube.com/watch?v=AkMkGOpAF4s
17. http://www.dashes.com/anil/2006/07/zidane-world-cu.html
18. http://www.youtube.com/emergencycheese
19. http://www.youtube.com/watch?v=8BfNqhV5hg4
20. http://www.youtube.com/watch?v=GEtZlR3zp4c&e
21. http://www.youtube.com/watch?v=pWe7wTVbLUU
22. http://www.youtube.com/press_room_entry?entry=c0g5-NsDdJQ
23. http://newteevee.com/2007/10/15/more-people-watching-tv-shows-online/
24. http://www.tvb.org/rcentral/adrevenuetrack/revenue/2007/ad_figures_1.asp
25. http://www.jupiterresearch.com/bin/item.pl/research:concept/1215/id=99419
26. http://newteevee.com/2008/05/14/cbs-will-lonelygirlize-its-tv-shows/
27. http://newteevee.com/2008/05/05/iab-approves-new-video-ad-formats/
28. http://newteevee.com/2008/05/13/youtube-targets-ads-to-vids-about-to-go-viral/
29. http://www.comscore.com/press/release.asp?press=2223

Chapter 11
Digital Archiving in the Entertainment and Professional Media Market

Thomas M. Coughlin*

Abstract This chapter explores the current trends and drivers for digital archiving in the entertainment and professional media markets. Methodology and technologies utilized in digital archiving as well as future requirements will be explored. We will also examine the requirements for long-term content storage, look at various storage options and discuss how content administrators can create a reliable long-term archive.

Growth in the Entertainment and Media Market

To understand the demand for archiving in the Entertainment & Media (EM) market, it is important to begin with a discussion of the growth in content attained by all forms of EM companies from broadcast to post, animation to digital imaging and pre-press.

For companies participating in the entertainment and professional media markets their assets are primarily the rich content that they create and manage. A movie, a piece of music, a television program, a documentary, a video or audio file for web download and news or advertising pieces all generate revenue. They also contain large amounts of data and consume storage capacity. It is important to note that the raw data collected to make these assets is much greater than what will be used in an actual product.

For instance, a professional animal videographer told me that he shoots 10 h of high resolution video to finally get 5 min of selected and edited footage for a television documentary. Those 10 h of video were captured in 10–40 min periods over the course of many months while waiting in the open for hours at a time. There have been days when he did not get any images at all. Obviously, for content creation professionals there is a tremendous investment in the raw content.

---

*The material presented in this report was largely extracted from the *2007 Entertainment Content Creation and Digital Storage Report* or from the data set created in putting together that report. For more information or to order a copy of this report, please go to http://www.tomcoughlin.com/techpapers.htm.

D. Gerbarg (ed.), *Television Goes Digital*,
© Springer Science + Business Media, LLC 2009

These pieces of content are also unique and can never be recreated exactly – time moves on. As a result, raw and edited content are of inestimable value in preserving a record of natural history, historical events, hits and fads of a particular age and generally serve as a cultural record of who we were and what mattered to us.

For the videographer to maintain this 10 h of raw content he would need 648 GB of storage at HD-cam resolution. Retaining raw content can get expensive as it is continuously acquired and maintained. Of course this problem is not unique to videographers. From broadcast to post to imaging, all media and entertainment artists have to deal with storage of growing collections of raw content.

The effect of this is that professionals are creating and storing more content than ever before. Figure 11.1 shows projections out to 2012 for the growth of annual storage capacity requirements for the creation of professional moving image content. In 2007, over 700 petabytes of storage hardware were required while in 2012 this is estimated to climb to about 2.4 exabytes.

One of the drivers of this increase in storage capacity is the move to higher resolution content. As the resolution of video content increases the digital storage required increases. Table 11.1 shows the bandwidth and 1-h storage capacity demands of typical professional media formats (including sound) and the primary applications that they are used in. The move from SD to HD has resulted in 6X higher data rates and storage capacities while 2–4 K has resulted in 4X higher data rates and storage capacities. Bandwidth increases result in greater production of storage content and thus more demand for storage capacity.

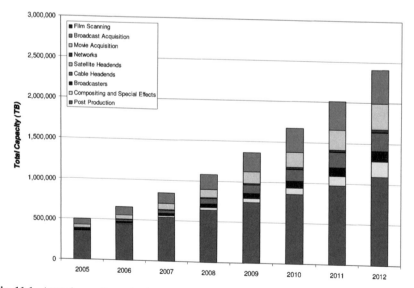

Fig. 11.1 Annual capacity projections for creation of professional moving image content. *Source:* T. M. Coughlin, *2007 Entertainment Content Creation Digital Storage Report,* Coughlin Associates, http://www.tomcoughlin.com/techpapers.htm

Table 11.1 Example raw data rates, professional media standards

Resolution	Application	MB/s	Storage (GB, 1 h)
Uncompressed audio (48 kHz/24-bit)	All	0.15	0.540
MiniDV/DVCAM/ DVCPRO (digital video)	Consumer, Corporate, Broadcast & News	3.6	12.96
IMX D10	Broadcast & news	6	21.6
HD Cam (compressed hi-def)	Broadcast, post production	18 (max.)	64.8 (max.)
SD Video (8-bit, uncompressed)	Broadcast, post-Production	20	72.0
Uncompressed 601 (SDI) (10-bit standard def.)	Broadcast, post-production	34	122.4
High Resolution HDTV (8-bit, 1080i)	Broadcast, post-production	120	432
Uncompressed 2 K (10 bit-log)	Film production, television	300	1,080
Uncompressed 4 K (10 bit-log)	Film production, some television	1,200	4,320

It should be realized that Fig. 11.1 gives an estimate for hardware storage assets required to make digital content in each year. The actual digital content generated using this hardware will tend to be even greater. Raw content stores alone can be considerable since a movie producer might edit hundreds of hours of content to come up with a 2 h final product. Then there is the unused content saved for outtakes or even sequels and the digital intermediaries and effects created during production. Producers, who make a practice of saving their entire source raw material can in some cases, end up with several petabytes of content.

When the digital content created and retained from prior years is added in, the cumulative digital storage required for a company to maintain its revenue generating content for the long term can become very great indeed. This is especially true as more ways to use and distribute captured content are identified (e.g., Internet and mobile phones) and the demand for richer and richer content increases.

Figure 11.2 shows estimates for storage capacity required to retain digital cumulative content created since 2004. These estimates assume that only a part of the total raw content is preserved. If the percentage of raw content retained over the long term is greater than assumed here the total cumulative storage capacity could increase by 50% or greater.

To these estimates must also be added the digital storage required for the retention of digitally converted, formerly analog content such as old movies and television programs as well as music and digital still images. Furthermore, extra copies of content such as are needed for disaster recovery will add to the total storage requirement. *As of 2007 the total unconverted analog video and movie content that could potentially be converted to digital form is on the order of 200 exabytes.*

The growth of converted content depends upon the assumptions made about the conversion rate and resolution requirements as well as the continued rate of

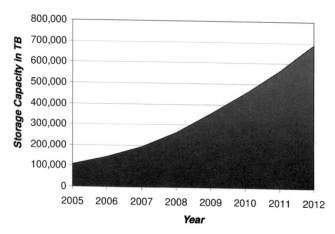

Fig. 11.2 Cumulative digital storage projection for professional video digital content preservation. *Source*: Produced from background data for T. M. Coughlin, *2007 Entertainment Content Creation Digital Storage Report*, Coughlin Associates, http://www.tomcoughlin.com/techpapers.htm

creation of analog content that may need to be converted. Together with copies made of content archives for disaster recovery the total digital storage required for the cumulative preservation of professional digital content by 2012 is estimated to be many exabytes.

As can be imagined, storing all of this content on disk is not feasible. For this reason, the entertainment and media industry is at the forefront of using archiving to cost-effectively retain and manage this content.

Archiving in the EM Market Defined

An *archive* is a copy of data that is being retained for very long periods of time, usually for years and in some cases centuries. Archives are used throughout the entertainment and media industry for storing content that is not being used in ongoing projects, but could be re-purposed or referenced in the future. An archive may be *active*, online, where it can be accessed relatively quickly or *cold*, offline, where it can be stored safely and economically; but it may take a considerable amount of time to mount the digital storage medium and read the archived data. The average time to access archived data is the archive latency.

Editing and some other content industry segments also keep *working archives* of content on storage networks during the course of their work. These working archives are raw content and edited content that are protected during active work on a project. They are often kept in storage area networks (SAN) or network attached storage (NAS) systems used in the working studio. After a project is completed, the content of a working archive may be retained in a long-term archive depending on the value and time to create intermediaries, certain effects and other content used to develop the final cut.

Status of the Professional EM Archiving Market

Archiving within the EM market is currently driven by two factors: The need to cost-effectively retain content for re-use and the need to convert historical analog content to digital form to prevent degradation of content. Many sorts of facilities keep content for varying periods of time. Keeping completed content in long-term archives is common practice among content owners, including movie and television producers. Raw content retention is not so complete and varies depending upon the policies and budgets of the facilities. Post, special effects and computer generation houses may keep some of their unique content for extended periods. As the cost of archiving declines more content will be retained by all of these facilities.

For preservation of new content, deciding what to archive can be difficult. The retention of digital entertainment and professional media involves costs in real estate, operation, management software and hardware. In practice data managers handling large and even small volumes of raw and edited content must make choices in what they will preserve for the long term because they often do not have the resources or budgets to save everything.

Preservation of source media containing the original content is almost always a stringent requirement since it is difficult, if not impossible to recreate. However, this alone is often insufficient, as raw source material does not capture any edits or metadata generated during the processing of the raw content to create a finished product. As a result, more content must be archived than the source material.

To this end, many movie studios and editing facilities will save a set of master movie films (with color separation preserved) as well as managed digital tapes of the content in a cold archive. In addition, many of these facilities will keep copies of content on-line in an active archive on a disk array or tape library for some period of time.

Many television networks, including major news networks, retain their library of analog video tape with a digitized index and metadata database of their analog tapes. They convert the analog content to a digital form and store it on a combination of disk arrays and tape libraries as they are accessed and used for historical content for current projects. Networks tend to keep cold as well as active archives so that they can improve their odds of rapid content retrieval and successful long-term content retention.

Smaller organizations, including smaller post-production shops and other facilities, may not have the resources to set up a complex and expensive archiving system. For these users it is advantageous to retain the source media and players to play them back later. Careful logging and management of these physical media combined with retention of the most valuable content in disk arrays or tape libraries may be a more affordable option.

While archiving will be driven in the long term by new content creation, there is also a sharp increase in digital storage capacity used for digital conversion and preservation of analog historical content. Costs for digital conversion are being reduced with the development of service providers who can do the conversion of bulk material at an attractive price and with the decline in the overall cost of storing digital archives.. *We project that several exabytes of digital storage will be used for digital archiving and content conversion and preservation by 2012!*

Long-term retention of digital files is not merely a need of the entertainment and professional media industry. Regulatory and other pressures are driving many industries and companies to turn to long-term data retention as well. The Storage Networking Industry Association (SNIA) started a 100 year archive project in 2004 and in August 2007 it released a survey of business professionals speaking on their long-term archiving needs. In that survey it was found that 80% of respondents have information that they must keep for over 50 years, and 68% of respondents said they must keep this data for more than 100 years. Thus there is a strong incentive to develop hardware and management software to support long-term retention requirements for several industries.

Solutions and Products for the EM Archiving Market

Solutions and products for archiving vary depending on the overall size and needs of an organization.

For smaller organizations, archiving may be a simple process in which final cuts from working storage is written out in digital format to media and placed in a cold, offline archive along with source tapes. Products used for data movement are typically asset managers but may also include backup applications. For digital content written out from working storage, archive media uses "commoditized" IT storage like digital tape, optical storage and even disk drives and disk drive cartridges. These commoditized products could include LTO and DLT tapes, DVD or blue laser DVD write one or rewritable media as well as Iomega REV drives or disk drives in removable modules.

Factors in the choice of cold archive storage formats include not only cost, $/GB, but the expected life of the archive media. Media life depends upon the quality of that media as well as the environment that it is stored in. It is likely that inexpensive off-the-shelf optical disks, for instance, may not provide long-term data preservation (many tens of years). However, disk while being an easy to use format, is not suitable for cold archives because of its life span. For this reason, most cold archives use tape (e.g., LTO) due to its portability, quality and long shelf life – upwards of 30 years. In any event, media should be stored in a climate controlled vault for high quality preservation.

Larger organizations will also use cold archives but in conjunction with some form of active archiving. In real world deployments, active archiving tends to include a hierarchical system consisting of multiple storage tiers. A disk storage array may be used on the front end to provide faster content transfers between artists during ongoing and recently completed projects. Less frequently used files will reside on a local tape or even optical disk library system for near line access.

Disk arrays used for active archiving typically use SATA hard drives since these provide higher storage capacity for a given price and provide good reliability under less frequently accessed conditions expected in an archive application. There are even SATA storage arrays called MAIDs (*massive array of inactive disks*) that keep most of the SATA drives in the array powered down most of the time, providing significant power and heat load savings for a data center.

Data movement between tiers in an active archive can be accomplished via administrative action (manually moving files to different storage locations) but this is a cumbersome process and can result in data loss. To alleviate this issue, most organizations that use active archiving rely on products that automate data movement between tiers. These products often also include the ability to protect content by cloning of files and allowing them to be placed in a cold archive. Active archiving products are built to include or work side by side with content asset managers.

Some of the companies making software used for asset management and digital archive management in the entertainment and professional media markets (either by themselves or in combination) include: Dalet, Etere, Front Porch Digital, Masstech Group, Quantum, SGI, SGL and XenData. Cold archiving is done by companies such as Iron Mountain that specialize in retaining records and assets in controlled environments.

Issues and Opportunities in EM Archiving

In this section we shall examine some important issues in the archiving of digital entertainment and professional media content in order to get a better understanding of them and to understand how they can be managed. This will include what is involved in dealing with format conversions, protection of archived data from disasters at the primary data center, longevity of various possible storage media and total operating costs in maintaining a digital media archive.

Format Conversion and Long-Term Archive Management

Over the course of time storage media formats and interfaces become obsolete. This poses special problems for a long-term digital archive. In the case of retained source media extra copies of the reader devices for the media as well as systems that these readers can attach to are required to access these media in the future.

If the retention time is especially long this could even include a string of devices that can be used sequentially to convert older media contents into then current formats and with interfaces that then current devices support.

Thus to be secure in the future use of source media an archivist needs to also keep all the hardware and other software needed to read and convert that content into a form that will be readable to future hardware and software. Over the course of time this can become quite a collection of devices and can become a serious management issue itself.

Regardless of whether the original source media are retained if the content data is transferred into a media archive system using hard disk drives, optical disks or magnetic tape format obsolescence still forces the administrator to convert older storage formats into newer ones as time goes by. Storage formats that include backwards compatibility mitigate this issue, but do not solve it.

This issue becomes more pronounced as the size of the digital archive increases. As the size of an archive grows the time to transfer or convert digital content from the old media to the new can be overwhelming unless there are sufficient old and new resources on hand.

In a sense, archiving (even cold archiving) should not be a static process. When the archive load becomes too large choices will have to be made about which content to transfer and preserve on the new format. Format choices should always be made with a consideration of backwards compatibility. Otherwise archive transfers could become a constant process.

The rate of obsolescence for storage device formats varies with the devices. For hard disk drives the stability of the interface and the drive specification that controls that interface sets the backward compatibility. For SCSI drives and for fiber channel disk drives that use the SCSI specification there is very long format stability (backward compatibility) on drive commands.

On the other hand the SCSI hard drive connection interface evolves to a faster version, roughly every 5–7 years. Recently both SCSI and ATA, found in the past in personal computers, made a conversion from parallel to serial connections. The resulting SAS and SATA interfaces are completely different from the interfaces used in older format drives. Thus disk drive interfaces change relatively frequently with time from an archivist point of view.

An archival system built around the use of disk drives must take this into account and either have a means to migrate to newer drives using adapters as the old drives wear out or eventually to move data from the older drive arrays to a new set. Thus the useful life of an active disk array is probably somewhere in the range of 5–7 years (the actual functional life with appropriate spares could be as high as 10 years). This time frame will also be influenced by service contract costs. After 3–5 years service costs for arrays tend to go up dramatically resulting in the desire to swap an array, even if it is functioning adequately.

For a MAID system with less active disks, this time period could be longer than 10 years. Often disk storage systems (as well as tape and optical) are replaced not because they no longer work but because there is technology with much more storage capacity, better performance and lower operating costs available.

The format obsolescence rate for tape (a common digital archival media) is variable depending on the format and technology. Different tape standards take different approaches.

For example, the LTO Consortium's roadmap communicates the member's intention to provide read/write capability one generation back and read capability for two generations back. The intent is to provide that capability at each specific generation's original density and performance. Thus an LTO Gen4 drive which is capable of recording 800 GB per cartridge at 120 MB/s must be able to read and write up to 400 GB on Gen3 cartridges at the manufacturer's originally specified Gen3 performance and must also be able to read Gen2 cartridges, again at the originally specified performance.

The LTO Consortium has a track record of introducing new generations every 20–30 months (note that DLT tape technology roadmaps have similar prior generation read requirements). Thus archival tape systems have a total format life (for reading) of about 6 years. An existing tape system could last much longer and the media is rated to last up to 20 years. Tape storage systems (especially libraries) probably have a useful life of 10–15 years.

Optical storage media may be more stable in media development than tape but generally there is a major format change every 10 years and interfaces develop like those of other computer peripherals. Optical storage media of good quality can probably last about 10 years under the right storage conditions and optical archive libraries probably have a useful life of about 10 years.

Thus an 8–10 year life of an archival storage system is likely for all these storage devices. Sometime before an older system is to be retired, its content must be moved to a replacement storage system.

To handle this format conversion, manual processes could be used, but they are error prone and time consuming, taking staff away from other projects. Storage management software should include a way to automatically control the format refresh. Management software can read archive data from an older generation tape environment, verify that the content is still intact and then automatically rewrite to the latest generation of tape.

By having this process follow rules defined by the client, their specific data retention and protection needs can easily be factored into the process. This also allows for maximum reuse of tape media and ultimately minimizes long-term data retention cost. Over a 100 year archive life this process is liable to happen at least ten times. This operation benefits from active software management to make sure such media progressions occur according to a pre-set schedule and that transfers are successful before the older media and storage systems are retired.

Creating Better Metadata for Archived Content

Creating better metadata to represent the data in the archive and creating the means to manage this metadata are keys to better search and discovery of historical content. While today much metadata is entered manually, technologies are being developed to enable searching data based upon matches with audio, still or moving video content. As these technologies develop the resulting metadata could be incorporated into professional video metadata formats such as MXF to create powerful ways of accessing older content archives.

Storage devices and storage management software should be designed to make use of these automated metadata generation capabilities as they are developed. Archive management software should search through active archive content, creating new metadata based upon rich media attributes. In the absence of this, or in environments that use customized metadata formats, archive management software should be as tightly aligned with the asset manager as possible so that artists can track and manage content as they need.

Decreasing the Overall Costs of Archiving

The cost of archiving is a function of several factors. Some of the more important of these factors are storage media utilization and the costs of maintaining the data center where the storage assets are kept. Storage management software is a key element of reducing the overall costs of storage.

Storage management that can find unneeded duplication of data and not back up multiple copies of the same files is one method to reduce overall system digital storage capacity as well as reducing the bandwidth requirements for moving this data around.

Although generally higher in archive environments, storage capacity utilization is usually rather low. Disk storage utilization of less than 50% is not uncommon in many data centers. It is possible to improve storage utilization by creating virtualization of storage assets so that storage can be provided to the user as needed rather than relying on pre-provisioning storage. By reducing the overall hardware and facilities costs (which tend to be much greater over the long run) good storage management software can more than pay for itself.

The cost of maintaining storage facilities greatly exceeds the initial hardware costs. Heating and air conditioning are essential to successful operation of an active storage facility. Reducing the heat load from the storage systems will do a lot to reduce overall facility costs. The use of smaller disk drives in drive arrays (particularly if these are lower RPM SATA drives) will reduce the heat generated by these drives and as the drives can be packed tighter in an array than larger form factor disk drives, the overall storage array footprint can be smaller for an equivalent storage capacity. This reduces the size of the data center space required for the active archive.

For larger archives tape is an important format because it does not require a large amount of power. Media is offline except when in use, in a tape drive. The tape library itself requires no power except for the robotics and drives, which when not in use are idle. Tape libraries can scale to multiple petabytes of storage without requiring significant power consumption in comparison to a disk array of the same capacity.

Projections for Various Storage Media Used in EM Archiving

Table 11.2 gives projections for annual demand of new storage media (tape, optical or hard disk drive) for entertainment and professional media archiving of newly generated content. Digital conversion of analog content and its preservation can increase these numbers considerably but prediction of this trend is hard to do. Suffice it to say that the overall demand could easily be twice that shown here.

As can be seen in this table tape remains the most used archival storage media. The anticipated growth in optical media depends upon the development of advanced high capacity optical technology such as holographic media.

A constant problem with a cold digital archive is staying ahead of the obsolescence of the storage media used. As time goes on digital storage technology improves and the storage media and drives change. If the data storage on a cold archived media is not migrated to new storage technology when it becomes

Table 11.2 Projections for the use of various archival storage media in the media and entertainment industry

	2005	2006	2007	2008	2009	2010	2011	2012
Archiving new content (TB)	61,571	82,820	111,243	153,291	201,300	253,149	310,528	379,518
Capacity change (TB)	16,436	21,250	28,423	42,048	48,008	51,850	57,379	68,990
Digital tape (%)	88.0	86.0	84.0	81.0	78.0	75.0	76.0	70.0
Optical disk (%)	11.0	12.0	13.0	15.0	17.0	19.0	21.0	23.0
3.5″ ATA HDD (%)	1.00	2.00	3.00	4.00	5.00	6.00	7.00	10.00
Estimated half inch tape cartridges	43,830	46,859	47,750	56,765	53,495	48,609	48,453	48,293
Estimated optical disk units	51,657	54,255	57,734	66,392	58,296	54,730	54,771	61,030
Estimated 3.5″ ATA HDD units	548	1.062	1,705	2,803	3,429	3,889	4,463	6,899

available, there is a danger that the data will not be readable as time goes by. Thus successful preservation of archived digital content must also include data migration management to deal ahead of time with the risks of format obsolescence.

Broader Asset Management Systems

A final topic of discussion is how archiving fits into a larger asset management system. An asset management system is a set of processes designed to control digital assets used in active and inactive projects. Processes should cover every aspect of the content lifecycle from tracking metadata, physical location from active usage to archive, and handling data protection.

While there is no one catch-all product that covers asset management, some broad strokes can be made about the design of a system. A digital media archive management system should do the following:

- Protect the digital assets for many years through active management and checking of the hardware and storage environment.
- Perform systematic format updates and transfers of the digital content as needed to avoid potential access loss due to format obsolescence.
- Alert the administrator of problems with the content, environment or storage hardware early enough for the administrator to take action and if necessary shut down and protect assets in the event of a crisis.
- Provide organized access to the digital archives by retaining an appropriate database of content metadata and perhaps indexing of the actual content on those assets.
- In case of an active archive, control the access and delivery of digital content when needed and in a timely manner.
- In case of a cold archive, initiate delivery and mounting of the media from the cold archive and delivery of the content where it is needed.
- Manage disaster recovery requirements such as mirroring or backup of managed data to remote data centers to make sure content can be recovered if the original copy is somehow damaged.

New developments in long-term archive management include:

- Active indexing of still and moving digital images during the archiving process – more advanced metadata creation and management allowing easier search and use of this content.
- More active and continuous checking of archived content to make sure the data integrity is OK and to detect growing problems.
- File-based access to digital content from the storage media to enhance content access.

Conclusions

This report has explored the important trends and drivers for the archiving of entertainment and professional media content. Management software as well as hardware play an important role in digital media archives. We have looked at the requirements as well as future expected developments in storage management. We have also looked at some of the providers of digital media management software.

The decreasing cost of digital storage and the capture and editing of content enabled by digital technology has increased the number of facilities and producers of content.

Digital technology and increased available communication bandwidth have also allowed the development of new ways to distribute content such as the internet and mobile phone networks. This has also increased the supply of new professional (as well as non-professional) content. Higher resolution is being required in professional content and the amount of digital footage being acquired for the final produced product has increased considerably. In addition, older analog content is being digitized in greater amounts with time. All of these factors have caused digital storage capacity requirements to swell.

As total content capacity increases so does the amount of content that is being archived in either cold or active archives (or both). Long-term preservation of large digital archives will lead the industry to solve new issues associated with format conversion, metadata creation and management as well as methods to reduce the total cost of operating a digital media archive. Preservation of digital data from the possible destruction of the primary storage system can be dealt with by having off-site copies of the content or by maintaining remote mirrors or backup of the content.

Part IV
Legal and Regulatory Issues

Chapter 12
Spectrum Policy and the Public Interest

Ellen P. Goodman

Abstract This chapter examines how spectrum policy priorities came to shape today's television broadcast system and the issues that will influence the future of wireless video. As video services come to migrate freely between wired and wireless platforms and as broadcast television merges with other forms of wireless video, spectrum policy and the public interest values that it reflects will shape the video value chain. These values are often cross-cutting and require tradeoffs among such interests as maintaining existing communications services, technical innovation, spectrum efficiency, universal service, media diversity and competition. What tradeoffs are made and what they cost, is too frequently hidden from public view.

Introduction

The provision of video services in the United States has long been linked to spectrum policy. In particular, the structure of broadcast television – its system of local stations and national networks – is a direct result of policy decisions in the early part of the twentieth century that produced a particular allocation of spectrum usage rights. The transition from analog to digital broadcasting in the first decade of the twenty-first century similarly reflects specific policy choices grounded in visions of the public interest and the pressures of interest group politics. So too, how video services develop in the future will depend in large part on battles currently being fought over the distribution of spectrum rights.

Spectrum Policy

The term "spectrum" refers to an intangible natural resource – the capacity of the environment to carry electromagnetic waves of various frequencies. Waves with frequencies between 3 kilohertz (kHz) and 300 gigahertz (GHz) travel in a subset of spectrum called the "radio spectrum." Until recently, the only commercially useful

D. Gerbarg (ed.), *Television Goes Digital*,
© Springer Science + Business Media, LLC 2009

spectrum was located below 3 GHz, but technical advancements now allow services to use ever shorter wavelengths well above 3 GHz.

Spectrum policy debates arise whenever there is rivalry among parties (both public and private) seeking to use what US law calls the "public spectrum resource."[1] The potential for interference between signals creates such rivalry for the most desirable frequencies. There are essentially two ways to deal with the threat of interference. The first and most common, is to license mutually exclusive rights to use the spectrum in a way that separates users by space, time or frequency. The second is to allocate spectrum for shared (often known as unlicensed) use and to rely on technological measures to reduce harmful interference. Such measures include smart radios that are able to adjust signal levels to avoid interference, low power transmissions and technical protocols that prioritize some transmissions over others. These technological measures have, to date, been capable of managing interference only for a limited set of low power applications, such as WiFi service and cordless telephones. For that reason, they have not supplanted exclusive spectrum licenses as the dominant form of interference control for wireless services. Unless and until technology enables much more widespread use of shared spectrum applications, there will be spectrum scarcity and rivalry among users.

In order to manage and allocate rights to the scarce spectrum resource, the Radio Act of 1927 asserted federal control over "all the channels of interstate and foreign radio transmission" and authorized federal licensing authorities "to provide for the use of such channels, but not the ownership thereof, by individuals, firms, or corporations, for limited periods of time." Management of the spectrum resource thus became (and under subsequent legislation remained) the job of the federal government.

The Communications Act of 1934 created an independent Federal Communications Commission ("FCC") to manage spectrum use by private entities (such as broadcasters) and non-federal public entities (such as police and fire departments). In 1993, Congress gave the FCC the authority to auction spectrum instead of assigning it by lottery and other methods.[2] The government's ability to gain financially from the sale of spectrum rights, combined with the explosion of mobile communications, made spectrum controversies of ever greater interest to Congress. As a result, spectrum policy can be highly political and subject to vigorous lobbying by groups that include technology firms, broadcasters, the wireless and satellite communications industries, state and local public safety providers and consumer advocates.

Spectrum is divided into blocks or "bands," which are then further divided into channels of varying bandwidths. Spectrum allocation is the process of defining particular bands and designating services that may be provided in those bands. In practice, since all the commercially usable spectrum in the United States has already been allocated to some service, it makes sense to think of this process as a resource *re*-allocation – one that can easily lead to contests between incumbent service providers and prospective new entrants competing to unseat the incumbents. In allocating spectrum, the FCC typically determines not only the type or types of service for which spectrum can be used (*e.g.*, cellular, broadcast television, etc.) but also stipulates how many licenses will be issued and the technology that may be deployed, as well as whether operators will be private or common carriers.

The FCC must conduct the allocation process in furtherance of the "public convenience, interest or necessity."[3] Although there is increasing reliance on market forces to dictate the allocation and use of spectrum, the FCC continues to define spectrum rights (that are then allocated through market mechanisms such as auctions) in accordance with particular values. Spectrum-related public interest goals typically fall into two basic categories: economic and social goals. Economic goals include the public interest in efficient spectrum use, innovation and competition. Social goals include the public interest in telecommunications access, diverse programming and emergency telecommunications services. Both types of goals – and the tradeoffs among them – were instrumental in determining what kind of broadcast television system emerged and what kind of wireless video services will thrive in the future.

Spectrum Policy and the Development of Television

The FCC created what it called "a table of allocations" for television in 1952. This table specified what channels were available for television broadcasting in each of the 210 local television markets across the country. The table of allocations implemented the FCC's statutory mandate to make radio services broadly available throughout the nation and in large and small communities on an equitable basis.[4]

The design of the table of allocations dictated the structure of broadcasting and for several decades, the nature of video services in the US. Although many take for granted that television broadcasting should be offered on a localized basis, there was nothing natural or inevitable about the decision to allocate television channels to smaller communities like Paducah, Kentucky or Altoona, Pennsylvania. As a technical matter, these communities could have been covered by signals transmitted from larger neighboring cities. Indeed, in most countries, this is exactly how broadcast television is structured.

An allocation table with fewer stations covering larger areas would have been much more spectrally efficient. Television stations cannot operate on the same channels or even on adjacent channels in close proximity. Thus, many more channels must be allocated for television broadcasting within a given area than are actually used to transmit signals. Suppose, for example, that 20 channels are set aside in order to provide five channels of broadcast television within a local community. Because of interference concerns, additional channels must be reserved in a neighboring community. As a result, more of the spectrum must be allocated for television in a system that seeks to accommodate multiple stations covering smaller areas within the same region. A system that provides for hundreds of local stations (more than 1600 in the American system) will require more channels to be set aside for television broadcasting than one that provides for fewer, more powerful regional stations. Fewer people will be reached for every hertz of spectrum that is allocated for television. Thus, the choice to support a system of local, as opposed to regional or national broadcasting, sacrificed spectrum efficiency for the benefits of what is often referred to as "localism."[5]

Another spectrum policy choice at the dawn of broadcast television turned out to be as important as the spectrum allocation choice. This was the decision to allow the holders of broadcast facility licenses to control the content that they transmitted. There were other options. Television broadcasters could have been regulated as common carriers. Licensees could have been required to carry the programming of content providers on a nondiscriminatory basis, opening up their broadcast transmission capabilities to all comers. The elaborate regulatory apparatus that developed in the 1960's and 1970's in order to influence the content of television programming was in large part a byproduct of the decision not to regulate broadcasters as common carriers.[6] In place of nondiscrimination principles, the Communications Act and implementing FCC regulations substituted a substantive vision of desirable broadcast content and broadcast structure.

Broadcast content regulation, such as requirements that broadcasters transmit political advertising and children's programming, are alternatives to the non-discrimination rules that apply to common carriers. Where the owner of the physical transmission capacity necessary for communications is under a non-discrimination requirement, we assume that communications will flow freely for the benefit of consumers and society at large. However, where network owners also have the right to control the content they transmit and are under no non-discrimination obligations, other rules may be needed to ensure the delivery of certain forms of content. Structural regulations such as ownership limits to prevent undue media concentration perform a complementary function. They seek to influence the content that licensees transmit by controlling who the licensee is, rather than by imposing non-discrimination requirements. The object, however, is much the same: to expand opportunities to access the airwaves and to expand the pool of voices that individuals receive.

As part of a survey of the regulatory actions that shaped the broadcast system we have today, we should not overlook the inactions. In the prevention of radio interference, both transmitters and receivers have a role. Transmitters can be sited, or can manage signals, in such a way, that the transmitted signals are less likely to interfere with each other. Alternatively, receivers can be built that are more capable of rejecting undesired signals. Arguably one of the greatest inefficiencies in today's system of broadcasting is that television receivers perform relatively poorly in rejecting signal noise. As a result, the broadcast television system is more prone to signal interference than necessary, given state of the art technology. The FCC, by not mandating better receiver performance, chose to build interference protection into transmitter, rather than receiver, design. It did this principally by reserving buffer channels between television stations, thereby effectively reducing interference, but at the price of inefficient spectrum use. In other words, the decision not to regulate receiver quality reduced burdens on receiver manufacturers at the expense of would-be users of the reserved spectrum who cannot use the reserved channels.

Another regulatory policy the FCC might have adopted was to give broadcasters the right to use their licenses flexibly to provide alternative, non-broadcast services. Instead, broadcast spectrum is allocated exclusively for broadcast services. As discussed below, broadcasters can use their digital channels for ancillary services, but they cannot freely alienate their licenses or parts of their licensed spectrum to non-broadcasters or use it entirely for non-broadcast purposes. The rigidity with which broadcasting is regulated stands in marked contrast to the increasing flexibility in the regulation of other wireless services. Spectrum allocated for commercial mobile radio services, for example, can typically be used for a wide array of services and technical architectures. So long as operators stay within prescribed power limits and control the interference they cause to other users, they have the freedom to innovate and to alienate spectrum resources they cannot exploit. Use and alienation restrictions on the broadcast spectrum reduce the incentives of broadcasters to improve the efficiency of their spectrum use and to make associated technical innovations because the licensees cannot extract full value from the spectrum resources they save.

Although efficiency interests might be served by permitting more flexible use of the broadcast spectrum, such a relaxation on use restrictions is not politically feasible. In the politics of spectrum management, the fact that broadcasters did not bid for their spectrum at auction shapes the ways in which they are regulated and therefore, the structure of the broadcast system. Restrictive broadcast regulations have come to be seen as a quid pro quo for operation on spectrum that was not auctioned.[7] In other words, broadcasters pay for their spectrum by serving the public interest in various ways. Any expansion of the rights that broadcasters have under their licenses, including the right to use those licenses for non-broadcast purposes, would be seen as enriching broadcasters at the expense of the public.[8]

I have suggested that broadcast television policy reflects a particular vision of the public interest and has required tradeoffs between various public interest goals like efficiency and localism. Regulatory paradigms, such as a common carrier or broadcast model of regulation, establish limitations on the wireless licenses they govern. These limitations in turn affect how the spectrum is used, how highly it is valued, what spectrum markets develop and what the demand is for alternative spectrum allocations in the future. In other words, the regulation of wireless services is closely bound to the underlying spectrum policy regime. This interrelationship between spectrum policy and service offerings is apparent in the evolution of digital broadcast television.

DTV and the Public Interest

The creation of a digital broadcast television system in the 1990's can be seen either as a colossal failure or a tremendous success of spectrum policy, depending on the public interests that one values most highly.

When the push for digital television began in the late 1980's, broadcast television had existed for more than 30 years without having made any substantial technical advancement other than the shift from black and white to color.[9] And this advance had been achieved in a way that was backwards compatible so that existing service was not interrupted; no consumer had to purchase a color television set in order to continue to receive the legacy black and white service.

Incremental innovation in the broadcast industry has always proved difficult in part because of the public interest goals the system was meant to serve. There is an expectation that broadcasting, unlike other forms of mass media, should be universally available and for free. In addition, there is an expectation that broadcast receivers, unlike handheld devices and computers, will be long-lived, inexpensive and interoperable nationwide. These characteristics are much more attainable if there is a single broadcast technology that facilitates scale in equipment production, as well as interoperability. That means that significant technical changes must be system-wide. Broadcast ownership restrictions that were adopted to enhance broadcast diversity make systemic change difficult and costly to coordinate by preserving a diffuse ownership structure with hundreds of broadcast station owners. It is thus as a byproduct of a locally-based, but nationally interoperable system, that major technical adjustments are difficult to achieve.

Technical alternations are made more difficult by the fact that the FCC mandates the transmission standard and other technical parameters of the broadcast service. Therefore, if broadcasters want to make a major technical change, such as to convert from analog to digital broadcast technology, they need FCC approval. And approval will be difficult to obtain where the change threatens widespread disruption to existing service. This commitment to the seamless, undisrupted provision of free over-the-air broadcasting is rooted in the treatment of broadcast service, unlike cellular telephone service, as a public entitlement with special importance for democratic discourse and the public sphere. The quasi public service characteristic of broadcasting has meant that regulators are unwilling to leave the fate of the broadcast service entirely to market forces.

In the U.S. as in other industrialized countries, the government initiated the shift from analog to digital broadcasting in anticipation of, but without any clear direction from, market demand for higher quality, more flexible and more abundant broadcast television services. The government had a choice among public interest goals to pursue when it began to implement the digital transition in the 1990's. In selecting from among these public interest goals, the FCC yoked spectrum policy to a particular vision of the role of broadcast television in the media landscape.

The federal government announced several public interest goals for the transition from analog to digital broadcasting. Of these, the two most important were the recovery of spectrum for other, non-broadcast uses and the delivery of a more advanced broadcast television service with all the traditional public benefits of existing service.[10] There was widespread consensus among stakeholders that these were appropriate public interest goals, but they were in tension with each other. All other things being equal, the more robust the broadcast television service, the more is the spectrum required. Moreover, the articulated spectrum policy goals left many details to be worked out, such as who should provide the television service, where in the large swath of broadcast spectrum the new digital service should be located, what regulatory steps are required to speed the transition to digital and free up analog spectrum for other uses and what the government's role in defining and effectuating advanced television services should be.

There were three basic fault lines in the policy debates over how to replace analog with digital broadcasting: (1) whether the existing structure of broadcast television, including the spectrum holdings of incumbent broadcasters, should be replicated in digital; (2) whether broadcasters should have to use their digital spectrum for bandwidth-intensive high definition television, or should have the flexibility to provide other digital services; and (3) what the role of the government should be in structuring the relationship between digital broadcasters and their partners in the delivery of digital television, namely consumer equipment manufacturers, cable and satellite. Although the federal government adopted compromise positions among the contending forces on each of these issues, in all cases, it acted conservatively to preserve the status quo of a local, over-the-air, advertising-based broadcast system.

On the first issue – the structure of broadcast television in the digital spectrum – there were many options. Through the early 1990's, the FCC considered proposals that would have changed the composition of broadcast station ownership and broadcast station coverage. The most radical of these proposals was to auction the digital broadcast spectrum to the highest bidder. This option was quickly rejected because there was no assurance that the high bidder would want to use the spectrum for broadcasting. The decision to not open up the spectrum to new, non-broadcast entrants was a decision to not allow the spectrum to migrate to what might be its most economically efficient use (something other than the status quo), but rather to preserve it for broadcasting.

It would have been possible, consistent with the commitment to broadcasting, to auction the spectrum with a stipulation that it be used for broadcasting services only. The government rejected this proposal for reasons of equity, politics and technical feasibility. Incumbent broadcasters insisted that the digital licenses were not new licenses at all, but rather replacements for the analog licenses they would return at the end of the transition. Broadcasters argued that it would not be fair for the government to mandate that they transition to a new technology, at the collective cost of about $10 billion and require them to pay for new licenses in addition. Moreover, they made the case that the best way to ensure a seamless transition from analog to digital broadcast technology, without creating additional interference and loss of service, was to physically collocate analog and digital broadcast services on the same tower and on adjacent channels. This would be most easily accomplished if the same entities owned both analog and digital channels. Broadcasters and the FCC used the principle of "replication" as shorthand for the proposition that digital channels should replicate the properties (location, bandwidth, coverage) of and bear the same ownership as, the analog channels.

One of the consequences of this commitment to replication was that more frequencies were allocated to digital broadcasting than might have been necessary had the government not tried to replicate analog service. Again, there was a tradeoff between the public interest goals of improving spectrum efficiency and maintaining features of the existing broadcast service. Ultimately, the FCC reallocated channels 52–69 – a total of 108 MHz – for non-broadcast services. This left just under 300 MHz of spectrum still allocated for television broadcasting.

The broadcast allocation could have been much smaller and more spectrum could have been reallocated for other purposes, had the FCC been willing to shrink broadcast service areas (thereby disenfranchising a certain number of viewers at the fringes of broadcast coverage), or require broadcast stations to share 6 MHz channels.

A principal reason broadcasters were not required to share 6 MHz channels was because the FCC early on committed the digital broadcast future to high definition television. HDTV requires that each broadcast station use a single 6 MHz channel to accommodate the nearly 20 megabits per second of data that comprise the HDTV signal. Other industrialized countries in Europe and Asia making the shift from analog to digital broadcasting did not embrace HDTV.[11] In the United States, by contrast, the early enthusiasm for digital television focused almost exclusively on the excellent sound and video quality that HDTV would deliver. Lower definition formats would enable broadcasters to transmit four or five video streams in a 6 MHz channel, permitting multiple stations to share a channel or a single station to broadcast multiple programming streams. The commitment of the FCC and ultimately Congress, to the broadcast transmission of at least some HDTV ruled out the possibility of shared channels. The debate then moved to whether broadcasters should be allowed to transmit anything other than HDTV.

The question of whether broadcasters should be mandated to transmit in HDTV and if not, whether the public should be compensated for any additional value broadcasters receive from transmitting multiple streams of broadcast programming, or a combination of broadcast and other services, raised issues that are central in most spectrum policy debates: what are the respective roles of the market and the government in ensuring public value from use of spectrum. The digital television transition, like most spectrum policy initiatives, involved governmental bets on technologies and public communications needs, as well choices among desirable services and service providers. Notwithstanding the clear and inevitable governmental intervention in the market to create digital television, policymakers wanted the market to shape the emergent DTV services. To this end, when the FCC finally authorized DTV service in 1996, it did not mandate that broadcasters transmit in the HDTV format that the channels were designed to accommodate. Indeed, Congress legislated that broadcasters should be permitted to offer not only multiple broadcast formats, but even non-broadcast services. Wireless service providers cried foul that broadcasters should be allowed to compete in non-broadcast businesses on spectrum that they did not have to pay for. In response, Congress mandated that broadcasters would have to pay a spectrum fee of 5% on the gross revenue of any ancillary (presumably subscription-based) service.[12]

DTV spectrum use issues and the hybrid regulatory-market model that was developed to deal with them, implicated the relationship between broadcasters and other entities in the broadcast delivery chain. One might not ordinarily think of issues like copyright policy, cable must-carry rules and consumer equipment mandates as being part of spectrum policy. But in the case of digital broadcasting, all these issues were tied to the central question of when and how consumers could begin receiving the full complement of digital signals and therefore when the analog channels could be turned off and the spectrum reallocated for other uses. In the context of analog broadcasting, there were federal rules requiring cable systems to carry local broadcast signals without degradation and requiring television manufacturers to include tuners that could receive all television channels on their sets. These rules were premised on the spectrum policy commitment to free, locally-based broadcast television. Once government had committed the spectrum resources to the broadcast service and consumers had come to rely on it, government felt compelled to take the further steps to ensure that third parties did not obstruct it and even facilitated the reception of over-the-air signals *even if* such reception was not over the air (such as through cable).[13]

In the digital world, it had to be decided whether similar kinds of rules were necessary to further reception of the DTV signals and therefore effectuate the digital transition. Although the issues were not new, the circumstances were. There was a well-developed market for the analog television product that the must-carry regulations supported. There was also evidence in the analog world that, in the absence of regulation, many consumers would not receive broadcast programming. By contrast, there was no established market for digital broadcast signals in the early part of the twenty-first century when the FCC was considering what rules were necessary to facilitate DTV reception. There was scant evidence that the market would fail to deliver digital signals through cable or any other distribution medium. There was no evidence that when the time came to turn off the analog signals – a date that moved from 2006 to 2009 – there would be any shortage of DTV receivers. The strong inclination of regulators to allow parties to work out signal transmission arrangements in the marketplace ran squarely into the articulated spectrum policy interest in recovering spectrum and replicating free over-the–air television (and the existing transmission pathways).

There was much at stake in FCC decisions regarding cable carriage. Because more than 70% of American households receive broadcast programming through cable, and another 15% through satellite, the manner in which the DTV signal was carried through these media would have a significant impact on broadcaster use of the DTV spectrum. For example, if cable operators declined to carry DTV signals in full HDTV quality, then broadcasters would have little incentive to undertake the expense of broadcasting in HDTV. If multiple streams of broadcast programming were not carried on cable or satellite, then broadcasters might find something else to do with this spectrum. Indeed, there was a good argument that if broadcasters failed to obtain HDTV or other carriage arrangements with cable operators, it would be because the market had spoken and the DTV spectrum would be better used for other purposes. But because the DTV transition was in no way market driven to begin with, there was also an argument that consumers could not know what DTV services they wanted until such services were available – something that would not happen without the full cooperation (even if government-mandated) of cable and other partners.

The argument for regulation ultimately won out starting in 2002, with the FCC mandating that cable operators carry at least one stream of DTV programming and then in 2007 further requiring that cable operators install the necessary equipment to ensure that at least one stream of DTV programming will be viewable in its original format in subscriber households. These decisions are a direct result of the chain of spectrum policy choices carried over from analog broadcasting, including the value invested in over-the-air broadcasting, the structure of broadcasting around local signals and multiple overlapping stations, the enlistment of broadcast distribution partners to compensate for poor reception and the interest in recovering analog spectrum relatively quickly.

The regulation of television sets presented old and new issues, all pitting the commitment to market solutions against the interest in speeding the digital transition. The old issue was one that had presented itself in the 1960's when UHF television broadcasting was just getting off the ground: since broadcasters do not control the design and manufacture of receivers, government mandates may be required to ensure that consumer products will be able to receive newly available broadcast signals. In 1967, Congress stepped in to legislate that television receivers be able to receive all broadcast channels, including UHF channels.[14] The corollary issue in the DTV world was whether receivers should be required to receive DTV signals, lest consumers continued to buy analog receivers and found themselves without DTV reception capacity when analog service ceased. Although it had not been willing to mandate receiver performance standards, the FCC did mandate the phase-in of DTV tuners.[15] It later required consumer electronics retailers to ensure that consumers were informed, at the point of sale, about the uselessness of analog tuners after February 17, 2009, when the analog signals would go dark.[16]

The new receiver issue involved copyright concerns. While the ability of consumers to record and retransmit broadcast programming had always bothered content producers, analog recordings were so flawed and modes of retransmission so cumbersome that the threat to producer control and revenues was minimal. Digital technology changed the equation. Content producers feared that once they began to make digital programming available over the air, they would lose control of the content to "pirates" who could easily record and retransmit perfect copies of the programming. Producers, in many cases owned by the same companies as the broadcasters themselves, were inclined to use copy control technology that would restrict the copying of certain programming. In order to function properly, the control technology would have to be recognized and effectuated by television receivers. Uncertain that they would be able to get receiver manufacturers to support the copy protection technology, producers and some broadcasters urged the FCC to regulate television receivers so that they would have to recognize what came to be known as the "broadcast flag." The FCC ultimately agreed to do this, but the regulation was overturned in court for lack of jurisdiction to regulate television receivers in this way.[17]

Future Battles

Just as the existing analog and new digital broadcasting services have been shaped by spectrum policy values, so too will the future of wireless video. We can expect spectrum policy battles to play out in three general areas: (1) what new services existing broadcasters will be allowed to offer; (2) what new services will be allowed to operate in the broadcast spectrum; and (3) how spectrum policy will evolve to shape relationships in the video value chain.

Broadcasters recognize that their future may well depend on the ability to offer consumers a mobile product. To that end, they are establishing a mobile broadcasting standard that will allow broadcasters to roll out mobile services to handheld devices on spectrum otherwise devoted to broadcast television.[18] To the extent that these services are subscription based, broadcasters will have to pay a fee on gross revenues. To the extent that they are advertising-based, there will be a question as to what public interest requirements should apply in return for the "free" use of the spectrum. These debates will implicate the question of whether mobile broadcasting is broadcasting that should serve the same localism and diversity functions as traditional broadcasting and be subject to the same kinds of requirements. There will also be the question of whether mobile broadcasting should receive the same regulatory solicitude as traditional broadcasting. Consider, for example, the possibility that a new service could be introduced in the broadcast band that would not interfere with fixed broadcasting services, but would interfere with mobile services. Broadcasters would likely seek interference protection for their mobile offerings. The protection of mobile services would in essence expand the spectrum entitlement that broadcasters have and a case would need to be made for why the spectrum should be allocated for this purpose as opposed to another.

The time is already ripe for the introduction of new services into the broadcast band, whether by broadcasters or new entrants. The use of the broadcast spectrum for new wireless services will impact the scope of DTV services incumbent in the band and will also provide new sources of competition for video transmission. Because so many buffer channels have been left open to prevent high power television transmissions from interfering with each other, there is a considerable amount of broadcast spectrum that is not actually being used to carry broadcast signals. The FCC has dubbed this spectrum "white space." In 2002, the FCC floated the idea of permitting the operation of low power unlicensed devices on broadcast white space. The technology community, particularly Intel, favored the proposal, along with public interest advocates of unlicensed use such as the New America Foundation. Television incumbents opposed the idea, arguing that the channels, while vacant, were not in fact unused because they served as buffers between high power television channels. To the extent that there were white spaces, the incumbents argued that this available spectrum should be allocated for licensed uses. What services can be offered in the white spaces, by whom and under what regulatory regime is still up in the air. In addition to disputes over technical details about the interference effects of new wireless devices on broadcast television, there is a deeper policy debate about the relative merits of broadcasting and other services and the role of the market in allocating spectrum rights.

The core of the debate over white space usage transcends the technical and policy details of the broadcast band. Both sides – broadcasters and prospective new entrants – assert that the spectrum can be put to more intensive use. The debate is really over whether incumbents should be granted additional rights to exploit adjacent spectrum, whether these rights should be licensed on an exclusive basis to the highest bidder, or whether the frequencies should be opened up to unlicensed devices. While the debate has been framed in technical terms about interference, it is as much about the course of innovation and governance of the spectrum resource. Centralized control of spectrum through licensing spurs innovation of a kind, as evidenced by the dramatic growth of cellular services. Decentralized control of spectrum through unlicensed usage spurs innovation of another kind, as evidenced by the flourishing of WiFi connections. Even with respect to the single public interest parameter of innovation, spectrum policymakers must make bets as to which kind of innovation is most likely and most productive.

If the vacant space between broadcast transmissions is the white space in the broadcast band, the frequencies that carry broadcast signals are the black spaces. After the transition to DTV, there will be at least 30 MHz, and sometimes closer to 100 MHz, of spectrum that is used for television broadcasting in each U.S. market. To provide some sense of the value of that spectrum, AT&T recently paid over $55 million for a 12 MHz license covering the Denver metropolitan area.[19] Given the availability of cable, satellite and fiber television transmissions and Internet broadband capability, there will be pressure on the FCC to reallocate broadcast spectrum in its entirety to new wireless uses. This pressure may come from broadcasters themselves who want the chance to sell their spectrum for non-broadcast purposes or to provide new services themselves under a different regulatory regime. At some point relatively soon, there will have to be a reassessment of the continued value of over the air broadcasting and the tradeoffs between preserving this system and the spectrum cost. This calculation will recapitulate the DTV debate over whether it is more important to support existing models or to free up spectrum for new services and secondarily, whether an administrative agency or the market should make this decision.

A third and perhaps most significant, influence on the future of wireless video will be policy choices about the conditions to place on spectrum entitlements used to distribute video and other wireless services. We saw in the case of digital television how FCC actions and inactions with respect to cable operators, receiver manufacturers, and broadcasters structured the rights and responsibilities of these actors. As more of the spectrum is allocated to new kinds of video service providers, the FCC will inquire how the public interest can best be served. In the case of broadcasting, the government has privileged social goals such as diversity, universal service and democratic discourse over economic ones, such as innovation and competition. In all likelihood, the highest ranked public interest values going forward when new spectrum is allocated for video services will be competition and innovation. This was certainly the case in the recent 700 MHz auction in which the government auctioned 52 MHz of analog broadcast spectrum for new nationwide broadband wireless services for just under $20 billion.

And yet, because communications services are involved, the importance of free communication in a democracy will push the FCC to look more closely at the power of gatekeepers and to consider special public interest obligations for spectrum licensees than might otherwise be required to advance innovation and competition. This was true in the 700 MHz auction. There, even in the absence of evidence that non-discrimination requirements were necessary to foster competition and innovation, the FCC imposed obligations on the licensees to open their networks to all applications and all devices without discrimination. In other words, the network operator would be required to "carry" third-party applications and give consumers choices about the devices they want to use to receive signals. The arguments for such restrictions on licensee operations are grounded in both economic and social values, with leading advocates emphasizing the free speech benefits of mandating unfettered access to broadband transmission pipes.[20]

In the future, there will undoubtedly be questions about whether broadband video providers, particularly when they have spectrum rights, should be subject to broadcast-like public interest requirements. The FCC will be put to the question of whether it should regulate via non-discrimination requirements, substantive requirements, or not at all. Particularly if broadcast television ceases and the spectrum is reallocated, the public interest impulses that have shaped ownership limits, programming requirements, must-carry and other regulations will turn towards the new spectrum and services. In place of or alongside broadcasting, there will be new "regulable spaces" where, as was true at the dawn of broadcasting, and then again with the creation of DTV, government will seek to express public interest values in the allocation of spectrum rights. And as was true with respect to the broadcast spectrum, these values will require tradeoffs among both social and economic goals that are invariably less explicitly stated than they ought to be.

Notes

1. 47 U.S.C. § 309(j)(3)(c).
2. 47 U.S.C. § 309(j).
3. 47 U.S.C. § 303.
4. 47 U.S.C. § 307(b) (2000) ("[T]he Commission shall make such distribution of licenses, frequencies, hours of operation, and of power among the several States and communities as to provide a fair, efficient, and equitable distribution of radio service to each of the same."). The FCC dispersed television station permits throughout smaller towns as well as urban centers within larger regions in order to "protect[ ] the interests of the public residing in smaller cities and rural areas ... [and ensure that] as many communities as possible ... have the advantages that derive from having local outlets that will be responsive to local needs." Sixth Report and Order, 17 Federal Register 3905, 68, 79 (1952).
5. Deregulation of Radio, 84 FCC 2d 968 58 (1981) ("The concept of localism was part and parcel of broadcast regulation virtually from its inception."); Cable Act, S. Rep. No. 92, 102d Cong. 42 (1992), reprinted in 1992 U.S.C.C.A.N. 1133, 1175 ("There is no doubt that, over the past forty years, television broadcasting has provided vital local services through its programming, including news and public affairs offerings and its emergency broadcasts."); *Turner Broadcasting System, Inc. v. FCC*, 512 U.S. 622, 663 (1994) ("[The importance of local broadcasting outlets 'can scarcely be exaggerated, for broadcasting is demonstrably a principal source of information and entertainment for a great part of the Nation's population.'"); *National Broad. Co. v. United States*, 319 U.S. 190, 203 (1943) ("Local program service is a vital part of community life. A station should be ready, able, and willing to serve the needs of the local community.")

6. McChesney, Robert M. *Telecommunications, Mass Media, and Democracy: The Battle for the Control of U.S. Broadcasting, 1928–1935*. New York: Oxford University Press, 1993; de Sola Pool, Ithiel. *Technologies of Freedom*. Cambridge, Mass.: Belknap Press, 1983.
7. Logan, Jr., Charles W. "Getting beyond Scarcity: A New Paradigm for Assessing the Constitutionality of Broadcast Regulation." *California Law Review* 85, no. 6 (Dec. 1997): pp. 1687–1747.
8. Goodman, Ellen P. "Spectrum Equity." *Journal on Telecommunications and High Technology Law* 4 (2005): 217–248; Snider, J.H. *The Art of Spectrum Lobbying: America's $480 Billion Spectrum Giveaway, How it Happened, and How to Prevent It From Recurring*. Washington, DC: New America Foundation, 2007.
9. Brinkley, Joel. *Defining Vision: The Battle for the Future of Television*. San Diego: Harcourt Brace, 1998.
10. Advanced TV Systems and Their Impact on the Existing TV Broadcast Service, Fifth Report and Order, 12 F.C.C.R. 12809, 12811 (1997) The FCC's goals in authorizing DTV were to "(1) preserv[e] a free, universal broadcasting service; (2) foster[] an expeditious and orderly transition to [DTV]…; (3)…recover[] contiguous blocks of spectrum; (4) ensur[e] that the spectrum…will be used in a manner that best serves the public interest." The FCC also set forth the following **goals** (1) to ensure confidence and certainty in the **DTV** transition; (2) to increase the availability of new products and services to consumers; (3) to encourage techno-logical innovation and competition; and (4) to minimize regulation and to ensure that those regulations that are adopted do not last any longer than necessary.
11. Galperin, Hernan, *New Television, Old Politics: The Transition to Digital TV in the United States and Great Britain*. Cambridge: Cambridge University Press, 2004.
12. 47 U.S.C. § 201(b) (2006); 47 C.F.R. § 73.624 (c) (2006).
13. *Turner Broadcasting System, Inc. et al. v. FCC*, 520 U.S. 180, 189 (1997) (articulating goals of statutory mandate that cable systems carry local broadcast signals).
14. All Channel Receiver Act of 1962, Pub. L. No. 87-529, 76 Stat. 15 (codified at 47 U.S.C. §303(s) (2000)).
15. In re Review of the Commission's Rules and Policies Affecting the Conversion to Digital Television, Second Report and Order and Second Memorandum Opinion and Order, 17 F.C.C.R. 15,978 (2002); *Consumer Electronics Association v. FCC*, 347 F.3d 291, 295 (D.C. Cir. 2003) (upholding rules on appeal).
16. Second Periodic Review of the Commission's Rules and Policies Affecting the Conversion To Digital Television, 22 F.C.C.R. 8776, 8777 (2007) (requiring Consumer Alert label on televi-sion receiving equipment that contains an analog-only broadcast television tuner).
17. American Library Association v. FCC, 406 F.3d 689, 692 (D.C. Cir. 2005).
18. "ATSC to Develop Standard for Mobile and Handheld Services" Advanced Television Systems Committee, Washington, DC, April 9, 2007 Last Accessed at http://www.atsc. org/news_information/press/2007/Mobile_07.html on June 26, 2008 (announcing the com-mencement of work of the Advanced Television Systems Committee on a mobile broadcast standard).
19. "Auction of 700 MHz Band Licenses Closes," FCC Public Notice DA 08-595, May 20, 2008, Attachment A pp. 14; Weiser, Philip & Hatfield, Dale "Spectrum Policy Reform and the Next Frontier of Property Rights" *George Mason Law Review* 15, no. 3 (Spring 2008): 549–610.
20. Lessig, Lawrence. "In Support of Network Neutrality" *I/S: A Journal of Law and Policy for the Information Society* 3, iss. 1 (Spring 2007): 185–196; Wu, Tim. "Network Neutrality, Broadband Discrimination." *Journal on Telecommunications and High Technology Law* 2 (2003): 141–176; Wu, Tim. "Why Have a Telecommunications Law?: Antidiscrimination Norms in Communications." *Journal on Telecommunications and High Technology Law* 5, iss. 1 (Fall 2006): 15–46.

Chapter 13
Cognitive Radios in Television White Spaces

Monisha Ghosh

Abstract On February 17, 2009, the transition to digital television broadcasting in the US will finally be complete. All full power television stations will cease their analog (NTSC) broadcasts and switch to digital (ATSC) broadcasts. This transition will free up channels in the VHF and UHF frequencies that can potentially be used for other wireless services and applications. Among the various possible scenarios is one which is being pursued most actively: that of secondary usage of the TV spectrum by unlicensed devices. In order to enable such usage, "cognitive radios" i.e. radios that are aware of their spectral environment and can dynamically access available spectrum without causing interference to the primary user are essential. In this paper we describe recent developments in cognitive radios that make them suitable for use in the television bands.

Introduction

Historically, spectrum allocation for various services: radio, television, public safety, cellular etc. has been based on a command and control regulatory structure, i.e. spectrum is allocated by the FCC for a certain service with accompanying rules of usage and no other legal use of the spectrum is permitted [1]. For example, UHF and VHF bands from 54 to 806 MHz have been allocated for terrestrial television broadcasting with each television channel occupying a 6 MHz bandwidth. As television channels are allocated, in a particular way in a given geographical area many channels may be unused. However, current FCC rules do not allow any other service to utilize that spectrum for any other purpose. Historically, reasons for doing so were based on interference caused to adjacent and co-channel television receivers. However with improvements in technology, it is now possible to build "cognitive radios" [2–4] that are aware of their spectral environment and can adjust their transmissions so as not to create unwanted interference to incumbents. This advancement, coupled with digital television transition that will free up large swathes of spectrum, creates an unprecedented opportunity for the FCC to change rules and allow spectrum-sharing and thus open up a whole new area of applications. In this paper we describe how cognitive radios can be used to harness the promise of television white spaces.

D. Gerbarg (ed.), *Television Goes Digital*,
© Springer Science + Business Media, LLC 2009

This chapter is organized as follows. The first section discusses the spectrum regulatory scenario and recent efforts to open up the white-spaces. Section "White Spaces: What, When, Why" introduces the topic of cognitive radios and the requirements that need to be met to satisfy goals of no interference. The next section describes a standardization effort being pursued in IEEE 802.22 for developing a wireless regional-area-network (WRAN) using cognitive radios in the television band and sensing algorithms that can be used to protect incumbents. The next section describes some lab and field tests that have been performed to test sensing algorithms. The final section concludes this paper.

White Spaces: What, When, Why

In the US, terrestrial television broadcasting is over Channels 2–69, covering frequencies 54–806 MHz as follows: Channels 2–4 (54–72 MHz), Channels 5–6 (76–88 MHz) Channels 7–13 (174–216 MHz), Channels 14–69 (470–806 Hz). Channel 37 is allocated nationwide for radio astronomy and medical telemetry. There are other services in the gaps in this frequency range such as land-mobile radio and FM radio [1]. With the introduction of digital television broadcasting beginning in 1997, the FCC allocated one channel for digital broadcasting to every existing licensed analog channel. Thus it is clear that "white spaces" or empty spaces in television frequencies have existed as long as television spectrum has been allocated and these were used fruitfully in the transition from analog to digital broadcasting. The first digital channel on the air was KITV in Honolulu in fall 1997 and initially the digital transition was supposed to have been completed by 2006. This digital transition is expected to finally be complete in 2009. On February 17, 2009, all analog television broadcasts will cease, which means that those channels will now become "white spaces". Why, one may ask, should one consider these channels as available, when these white spaces have existed in the past as well and not been considered for alternate uses? The reason is that, unlike analog television, digital television signal does not suffer from interference when there is an adjacent signal in an adjacent frequency band and hence guard frequency bands are not required. Moreover, the total number of channels allocated for television broadcasting is the same nationwide, even though in rural and less-populated areas of the country most of these do not have actual broadcasts, creating almost an 80% vacancy rate [5].

There are at least two ways that one might use this spectrum: licensed or unlicensed. In order to license any spectrum and auction it to the highest bidder, there has to be nation-wide availability of that spectrum. However, television allocations vary across the nation and a certain channel would not necessarily be unused in all television markets across the nation. The unlicensed model would be more flexible but would require the use of cognitive technology that could dynamically detect available spectrum in a certain region. The unlicensed model in the ISM (900 MHz, 2.4 GHz) and U-NII (5 GHz) bands have proved enormously beneficial over the past decade in spawning applications such as Wi-Fi, Bluetooth, wireless internet etc. Hence, as far back as 2002, following the release of the report on improving spectrum efficiency by the Spectrum Policy Task Force [6], the FCC issued a Notice of Inquiry (NOI) regarding alternate uses of TV white spaces. Based on responses, a Notice of Proposed Rule Making (NPRM) was issued in May 2004 to allow unlicensed devices to utilize vacant television channels [7]. It was recognized that the superior propagation characteristics of these frequencies will enable a whole host of new applications that would require greater service range than that provided by existing Wi-Fi and cellular services. Two classes of devices were proposed: low-power personal/portable devices such as Wi-Fi, and higher power fixed access services that will cover a larger region with broadband access. Both kinds of devices would need some measures for ensuring protection to incumbent television stations in these bands, as well as wireless microphones that operate as licensed secondaries under Part 74 rules [8]. Following this, a first report and order and NPRM was issued in October 2006 inviting more comments on the proposal to allow unlicensed services in the television bands [9]. Channels 52–69 (698–806 MHz), which had no television broadcasts nationwide, were reallocated for other applications, with some parts of the spectrum being set aside for auction [10]. This auction concluded in March 2008 with bids totaling about US $19 billion. This value indicates the premium companies were willing to put on this spectrum.

Measurements and analysis made by different groups [11, 12] over the last few years indicate that even in the crowded metropolitan areas such as New York city, 18–30% of channels would be available as white spaces after the DTV transition. If we consider only UHF channels 21–51, that would be about ten channels, each 6 MHz wide which is 60 MHz of spectrum. This is equivalent to the amount of spectrum available in the 2.4 GHz band, where there are three non-overlapping channels, each 22 MHZ wide. In rural markets, the percentage of vacant channels could be as high as 70%. Hence it is clear that significant services can be provided with the white spaces.

Cognitive Radio

It is well accepted in academia, industry and regulatory bodies such as the FCC that due to the legacy command-and-control method of allocating spectrum, spectrum access appears to be more of a problem than spectrum scarcity [4–6]. In many frequency bands there are "spectrum holes" i.e. frequency bands that are allocated but unused in certain geographical areas and certain times. Cognitive radios have been proposed as a solution to this problem. Various definitions of cognitive radio exist in literature, but in its simplest form, a cognitive radio is one that that can adapt its transmission characteristics such as power, bandwidth, frequency of operation etc. in response to the RF environment it detects. This method is also sometimes referred to as listen-before-talk. A true cognitive radio is more than just a software-defined-radio: it needs to smartly sense spectrum availability and react accordingly, based on existing policies, FCC rules etc. for that frequency band. In a network of multiple such radios, other issues need to be addressed as well: network coordination of spectrum sensing, dynamic spectrum access and sharing, coexistence between multiple cognitive networks competing for the same spectrum, as well as quality-of-service (QoS) considerations. The October 2006 NPRM [9] mentioned three ways in which one could use the television bands for unlicensed services in a way that incumbents would be unaffected by interference:

1. Use of a database, based on location information of the unlicensed device that would inform unlicensed users of incumbents of the need for protection. The problem with this approach is that while it may work for television stations that are fixed in frequency and location, wireless microphones that are also using this band would not be protected. Moreover, the database needs to be up-to-date and accurate in terms of coverage of television stations, and every unlicensed device would need a GPS receiver to accurately determine location as well as have access to the database. This would preclude applications which rely on ad-hoc networking.
2. Use a control signal that is issued when a certain frequency is available for use by unlicensed devices in a service area. This control signal could be transmitted from a TV transmitter, or possibly from an unlicensed device itself. This would require separate infrastructure to generate and receive this control signal. The wireless beacon signal being developed by IEEE 802.22.1 [13] to protect wireless microphones falls under this category.
3. Use cognitive radios that employ signal processing methods to detect spectral occupancy by either television or wireless microphones.

Of the above, the cognitive radio option offers the most flexible solution to the problem, provided adequate protection parameters could be defined for sensing TV signals and wireless microphones. Cognitive radios would need no additional infrastructure like GPS to detect spectrum holes and could easily adapt to different policies in different regulatory domains. DARPA's Next generation (XG) program started in 2006 has successfully tested cognitive radio technologies such as spectrum sensing and dynamic spectrum access in the context of establishing ad-hoc wireless mesh networks [14].

Overview of IEEE 802.22

Spurred by the NPRM in May 2004, the IEEE 802.22 Working Group was started in November 2004 [13] as the first worldwide group with the charter of developing an air interface specification based on cognitive radios for unlicensed operation in the television bands. Television broadcasters, wireless microphone manufacturers, research labs and wireless companies worldwide came together to begin the task of drafting a physical layer (PHY), medium-access-control (MAC) protocols and, unique to IEEE 802.22, sensing mechanisms that would enable unlicensed operations in the television bands. The primary application being targeted here was wireless broadband access in rural and remote areas where broadband access via cable and DSL was either scarce or non-existent. In recent years the US has fallen behind both in terms of percentage of population with access to broadband connections as well as speed of these connections. According to the ITU, the US is 15th in the world in broadband penetration [15] and one of the reasons is the cost of providing services to populations in rural areas. Since IEEE 802.22 would be implemented in the unlicensed television bands, the cost of offering services would be a lot lower than, for example WI-MAX based on 802.16 which would offer services over licensed bands. Moreover, superior propagation characteristics of the television frequencies allow much larger service areas as compared to WI-MAX. Other application areas for IEEE 802.22 would be in single-family residential, multi-dwelling unit, small office/home office (SOHO) and campuses. Services offered would include data, voice as well as audio and video with appropriate QoS. While immediate applications are in the US, IEEE 802.22 is being designed as an international standard that would meet regulatory requirements elsewhere in the world and can be used in 6, 7 and 8 MHz channels.

Topology, Entities and Relationships

The IEEE 802.22 system specifies a fixed point-to-multipoint (P-MP) wireless air interface whereby a base station (BS) manages its own cell[1] and all associated Consumer Premise Equipments (CPEs), as depicted in Fig. 13.1. The BS (a professionally installed entity) controls the medium access in its cell and transmits in the downstream direction to the various CPEs, which respond back to the BS in the upstream direction. In order to ensure protection of incumbent services, the 802.22 system follows a strict master/slave relationship, wherein the BS performs the role of the master and the CPEs, the slaves. No CPE is allowed to transmit before receiving proper authorization from a BS, which also controls all the RF characteristics (e.g., modulation, coding, and frequencies of operation) used by the CPEs. In addition to the traditional role of a BS, of regulating data transmission in a cell, an IEEE 802.22 BS manages a unique feature of *distributed sensing*. This is needed to ensure proper incumbent protection and is managed by the BS, which instructs various CPEs to perform distributed measurement activities. Based on the feedback received, the BS decides which steps, if any, are to be taken.

---

[1] Here, we define an 802.22 cell (or simply, a cell) as formed by a single 802.22 BS and zero or more 802.22 CPEs associated with and under control by this 802.22 BS, whose coverage area extends up to the point where the transmitted signal from the 802.22 BS can be received by associated 802.22 CPEs with a given minimum SNR quality.

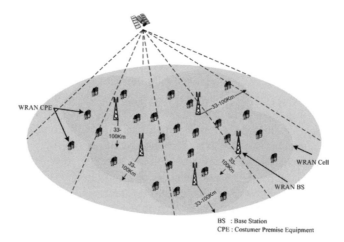

Fig. 13.1 Exemplary 802.22 deployment configuration

Service Capacity

The 802.22 system specifies spectral efficiencies in the range of 0.5–5 bit/(s/Hz). If we consider an average of 3 bits/s/Hz, this would correspond to a total PHY data rate of 18 Mbps in a 6 MHz TV channel. In order to obtain the minimum data rate per CPE, a total of 12 simultaneous users are considered which leads to a required minimum peak throughput rate at edge of coverage of 1.5 Mbps per CPE in the downstream direction. In the upstream direction, a peak throughput of 384 kbps is specified, which is comparable to Cable/DSL services.

Service Coverage

A distinctive feature of 802.22 WRAN as compared to existing IEEE 802 standards is the BS coverage range, can go up to 100 km if power is not an issue (current specified coverage range is 33 Km at 4 W CPE EIRP). As shown in Fig. 13.2, WRANs have much larger coverage range than today's networks, which is primarily due to its higher power and favorable propagation characteristics of TV frequency bands. This enhanced coverage range offers unique technical challenges as well as opportunities.

DFS Timing Requirements

The Dynamic Frequency Selection (DFS) timing parameters defines the requirements that the 802.22 standard must adhere to in order to effectively protect

Fig. 13.2 802.22 wireless
RAN classification as
compared to other popular
wireless standards

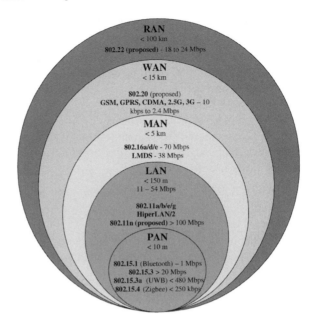

Table 13.1 Selected DFS parameters

Parameter	Value for wireless microphones	Value for TV broadcasting
Channel detection time	≤2 s	≤2 s
Channel move time (in-service monitoring)	2 s	2 s
Channel closing transmission time (aggregate transmission time)	100 ms	100 ms
Incumbent detection threshold	−107 dBm (over 200 KHz)	−116 dBm (over 6 MHz)
Probability of detection	90%	90%
Probability of false alarm	10%	10%

incumbents. These parameters serve as the basis for design of coexistence solutions, and are keys to understanding mechanisms presented later on.

Table 13.1 illustrates only key DFS parameters defined within 802.22, and which are based on the DFS model ordered by the FCC for the 5 GHz band [16]. Two key parameters are Channel Detection Time (CDT) and Incumbent Detection Threshold (IDT). The CDT defines the time during which an incumbent operation can withstand interference before the 802.22 system detects it. It dictates how quickly an 802.22 system must be able to detect an incumbent signal exceeding the IDT. Once the incumbent signal is detected higher than IDT, two other new parameters have to be considered, namely, Channel Move Time (CMT) and Channel Closing

Transmission Time (CCTT). The CCTT is the aggregate duration of transmissions by 802.22 devices during the CMT.

As will be shown later, these parameters are critical not only to the design of efficient PHY and MAC layer mechanisms for the sake of incumbent protection, but also to design schemes that cause minimal impact on the operation of the secondary network (e.g., QoS support).

The level of −116 dBm for sensing of digital television signals was chosen to be 32 dBm below the −84 dBm signal level required by an ATSC receiver to display a viewable digital signal. This was assumed to be enough clearance to account for the following losses:

1. *Antenna height.* The television antenna can be roof mounted and directional towards the television station whereas the unlicensed device will have an antenna lower in height.
2. Building penetration losses between external antenna and internal antenna.
3. Fading due to multi-path and shadow fading.

It is anticipated that with this threshold, hidden-node problems will be avoided. Similar argument hold true for the −107 dBm threshold for the detection of wireless microphones.

Spectrum Sensing Algorithms

The topic of spectrum sensing algorithms for detection of incumbent signals has recently been receiving a lot of attention [13, 17, 18]. Within IEEE 802.22, a number of techniques such as energy detection (full bandwidth and pilot), ATSC field sync detection, cyclostationary detection, spectral correlation, multi-resolution spectrum sensing and analog auto correlation have been proposed and evaluated via simulations using captured real-world ATSC signals. In this section we discuss a novel method based on detecting pilot energy and location that can be used with either one or multiple sensing dwells, and hence fits well with the MAC sensing architecture by allowing the QoS of secondary services to be preserved despite regularly scheduled sensing windows.

At the MAC layer, existing work has not addressed the implications of spectrum sensing and its impact on QoS to secondary users [19–21]. The IEEE 802.11h [22] standard includes basic mechanisms to quiet channels, but does not deal with the protocol mechanisms to synchronize quiet periods of overlapping networks or guarantee seamless operation in the presence of incumbents. The two stage sensing, incumbent detection and notification, and synchronization schemes described in this section, however, are designed for operation in highly dynamic and dense networks and have been adopted in the current draft of the IEEE 802.22 standard [13]. Variations of these schemes are also used in the Cognitive MAC (C-MAC) protocol introduced in [23].

TV Sensing Algorithms

In keeping with the general rule of IEEE 802, the 802.22 draft standard cannot specify receiver algorithms. However, 802.22 is a special case in that spectrum sensing is a very important feature of the standard even though its actual implementation will be in receivers. Hence, the objective of the 802.22 group is to define requirements for sensing that have to be met by all manufacturers. This specification of sensing requirements is ongoing [24, 32]. As presented above, the principal metrics for characterizing a sensing algorithm are Probability of Detection (P_D) and Probability of False Alarm (P_{FA}). In our discussion throughout the rest of this paper, we use Probability of Missed Detection (P_{MD}) instead of P_D. Both P_{MD} and P_{FA} are functions of received signal-to-noise-ratio (SNR) and threshold. Ideally, one would like to have $P_{MD} = 0.0$ and $P_{FA} = 0.0$. However, in a practical situation this will be hard to achieve and it might be more reasonable to allow a relaxed P_{FA} value of 0.01–0.1 and a P_{MD} of 0.05–0.10. From the incumbent protection point of view, a higher P_{FA} is more tolerable than a higher P_{MD}.

There are two main approaches to spectrum sensing: energy detection and feature detection. Energy detection is used to determine presence of signal energy in the band of interest, and is followed by feature detection to determine if the signal energy is indeed due to the presence of an incumbent. Since 802.22 will be implemented in TV bands, digital television incumbent signals could be ATSC (North America), DVB-T (Europe), or ISDB (Japan). In this paper we consider feature detection only for ATSC [25].

The ATSC signal has a number of features that can be exploited for feature detection algorithms:

- *PN 511 sequence.* The ATSC signal has a 511-symbol long PN sequence that is inserted in the data stream every 24.2 ms. Since averaging over more than one field would be necessary for detection reliability, the PN 511 sequence based sensing requires longer detection times.
- *Pilot.* The ATSC signal uses an 8-VSB modulation with signal levels (−7, −5, −3, −1, +1, +3, +5, +7). A DC offset of 1.25 is added to this at baseband to effectively create a small pilot signal to enable carrier recovery at the receiver.
- *Segment-sync.* The ATSC data is sent in segments of 828 symbols. A 4-symbol segment sync sequence (+5, −5, −5, +5) is transmitted at the beginning of each data segment. Detection of the segment sync sequence can be used in a feature detector.
- *Cyclostationarity.* Since the ATSC signal is a digital signal with a symbol rate of 10.76 MHz, cyclostationary detectors may be used as a feature detector.

The main problem with any feature-detection method for ATSC is the requirement of detection at very low signal level (−116 dBm). Most of the synchronization schemes designed for ATSC receivers fail at these low signal levels and the detector may require large number of samples to average over for a reliable detection.

The ATSC VSB signal has a pilot at the lower band-edge in a known location relative to the signal. For this description, we will assume that the signal to be sensed is a band-pass signal at a low-IF of 44 MHz with nominal pilot location at 46.69 MHz (assuming single stage conversion) and is sampled at 100 MHz. However, basic steps can be implemented with suitable modifications for any IF and sampling rate. Essential features of the proposed method are as follows:

1. Downshift signal to baseband by multiplying it by frequency, f_c = 46.69 MHz. Hence, if $x(t)$ is the real, band-pass signal at low-IF, then $y(t) = x(t)e^{-j2f_c t}$ is the complex signal at baseband.
2. Filter $y(t)$ with a low-pass filter of bandwidth e.g. 40 kHz (+/−20 kHZ). The filter bandwidth should be large enough to accommodate any foreseen frequency offsets.
3. Down-sample the filtered signal from 100 MHz to 53.8 kHz, to form the signal $z(t)$.
4. Take FFT of the down-sampled signal $z(t)$. Depending on the sensing period, length of the FFT will vary. For example a 1 ms sensing window will allow a 32-point FFT while a 5 ms window will allow a 256-point FFT.
5. Determine maximum value, and location, of the FFT output squared.

Signal detection can now be done either by setting a threshold on the maximum value, or by observing the location of the peak over successive intervals. Instead of the FFT, other well-known spectrum estimation methods, such as the Welch periodogram can also be used in step (4) above.

The basic method described above can be adapted to a variety of scenarios as described below:

1. Multiple fine sensing windows, e.g. 5 ms sensing dwells every 100 ms. The 256-point FFT outputs squared from each sensing window can be averaged to form a composite statistic as well as the location information from each measurement can be used to derive a detection metric.
2. If a single long sensing window, e.g. 10 ms is available, a 512-point FFT or periodogram can be used to obtain better detection performance.

Parameters of the sensor can be chosen depending on desired sensing time, complexity, probability of missed detection and probability of false alarm. Detection based on location is robust against noise uncertainty since the position of the pilot can be pinpointed with accuracy even if amplitude is low due to fading. Various combining schemes can be developed for both pilot-energy and pilot-location sensing.

1. *Pilot-energy sensing.* For a single sensing window, the FFT output is simply squared and maximum value is compared to a threshold. For multiple sensing dwells, there are two possibilities (a) decision from each dwell is saved and a "hard-decision" rule is applied to declare "signal detect" if the number of positives is greater than a certain number, or (b) the square of the FFT output of all dwells is averaged and the maximum level is compared to a threshold. Choice of threshold in all cases is determined by the desired probability of false alarm.

2. *Pilot-location sensing*. This is usually used for multiple dwells. Location of the maximum value of the FFT output squared is compared between multiple dwells. If the distance is less than a prescribed threshold, the signal is declared detected. Another method is to count the number of times a particular frequency bin is chosen as the location of the maximum: if greater than a certain threshold, the signal is declared detected.

Wireless Microphone Sensing Algorithms

Wireless microphones belong to the class of licensed secondary users of the TV band. Operation of these devices is regulated by the FCC under Part 74 rules [8]. The bandwidth of wireless microphone signals is less than 200 kHz with the center frequency at an integer multiple of 25 kHz starting at the lower edge of the TV band. Maximum transmit power is limited to 50 mW in VHF band and 250 mW in UHF band. There is no standard specification for generation of wireless signals. Therefore, different manufacturers use their own propriety technology to generate these signals, though analog Frequency Modulation (FM) seems to be more prevalent.

To design and verify wireless microphone signal detection algorithms, we have used procedures described in [26] to model wireless microphone signals. The reference describes three profiles viz. silent, soft speaker and loud speaker, each generated with a unique combination of tone and deviation parameters.

The challenge with wireless microphone signal detection is that these signals do not have a unique identifying feature. In addition, multiple wireless microphone signals could be present in a single TV channel and frequency separation among different wireless microphone signals is also not clearly defined. Since wireless microphone signals do not have a unique feature, detection methods have to rely on signal energy in the band of interest to detect/identify wireless microphone signals.

The proposed basic wireless microphone signal detection algorithm relies on detection of signal energy in frequency domain. In the absence of spurious tones, wireless microphone signals will manifest as a group of tones that could span 200 kHz range in frequency domain. By sufficiently averaging across time, wireless microphone signals can stand out even at low signal levels.

Since we use the DTV tuner to tune to the channel of interest, the front-end processing in this case will be similar to that described in section "Lab Test Results". Assuming that the IF signal is located at 44 MHz and sampling rate is 100 MHz, the detection steps are:

1. Downshift signal to baseband by multiplying it by frequency, f_c = 44 MHz. Hence, if $x(t)$ is the real, band-pass signal at low-IF, then $y(t) = x(t)e^{-j2f_c t}$ is the complex signal at baseband.
2. Filter down-shifted signal $y(t)$ with a low-pass filter of bandwidth 7.5 MHz.
3. Down-sample filtered signal from 100 to 7.5 MHz, to form signal $z(t)$.
4. Take 2048 point FFT of down-sampled signal $z(t)$ to form $Z_n(k)$.

5. Average FFT output squared across multiple FFT blocks to improve reliability of detection. $P(k) = \sum_{n=1}^{N} Z_n^2(k)$ where $k = 1\text{–}2{,}048$. Parameter N is determined by the sensing time.
6. Determine maximum value of $P(k)$ and compare it against a threshold.

Threshold can be varied to achieve required PMD. The drawback, however, is that it impacts the PFA.

As it relies on energy detection, the above method will trigger on TV signals as well as spurious tones. In the detection flow, wireless microphone detection is enabled only when the sensor does not detect TV signals in that channel. More advanced algorithms are required to avoid false detections due to spurious tones. These algorithms will be implemented in subsequent versions of the sensor prototype.

Spectrum Sensing at the MAC

In order to maximize reliability and efficiency of spectrum sensing algorithms described in the previous section, and meet CDT requirement for detecting presence of incumbents, the network can schedule network-wide quiet periods for sensing. During these quiet periods, all network traffic is suspended and stations can perform sensing more reliably. In 802.22, for example, the base station (BS) is responsible for managing and scheduling these quiet periods.

To meet these requirements while satisfying the QoS requirements of the secondary network, initially we propose a two stage sensing (TSS) management mechanism. The TSS mechanism enables the network to dynamically adjust duration and frequency of quiet periods in order to protect the incumbents. In the first stage, multiple short quiet periods are scheduled to attempt to assess the state of the sensed radio spectrum without causing impact to secondary network performance. In the second stage, more time consuming quiet periods can be scheduled in case target spectrum needs to be sensed for a longer period of time.

In addition to the TSS which provides timely detection mechanism, we also introduce a notification mechanism through which devices (e.g., consumer premise equipments (CPEs) in IEEE 802.22 terminology) can report results of the sensing process back to the BS. To ensure effective use of quiet periods to improve sensing reliability, nearby networks must also synchronize their quiet periods.

The TSS, notification, and synchronization mechanisms proposed here have been incorporated into current 802.22 draft MAC standard.

Quiet Periods Management and Scheduling

Quiet period management mechanism defined by the TSS mechanism has different time scales, namely, a short (or fast) sensing period that can be scheduled regularly with minimal impact on the users' QoS, and a long (or fine) sensing period that can be used to detect a specific type of incumbent signal. Short and long sensing periods correspond to first and second stage of the TSS, respectively. The TSS presented here is a more general and enhanced version of the MAC sensing scheme introduced in [23,27]. Within IEEE 802.22, the first stage of TSS is termed as intra-frame sensing, while the second stage is called inter-frame sensing.

- *Intra-frame sensing.* This stage uses short quiet periods of less than one frame size. The 802.22 MAC allows only one intra-frame quiet period per frame and it must be scheduled always at the end of the frame. This is important to ensure nearby 802.22 cells can synchronize their quiet periods. Based on results of spectrum sensing done over a number of intra-frame quiet periods, the BS decides whether to schedule an inter-frame quiet period over multiple frames in order to perform more detailed sensing.
- *Inter-frame sensing.* This stage is defined as taking longer than one frame size and is used when the sensing algorithm requires longer sensing durations. Since a long quiet period may degrade the performance for QoS sensitive traffic, allocation and duration of inter-frame sensing stage should be dynamically adjustable by the BS in a way to minimize impact on users' QoS.

The TSS mechanism in IEEE 802.22 is illustrated in Fig. 13.3. A first stage involving several intra-frame sensing periods can be followed by a longer inter-frame sensing period, if needed to detect the specific signature of a signal detected during the first stage. Considering the fact that incumbents in TV bands do not come on the air frequently, only the intra-frame sensing stage will be used most of the time; so QoS is not compromised. The longer inter-frame sensing stage will step in only when required.

In 802.22, the BS broadcasts schedule and durations of the intra-frame and inter-frame quiet periods in the superframe control header (SCH), which is transmitted at the beginning of every superframe.[2] This method incurs minimal overhead and allows scheduling of quiet periods well in advance, which enables tight synchronization

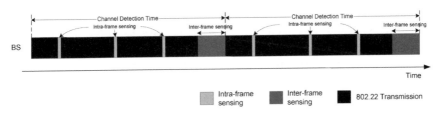

Fig. 13.3 TSS mechanism

---

[2] The 802.22 MAC is based on a periodic superframe structure. A superframe contains ten frames of 10 ms each for a total duration of 160 ms.

of quiet periods amongst neighboring systems. The BS can also schedule quiet periods on an on-demand basis using management frames specified in the 802.22 draft [28].

One of the major benefits of the TSS mechanism is allowing the CR network to meet stringent QoS requirements of real time applications such as voice over IP, while ensuring required protection to incumbents.

Incumbent Detection and Notification

Once an incumbent is detected on an operating channel, say channel N, or in an adjacent channel (e.g. $N + 1$ and $N - 1$), the secondary system must vacate the channel, while satisfying DFS requirements (CMT and CCTT) described in Table 13.1.

In a cell-based system, like 802.22, detection of an incumbent must be notified in a timely fashion to the BS, so it can take proper action to protect them.[3] A number of mechanisms are described in the 802.22 draft standard to deal with these situations. For example, a CPE may notify the BS by using the UCS (Urgent Coexistence Situation) slots available within the MAC frame. Since allocation of the UCS window is known to all CPEs, it can be used even when CPEs are under interference. As far as access method goes, both contention-based and CDMA can be used during the UCS window. Alternatively, the BS can poll CPEs to obtain feedback. In this case, the polled CPE can send a notification back to the BS, or else, if no response is received from CPEs, the BS can take further actions to assess the situation such as scheduling additional quiet periods or even immediately switching channels.

Synchronization of Quiet Periods

Self-coexistence amongst multiple overlapping CR networks is a key feature not only to efficiently share available spectrum, but also to ensure required protection to incumbents. For instance, multiple secondary networks may operate in the same geographical region, and in case overlapping, these networks share the same channel; it is paramount that they are able to synchronize their quiet periods, since transmissions during sensing periods could increase the probability of false detection considerably.

In the case of the 802.22 standard, it provides a comprehensive coexistence framework to enable overlapping networks to exchange information in order to

---

[3] In 802.22 this is referred to as incumbent detection recovery and is performed through the Incumbent Detection Recovery Protocol (IDRP). IDRP maintains a priority list of backup channels that can be used to quickly re-establish communication in the event of an incumbent appearance.

share the spectrum and also synchronize their quiet periods. At the core of this framework is the Coexistence Beacon Protocol (CBP), which is based on the transmission of CBP frames (or packets) by CPE and/or BSs. The CBP packets are transmitted during coexistence windows that can be open by the BS at the end of a frame. During these windows, CPEs in overlapping areas can send CBP packets. These packets may be received by neighboring BSs or by CPEs in neighboring cells, which forward them to their corresponding BSs. The CBP packets carry information needed for establishing time synchronization amongst neighboring cells, as well as schedule of quiet periods. For the purpose of synchronization, CBP packets carry relative timestamp information about their networks. Mathematically speaking, when BSi, responsible for network i, receives a CBP packet from network j, controlled by BSj, it shall only adjust the start time of its superframe if, and only if, the following convergence rule is satisfied:

$$\left| \begin{array}{l} (\text{Frame\_Number}_j - \text{Frame\_Number}_i) \times \text{FDC} + \\ \text{Transmission\_Offset} - \text{Reception\_Offset} \end{array} \right| \leq \frac{\text{FS} \times \text{FDC} + \text{GuardBand} \times \text{SymbolSize}}{2},$$

where Frame_Number is the frame number within the superframe, FDC is the frame duration code (equal to 10 ms), FS is the number of frames per superframe (equal to 16), GuardBand is a few OFDM symbols long to account for propagation delays, SymbolSize is the size of an OFDM symbol, and Reception_Offset and Transmission_Offset are the index of symbol number within the frame where the beacon was received/transmitted, respectively. By this mechanism, it has been shown [29] that co-channel networks are able to synchronize their quiet periods resulting in the arrangement depicted in Fig. 13.4. This way, sensing can be made with high reliability.

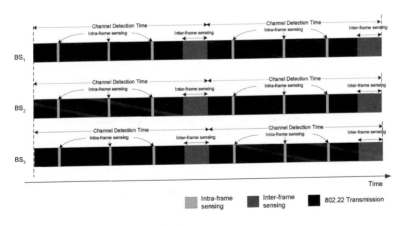

Fig. 13.4 Synchronization of quiet periods

Lab and Field Test Results

A prototype was built to test the spectrum sensing algorithms described above. This prototype used a consumer grade tuner for the RF front-end, followed by signal processing. The performance of this sensing prototype was evaluated in the lab using generated signals and field captured signals and in the field using over-the-air (OTA) signals.

Lab Test Results

We used an ATSC DTV signal generator to generate a clean (i.e. without any impairment) DTV RF signal. A RAM-based Arbitrary Waveform Generator (AWG) was used to regenerate RF signals from the low-IF field captured signals referred to in [30]. The RF signal was attenuated to the desired signal level by an external attenuator and then fed to the antenna input of the DTV tuner. Similar tests were performed by the FCC which are presented in [31], under the label "Prototype B". The sensitivity tests in Fig. 13.5 show a 100% detection capability at signal levels down to −115 dBm. The FCC recently released a report [33] with the results from the latest round of lab and field testing, showing that a sensing threshold of -123 dBm can be achieved with 100% detection capability.

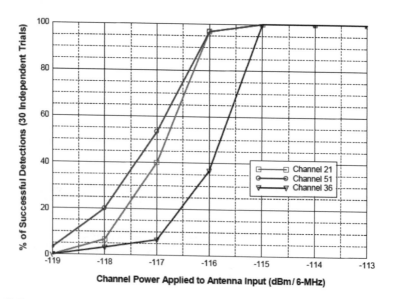

Fig. 13.5 Probability of successful detections vs. input channel power for three different UHF TV channels

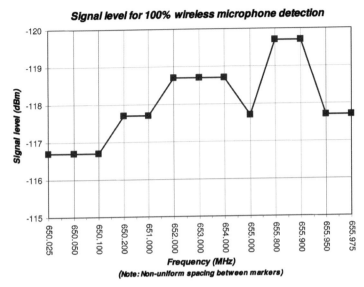

Fig. 13.6 Wireless microphone detection with a lab generated signal

To generate clean wireless microphone signals in the Lab we used an RF signal generator with FM capability. Different profiles were generated by adjusting the frequency deviation and tone frequency. The carrier frequency of the FM signal was placed at different frequencies in a 6 MHz UHF channel to measure performance variation within a TV channel. The input signal level to the tuner is controlled by an external attenuator. Figure 13.6 shows the detection capability of the sensing prototype in the presence of a wireless microphone signal. For this particular test, the wireless microphone signal was generated using a 1,000 Hz tone and 24 kHz frequency deviation. In this plot, Y-axis represents lowest signal level for which the sensor has 100% detection (averaged over 30 independent scans) and X-axis represents carrier frequency of input signal. The probability of false alarm was less than 0.1%.

Field Test Results

The sensing prototype was field tested in the New York metropolitan area in 18 sites, mostly residential structures such as single-family homes and apartments. While measurements were made on channels 21–51, we present results for Channel 22. The reason for this is that most of the sites tested were on or beyond the edge of coverage of Channel 22. Figure 13.7 shows coverage area (shaded portion) and sites where the sensor prototype was tested. Since power measurements at low signal levels such as −116 dBm are not very accurate, no attempt was made to actually measure power in the field.

Fig. 13.7 Map of New York metropolitan area locations used for OTA sensing

Table 13.2 Summary of OTA channel 22 detection at different sites in New York metropolitan area

Site #	Site	Latitude	Longitude	Successful detections	Total attempts
1	Briarcliff Manor, NY	Lat: 41 09 05.59 N	Long: 73 51 16.14W	18	18
2	Chappaqua, NY	Lat: 41 12 16.32 N	Long: 73 45 29.43W	16	16
3	New City, NY	Lat: 41 09 41.24 N	Long: 74 01 37.56 W	17	17
4	Tarrytown, NY	Lat: 41 03 50.98 N	Long: 73 5115.16W	22	22
5	Edison, NJ	Lat: 40 33 51.74 N	Long: 74 18 17.9W	8	8
6	Mt. Kisco, NY	Lat: 41 12 50.91N	Long: 73 44 36.07W	12	12
7	Chappaqua, NY	Lat: 41 11 11.39N	Long: 73 46 30.98W	10	12
8	Ossining, NY	Lat: 41° 8'50.88"N	Long: 73°51'27.79"W	18	18
9	Ossining, NY	Lat: 41° 8'46.59"N	Long: 73°51'27.99"W	16	16
10	Ossining, NY	Lat: 41° 8'50.88"N	Long: 73°51'27.79"W	15	15
11	Ossining, NY	Lat: 41 09 10.07 N	Long: 73 51 3066W	14	14
12	Briarcliff Manor, NY	Lat: 41 09 05.59 N	Long: 73 51 16.14W	6	6
13	Maplewood, NJ	Lat: 40 42 55 N	Long: 74 15 28W	10	10
14	NYC Apt. 8th floor, NY	Lat: 40 46 54.24 N	Long: 73 58 59.54W	11	11
15	Yorktownheights, NY	Lat: 41 17 17.78 N	Long: 73 49 58.26 W	8	8
16	Brookefield, CT	Lat: 41 29 55.19 N	Long: 73 23 55.29 W	12	12
17	Danbury, CT	Lat: 41 26 22.12 N	Long: 73 30 45.21	12	12
18	Pleasantville, NY	Lat: 41 07 35.87 N	Long: 73 47 12.02 W	8	8
19	Hillsdale, NJ	Lat: 41 00 28.22 N	Long: 74 02 17.99 W	16	16

At each test site, multiple measurements were made in various rooms and locations within rooms. No attempts were made to optimize position of the sensing antenna, which was a simple whip-antenna. Where possible, measurements were made in basements as well.

Table 13.2 shows the sensing results for the 18 sites. We see that out of a total of 235 measurements, the sensor missed detection of Channel 22 on only two measurements for a detection rate of 99%. The missed detections were in Site 7, which is outside the Channel 22 contour and measurements were in the basement. Other measurements in that house were able to sense Channel 22.

The latest field tests are described in [33] and demonstrate conclusively that 100% of television receivers that are able to receive viewable pictures will be protected by sensing, while only 84% will be protected by an approach using databases alone.

Conclusions

While research into cognitive radios has been ongoing for a few years and some military applications do exist, the first commercial applications have yet to be widely deployed. The television white spaces offer an unprecedented opportunity to develop this new technology and thus provide new wireless applications and services to consumers. The past couple of years have seen advancements in sensing technology required to make cognitive radios a reality, using low-cost components. Standardization efforts have already begun within IEEE and other industry groups. However, as of now, the FCC has yet to release the final rule and order that would make cognitive radios in television white spaces a reality. Hopefully, this valuable slice of the spectrum will not be allowed to remain unused, while other parts of the spectrum get increasingly crowded with demand for more wireless service. The next few years certainly promise to be interesting ones as cognitive radio technology and new regulations evolve to create whole new applications in television white spaces.

References

1. US Frequency Allocation Chart, http://www.ntia.doc.gov/osmhome/allochrt.pdf
2. J. Mitola et al., "Cognitive Radios: Making Software Radios more Personal", *IEEE Personal Communications*, vol. 6, no. 4, pp. 13–18, August 1999
3. J. Mitola, "Cognitive radio: An integrated agent architecture for software defined radio", *PhD Dissertation*, Royal Inst. Technol. (KTH), Stockholm, Sweden, 2000
4. S. Haykin, "Cognitive Radio: Brain-Empowered Wireless Communications", *IEEE JSAC*, vol. 23, no. 2, pp. 201–220, February 2005
5. P. de Vries, "Populating the vacant channels", August 2006, http://www.newamerica.net/files/WorkingPaper14.DTVWhiteSpace.deVries.pdf
6. Spectrum Policy Task Force Report, November 2002, http://hraunfoss.fcc.gov/edocs_public/attachmatch/DOC-228542A1.doc

7. Unlicensed Operation in the TV Broadcast Bands, NPRM, May 2004, http://hraunfoss.fcc. gov/edocs_public/attachmatch/FCC-04-113A1.pdf
8. Part 74 – Experimental Radio, Auxiliary, Special Broadcast and Other Program Distributional Services, http://www.access.gpo.gov/nara/cfr/waisidx_00/47cfr74_00.html
9. Unlicensed Operation in the TV Broadcast Bands, October 2006, http://hraunfoss.fcc.gov/ edocs_public/attachmatch/FCC-06-156A1.pdf
10. Revised 700 MHz Band Plan for Commercial Services, http://wireless.fcc.gov/auctions/data/ bandplans/700MHzBandPlan.pdf
11. M. Calabrese, "Measuring the TV 'White Space' Available for Unlicensed Wireless Broadband", January 2006, http://www.newamerica.net/index.cfm?pg=article&DocID=2713
12. M. Calabrese, "Broadcast to Broadband: Unlicensed Access to Unused TV Channels?" *Internet Computing*, vol. 12, pp. 71–75, March–April 2008
13. IEEE 802.22 Working Group on Wireless Regional Area Networks, http://www.ieee802.org/22/
14. M. McHenry, E. Livsics, T. Nguyen and N. Majumdar, "XG Dynamic Spectrum Access Field Test Results", *IEEE Communications Magazine*, vol. 45, pp. 51–57, June 2007
15. M.J. Copps, "America's internet disconnect", Washington Post, Nov. 8 2006, http://www. washingtonpost.com/wp-dyn/content/article/2006/11/07/AR2006110701230.html
16. Federal Communications Commission (FCC), "Revision of Parts 2 and 15 of the Commissions Rules to Permit Unlicensed National Information Infrastructure (U-NII) Devices in the 5 GHz Band", *ET Docket no. 03-122*, November 18, 2003
17. A. Sahai, R. Tandra, S. Mubaraq Mishra, N. Hoven, "Fundamental design trade-offs in cognitive radio systems", in *IEEE International Workshop on Technology and Policy for Accessing Spectrum (TAPAS)*, August 2006
18. S.J. Shellhammer, N. Sai Shankar, R. Tandra and J. Tomcik, "Performance of Power Detector Sensors of DTV Signals in IEEE 802.22 WRANs", in *IEEE International Workshop on Technology and Policy for Accessing Spectrum (TAPAS)*, August 2006
19. S. Seidel and R. Breinig, "Autonomous Dynamic Spectrum Access System Behavior and Performance", in *IEEE DySPAN*, November 2005
20. L. Ma, X. Han, and C.-C. Shen, "Dynamic Open Spectrum Sharing for Wireless Ad Hoc Networks", in *IEEE DySPAN*, November 2005
21. Q. Zhao, L. Tong, and A. Swami, "Decentralized Cognitive MAC for Dynamic Spectrum Access", in *IEEE DySPAN*, November 2005
22. IEEE 802.11 h Standard for Spectrum and Transmit Power Management Extensions, http:// standards.ieee.org/getieee802/download/802.11h-2003.pdf, 2003
23. C. Cordeiro and K. Challapali, "C-MAC: A Cognitive MAC Protocol for Multi-Channel Wireless Networks", in *IEEE DySPAN*, April 2007
24. G. Chouinard, D. Cabric and M. Ghosh, "Sensing Thresholds", IEEE 802.22, doc. no. 22-06-0051-04-0000, May 2006
25. Advanced Television Systems Committee, "ATSC Digital Television Standard, Doc. A/53," September 16 1995. http://www.atsc.org
26. C. Clanton, M. Kenkel, Y. Tang, "Wireless Microphone Signal Simulation Model", IEEE 802.22, March 2007
27. C. Cordeiro, K. Challapali, and M. Ghosh, "Cognitive PHY and MAC Layer for Dynamic Spectrum Access and Sharing of TV Bands", in *IEEE International Workshop on Technology and Policy for Accessing Spectrum (TAPAS)*, August 2006
28. IEEE 802.22 draft standard, "IEEE P802.22TM/D0.3 Draft Standard for Wireless Regional Area Networks," http://www.ieee802.org/22/, doc. no. 22-07-0086-01-0000, May 2007
29. C. Cordeiro, et al., "A PHY/MAC Proposal for IEEE 802.22 WRAN Systems", IEEE 802.22, doc. no. 22-06-0005-05-0000, March 2006
30. S. Shellhammer, V. Tawil, G. Chouinard, M. Muterspaugh and M. Ghosh, "Spectrum Sensing Simulation Model", IEEE 802.22-06/0028r10, August 2006
31. Office of Engineering and Technology, Federal Communications Commission, "Initial Evaluation of the Performance of Prototype TV-Band White Spaces Devices", FCC/OET 07-TR-1006, July 31, 2007, http://hraunfoss.fcc.gov/edocs_public/attachmatch/DOC-275666A1.pdf

32. S. Shellhammer, V. Tawil, G. Chouinard, M. Muterspaugh and M. Ghosh, *Spectrum Sensing Simulation Model*, IEEE 802.22-06/0028r10, August 2006
33. Office of Engineering and Technology, Federal Communications Commission, "Evaluation of the performance of protype TV-band white spaces devices Phase II, " FCC/OET 08-TR-1005, October 15, 2008. http://hraunfoss.fcc.gov/edocs_puplic/attachmatch/DA-08-2243A3.pdf.

Chapter 14
Digital Rights and Digital Television

Bill Rosenblatt

Abstract As media industry struggles with large-scale copyright infringement made possible by networked digital media, one of the most interesting – and most controversial – aspects of digital content distribution is control over content rights. In this paper, we examine the state of the market for digital rights technologies specifically for digital television and other manifestations of digital video. We also discuss the relationship between digital rights technologies and certain aspects of copyright law.

Introduction

In late 1993, an ad-hoc collection of academics, technologists, publishers, and policy wonks came together in Washington, DC, for a conference called *Technological Strategies for Protecting Intellectual Property in the Networked Multimedia Environment.*[1] The conference organizers were prescient in that they understood intuitively that the digital content revolution would in large part be about rights.

But the proceedings from this conference show – in 20/20 hindsight – a bunch of blind men attempting to describe the unseen elephant that they know is in the room. Few could truly foresee how markets for online content would develop and how technologies for both distributing content and controlling rights would take shape along with them.

The world has changed a lot in the last 15 years, and yet, it has not changed much with respect to the problems of rights management. The essential problems that content owners face when distributing their content in digital form persist. Bits are still easy to copy; the Internet is still essentially an open architecture; and many types of content rights are still accounted for with blunt instruments such as statistical sampling and blanket licensing.

The challenges associated with content rights for digital television are fundamentally no different from those associated with digital music, e-books, and other digitized media. Digital television (generally speaking) adds a few layers of complexity compared to other types of content, but inter-industry dynamics, market forces, and interfaces between law and technology remain substantially the same.

D. Gerbarg (ed.), *Television Goes Digital*,
© Springer Science + Business Media, LLC 2009

Purposes of Digital Rights Technologies

Technologies for controlling and tracking content usage are not new; they have been around for centuries. The physical characteristics of traditional media products serve as de facto "rights management technologies." Consider the printed book: books are easy to give and lend; they can be read by only one or two people at a time; they can be copied with some effort and expense; they are difficult to alter without detection. This "rights management" has been implicit in book industry business models for a very long time.

Early electronic media also had "rights management" attached to it, such as plastic "do not record" tabs on audio cassette tapes and serial copy management on VHS videotapes. Even some digital media products distributed physically, such as DVDs, are encrypted.

Of course, the more recent availability of "pure" digital files and ascendancy of open-access data networks such as the Internet have changed the game. These factors have shifted the balance between content owners and consumers so that the latter have much more power to use content in ways not contemplated by the owners and, in many cases, not permitted by law. As commercial content providers began to grapple with this monumental shift, technology vendors began to offer ways to approximate physical limitations on content use, that have been present for all these years. Thus the notion of digital rights management (DRM) was born.

As the market for digital content technology has developed over the past decade-plus, other purposes for digital rights technologies have emerged along side those emulating physical media usage constraints. These primary purposes are as follows:

- *Curb misuse of content.* We use the term "misuse" intentionally to cover both uses that are not approved by copyright law and those not permitted by licenses that consumers agree to abide by for content usage under digital distribution schemes. There is a current debate over whether pure digital distribution of content is governed by copyright law. Content owners generally hold that it is instead governed by license terms, often of the "clickwrap" variety.[2] We also use the term "curb" advisedly as the content industries have abandoned the notion that DRM can completely prevent misuse. This newer view of DRM is like a series of "speed bumps" intended to make misuse more trouble than worthy.
- *Enable new content business models.* Control over content access is thought to be necessary to enable multiple offers that lead to efficient markets.[3] In the digital realm, there are virtually no limits on new business models that can be created, though some of these are not feasible without digital rights technologies. The most prominent example of this is subscription services, such as Rhapsody for music or CinemaNow for movies and TV. In these, a user pays a monthly or annual subscription fee and gets on-demand access to any content in the services' subscription libraries. This model resembles neither of the two predominant legacy distribution models: physical products (CDs, DVDs) or broadcasting. Digital rights technology is needed to prevent a user from signing up for the service, paying for one month (or not), copying every item in the

library, and then canceling. Another example is advertising-based services like SpiralFrog and QTrax, in which users can download and listen to music as much as they want for free as long as they view ads on a periodic basis – i.e., limited rights to content in exchange for non-financial consideration.

- *Track content usage.* Digital rights technologies can be used to track consumers' use of content, not to limit their usage rights but to provide inputs to schemes for compensating rights holders. Use of digital rights technologies for this purpose is not yet widespread,[4] but similar technologies are currently used by media ratings agencies such as Nielsen to track content viewer-ship for advertising rate-setting purposes.
- *Lock consumers into technology platforms.* As we will see shortly, technology vendors need incentives to offset cost of incorporating digital rights technologies into their products and services. A powerful incentive for any technology vendor is that of consumer lock-in.[5] The most prominent – but by no means – onlyexample of this is Apple's iTunes, which has used FairPlay DRM to lock consumers in to the iPod for both audio and video content.

Types of Digital Rights Technologies

The term DRM has a range of meanings. The narrower definition refers to technology that encrypts content and requires special hardware or software to decrypt it and allow user to exercise rights, such as play or copy. This is the definition most commonly used in the press.

The broader definition encompasses any technology used to control, track, or manage use of digital content. We acquiesce to the use of DRM in the narrower sense and use the term "digital rights technologies" for the broader meaning. There are four basic types of digital rights technologies.

DRM

A "classic" DRM system[6] generally has the following components:

- A *content packager* that runs on a server, typically that of a content retailer. The packager encrypts content along with some metadata (information about the content).
- A *license server* that also runs on a server. A license server processes requests from user's software or device to obtain rights to encrypted content. It checks credentials, including the identity of the user and/or device, and if valid, creates a small encrypted file called a *license* and sends it to the user's software or device. The license contains content encryption keys and possibly a description of rights granted.

- Functionality on the user's device to process content usage requests, communicate with the license server to obtain a license; decrypt license; extract content encryption keys and rights; and exercise user's rights. Often this functionality is part of a media player such as iTunes (FairPlay DRM) or Microsoft Windows Media Player (Windows Media DRM).

Digital Watermarking

Digital watermarking refers to embedding data into content in such a way that the user does not perceive it.[7] Digital still images, audio, and video can be watermarked. Watermarking technologies have two parts: insertion (or embedding) and detection (or extraction).

Watermarking schemes are designed to trade off among several qualities, including:

- *Capacity*. The amount of data that can be embedded.
- *Robustness*. The ability of the watermark to survive file format conversion, digital to analog conversion, downsampling, etc.
- *Undetectability*. Lack of effect on the user's perception of the content.
- *Security*. Imperviousness to removal or alteration.
- *Efficiency*. Speed of insertion and detection.

Data included in an imperceptible watermark is generally limited to a few dozen bytes. But that information can be anything, including identity of the content owner or that of the user or device that downloaded it. Often a watermark is an ID number that is looked up in a database for further information about the content.

Watermarks can be used for forensic tracking of content as it makes its way through cyberspace; examples of this include Activated Content's watermarking scheme for pre-release music and Nielsen's Digital Media Manager for television content distributed on the Internet. They can also be used to take actions according to the identity of the content, such as serve a contextually related ad to the user or compensate rights holders; such business models are often discussed but are not yet common in real life.

Fingerprinting

Fingerprinting refers to examining data in a content file and calculating a set of numbers that represent its characteristics (the content's "fingerprint"), then looking those numbers up in a database to determine the content's identity. Audio and video can be fingerprinted.

Fingerprinting technique for music was first proposed around the time of the *A&M v Napster* litigation in 2001, when file-sharing service was searching for ways to control use of copyrighted material that satisfied the court.[8] The most common use of fingerprints is to block uploads of copyrighted files to file-sharing networks; the iMesh peer-to-peer (P2P) network began to use audio fingerprinting in 2005, with the blessing of the major music companies, for this purpose.

User-generated video content (UGC) sites like YouTube and MySpace are also using audio fingerprinting to block unauthorized content, such as music videos. More recently, the social networking site imeem is using it to serve contextual ads to users who upload files and send a portion of the ad revenue generated to rights holders.

Fingerprinting for video is a newer technique, considered by many to be experimental at this stage. Digital video is far more complex to analyze than audio. The primary applicability of video fingerprinting at this point is for UGC sites; see below.

Fingerprinting and watermarking are sometimes known collectively as *content identification*. There is some overlap between viable applications for the two technologies, but there are also important differences:

- Watermarking requires that some entity in the content value chain – content owner, distributor, retailer, or end-user device – insert watermarks into content files. Fingerprinting requires no analogous effort.
- Fingerprinting is not one hundred percent accurate at identifying content. Watermarking is, by definition.[9]
- Different copies of a given work can have different watermarks: for example, watermarks denoting the retailer where the file was purchased or the user who downloaded it, or watermarks denoting version of the content (e.g., North American vs. UK). In contrast, a given work always has the same fingerprint (provided that fingerprinting technology works properly).

Rights Information Management

The final digital rights technology is one that is (or ought to be) used within media companies rather than in distributing media to the public. It is desirable to track information about content rights holders, the rights that a company has to their content, rights that the company can pass on to third parties, terms under which that can be done, and so on.

This can be very complex information to manage, but doing so makes it easier to create content licensing deals, compensate rights holders, and mitigate legal risk. Some media companies have built customized databases to track rights information, while others have adopted off-the-shelf systems from a handful of vendors. Such systems can integrate with other systems within media companies, such as financial, ERP (enterprise resource planning), and royalties. Ideally, they can also integrate with digital rights technologies for consumer content distribution.

DRM for Digital Television

In this section, we examine DRM and related technologies specifically for digital television. These break down into two parts:

- Technologies used to protect content from transmitter or distributor to the consumer's gateway device, which could be a set-top box (STB), PC, etc.
- Technologies used to protect content from the gateway device to other devices in the consumer's home or personal network.

We also discuss how digital rights technologies – particularly content identification technologies – are being used with user-generated content sites.

Transmitter to Gateway Device

In general, digital television schemes feature some sort of a transmitter sending content to a consumer device. The transmitter could be a digital broadcaster, cable head end, satellite, or Internet server.

Basic concepts in protecting the link between transmitter and consumer's gateway device are to encrypt content over the link and pass along rights information. The latter is often taken from a subscriber management system; it can include identities of users or devices that are entitled to content rights, as well as descriptions of those rights. One example of such rights could be "allow the user to play this content for up to 48 h."

This type of technology can be thought of as a successor to traditional conditional access (CA) systems for analog cable television. CA systems descramble content on the user's device. In many CA systems, the user plugs a SmartCard into the STB, which provides a credential to decrypt the content. This is like a simple DRM system that supports a single right – that of "play this content right now."

More modern technologies of this nature are used with digital cable, satellite, and IPTV. An early technology from Widevine replaced physical SmartCards with a software solution, which eliminated the cost and logistical complexity of distributing SmartCards; subsequent technologies added the ability to process more sophisticated rights.

In addition, many modern technologies incorporate digital watermarking in addition to encryption, two examples being Verimatrix's VCAS system and integration of Cinea's Running Marks watermarking with Widevine's link encryption technology. In many cases, the type of watermarking used in this scenario is known as *transactional watermarking*, in which identity of the client device (e.g., STB) is embedded into content as a watermark at transmission time. This enables content to be traced forensically to the user who downloaded it, if it is found in an unauthorized place, such as a file-trading network.

An important criterion for technologies that encrypt digital television signals from transmitters to STBs is that they minimize the amount of extra hardware required on the STB. This encourages adoption of digital rights technology by STB vendors, which in turn makes it more attractive to digital TV service providers, who distribute STBs to users.

Gateway Device to Home Network

DRM-related technologies for digital television inside the home are far more complex and varied. They relate to the essential idea that consumers should be able to use legitimately obtained content anywhere in their home – or on any device in a *home network* or *personal network*, which theoretically includes portable and automotive devices. Many content owners have generally come to accept this idea and thus have evolved their attitudes from insisting that consumers pay separately for each version of content for different devices.

This more tolerant attitude aligns with that of much of the consumer electronics industry, which sees digitally connected home as the next great opportunity to sell new gadgets to consumers. From the DRM perspective, digital home architectures include a "control center" device, which functions as both a gateway device (in the sense described above) and as the controller of how content can be sent around to various other devices connected to the network. The boundaries of the network – often referred to as a *domain* – can be expressed as a maximum number of devices or all devices within a certain distance from the control center.[10]

Axes of DRM Power in the Digital Home

Thus the market for DRM for home media networks can be seen as a struggle among various factions for ownership of crucial control center. The owner of the technology platform for the control center can then dictate which devices can play on the network and under what conditions (e.g., by licensing technology from the control center platform providers).

The factionalism in this market is not among individual technology vendors; instead, the market has coalesced into ecosystems, or "axes of power," based on device types. Each axis has DRM technologies that the members of the axis attempt to assert as standards. It should be apparent how DRM is a strategic tool for technology platform owners to achieve lock-in, as described above.

The four axis of DRM power in the digital home are:

1. Set-top box (STB) axis
2. Media player axis
3. Mobile handset axis
4. PC axis

Apple may constitute a fifth axis of power if it opens its platform to third-party vendors or produces more (or more successful) products for the digital home.

Each of these axis of power is represented by a group of technology vendors and DRM technology that is either proprietary or based on specification from a standards body or consortium. Some vendors will participate in multiple axis. We now examine each of these axis of power.

The Set-Top Box Axis

The STB axis includes these vendors:

- *STB vendors.* Pace Micro, Humax, Maxian, ADB, Amstrad, Pace Micro, others
- *Incumbent CA technology vendors.* Thomson, NDS.
- *Semiconductor makers.* AMD, ARM, ATI, Broadcom, Conexant, STMicro-electronics, Texas Instruments

DRM technology for the STB axis is Secure Video Processor (www.svpalliance. org), a consortium that was started by NDS and Thomson in 2004. SVP enables content providers to set relatively simple rules for how content can be used in a home network once it reaches an STB. The complexity of SVP has been kept fairly low in order to minimize incremental cost of hardware on STBs that support it. The SVP Alliance has members other than the above companies, including major consumer electronics companies such as LG Electronics, Samsung, and Philips.[11]

While writing this, there are no actual SVP-based content services. After semiconductor makers STMicroelectronics and Broadcom introduced chips that implemented SVP, some STB makers adopted those chips in their designs.

The Media Player Axis

Media Player axis's major players are Sony, Philips, Panasonic (Matsushita Electric Co.) and Samsung. The other major player is Intertrust Technologies, a DRM research and development company that holds many core DRM patents and is now owned jointly by Sony and Philips.

The DRM technology for Media Player axis is Marlin (www.marlin-community. com). Marlin is a consortium-based technology whose primary inventor is Intertrust. The initiative was announced in early 2005, and it released its first spec the following year. Marlin is nominally intended for portable (or non-portable) media player devices that can connect to a network.

Users register with an online service as owners of Marlin-based devices; they also register with services as purchasers, subscribers, or other obtainers of content. When such a device receives content to copy or play, Marlin goes through a process of tracing conceptual links[12] from user's identity through devices and services to the content, in order to ensure that he does have the right to use the content.

Trials of Marlin have begun in Japan for IPTV to Internet-enabled television sets. Pioneer Electronics launched a Marlin-powered service in the United States through a spinoff company called SyncTV in late 2007. Sony intends to make Marlin a component of a new line of video products that it plans to launch in 2008.

The Mobile Handset Axis

The Mobile Handset axis has some obvious overlap with the media player axis; there are several vendors that are involved in both. As far as DRM is concerned, Nokia has been the nominal leader of this axis.

The handset axis's DRM strategy is based on a DRM standard from the Open Mobile Alliance, a pre-existing standards body that also creates and maintains standards in many other areas of mobile telecommunications.

There are two major versions of Open Mobile Alliance DRM (OMA DRM) – 1.0 and 2.0 – and they are very different. OMA DRM 1.0, released in 2002, is not relevant to home media networks; it was designed for low-end handsets with built-in media players but not much computational power. Its low cost of implementation has led to an installed base of over half a billion devices, though only a fraction of those are actually used with any OMA DRM 1.0-compatible content service.

OMA DRM 2.0 is a much more powerful and flexible DRM scheme that can support rich media, including digital video. It is capable of supporting a range of rights equivalent to DRM schemes for PCs, like Windows Media DRM from Microsoft. It has some hooks for home network applicability, such as the ability to use domain authentication – i.e., to allow use of content on all devices in a domain (personal or home network), as described above.

Although OMA DRM 2.0 has been around since 2004, it has gotten very little uptake in the market so far, just a couple of relatively small mobile content services in Europe. One of the obstacles has been contention over royalties from DRM patents held by Intertrust and other companies. At the time of this writing, OMA DRM 2.0 is expected to gain traction in mobile TV broadcasting, e.g., together with the DVB-H standard in Europe.

The PC Axis

Microsoft, not surprisingly, sits at the center of the PC axis, which is based on the idea of the Windows Media Center PC as control center device. The DRM for the PC axis is Microsoft Windows Media DRM (WM DRM).

WM DRM started around 2000–2001 as a DRM scheme solely for Windows PCs. With Version 10, introduced in 2004, Microsoft introduced WM DRM for Network Devices, a DRM technology that supports home media networks. Another important technology in the Microsoft platform is Microsoft Media Transfer Protocol (MMTP), which enables secure transmission of content from one device to another.

With WM DRM 10, Microsoft also permitted makers of non-Windows devices to license the technology, along with a "logo program" called PlaysForSure (www. playsforsure.com) that signifies WM DRM compliance. The semiconductor makers Cirrus Logic, Portal Player, and Sigmatel are embedding WM DRM into their chipsets for consumer devices.

As a result, the WM DRM ecosystem includes a large number of hardware makers, not just PC vendors like Dell and HP. Most of these are portable device makers (Archos, Audiovox, Creative Labs, iRiver, Rio, Samsung, Sandisk, etc.), but some are makers of devices for digital home such as Denon, Digitrex, D-Link, Netgear, Pioneer, and Roku, whose WM DRM-compliant products include streaming media servers, audiovisual receivers, flat-panel TVs, and adapters for existing television sets.

Unlike SVP, Marlin, and OMA DRM 2.0, many current content services use WM DRM. It is possible to obtain video downloads in Windows Media format from services like Amazon Unbox, Movielink, and CinemaNow, and transfer them to other WM DRM-compatible devices in the home as well as to standard TVs through adapters.

Apple

Apple is the wildcard in the digital home arena. The company has a strategy for digital home media networks, but it is very different from others. Instead of putting out a platform based on products and/or published specs in the market and trying to attract a critical mass of vendors, it is sticking to its usual strategy of only releasing its own products and not licensing its technology to third parties. iTunes, video-playing iPods, and Apple TV are its products for digital video.

Apple's DRM, FairPlay, is a rudimentary technology compared to the others described here. Apple licensed it in 2001 from a small company called Veridisc that has since disappeared. It has no ability, for example, to represent different types of rights that are being granted to devices or users; support for specific rights must be "hard wired" into surrounding technology such as software for iTunes, iPods, and Apple TV devices.

Apple has built the ability to offer time-bounded content rights in to the latest generation of iPods, Apple TV, and iTunes in order to support a 24-h movie rental service that it launched in January 2008. In this service, movies can reside only on a single device at a time (regardless of how many devices the user owns), and the software deletes each file 24 h after the user starts the first play.

As we will see shortly, Apple's strategy for the digital home may look hesitant and tentative compared with the others, but there is a strategic reason for that.

As a final comment on the axis of power, it is worth noting that four or five is too many. Most technology markets settle down to one or two dominant vendors, surrounded by a handful of niche players.[13] Although these axis of power represent distinct markets, convergence will lead inevitably to consolidation of DRM strategies.

The Internet and User-Generated Content

The foregoing two-part scenario pertains to content distribution systems that involve servers, gateway devices, and other client devices. But alongside this broadcasting-derived paradigm, there is a huge groundswell of activity around websites that feature user-generated content (UGC), such as YouTube, DailyMotion, and Veoh.

As mentioned above, most creators of so-called user-generated content are not interested in protecting their revenue opportunities (many are not interested in direct revenue at all). Yet a lot of copyrighted material from major media companies ends up on these websites, so the media industry has been trying to figure out how to either block such content or monetize its appearance on UGC sites.

"Classic" encryption-based DRM is a nonstarter in this scenario, because vast majority of content creators who post content on UGC sites would not be interested in it. So the media industry is increasingly turning to content identification technologies – watermarking and fingerprinting – as its putative solution.

Content identification technologies serve a very practical purpose in this case: they enable media companies to avoid spending untold time and money in scouring these websites for their content and issuing so-called takedown notices.[14] Instead, UGC sites can use content identification technologies to block unauthorized uploads of copyrighted material, or apply business rules to uploads, e.g., display a targeted ad to the uploader and give the content owner a piece of the ad revenue. This has two advantages as far as content owners are concerned: it shifts the cost burden to the UGC site operator, and it enables content to be blocked before damage is done.

Currently, fingerprinting is the preferred content identification technology because it requires least amount of effort from content owners and other players, though watermarking solutions are being developed. Video fingerprinting technologies have emerged over the last couple of years from several vendors.

It is fair to say that Hollywood views video fingerprinting as the "silver bullet" solution to its problems with UGC sites, despite the fact that the technology has yet to be tested very extensively in the real world. MovieLabs, the R&D joint venture of the major film studios, held a closely-watched competition of video fingerprinting technologies in September 2007. A dozen vendors participated; MovieLabs has kept the results confidential, in part because they were lab tests and do not necessarily reflect real-world behaviors.

Furthermore, Hollywood got together with several leading UGC sites in October 2007 and created a document called User Generated Content Principles[15] – a sort of "peace treaty" stipulating that movie studios and television networks would not sue UGC sites if they implemented content identification technologies in good faith. One company that is conspicuously absent from the UGC Principles is YouTube (Google), which is being sued by Viacom over this issue. On the other hand, while Viacom is participating, Time Warner and Sony Pictures are conspicuously absent on content owner side.

The UGC Principles document carefully allows for both watermarking and fingerprinting technologies to be used in identifying content. So far, the only entity that is implementing a watermarking-based solution for UGC sites is Nielsen, which is working with the watermarking technology company Digimarc. Yet even Nielsen's Digital Media Manager solution employs video fingerprinting in cases where technology cannot detect a watermark in a video file.

The DRM Tug-of-War

In many respects, and despite massive popularity of YouTube and other video UCG sites, the UGC scene is currently a sideshow to current focuses of media and electronics industries. Not far off in the background while the CE axis of power vie for supremacy, a tug-of-war among three factions: the consumer electronics and IT industry (taken as a whole), the media industry, and consumers is the essential conundrum of DRM.

Media industry has the primary incentive to promote the use of DRM. It has been fighting a battle against copyright infringement that gets increasingly difficult with new technologies. The industry's approach to anti-piracy has been one of "fight the battle on all fronts" – including law, technology, and consumer education – with relatively little coordination among the different approaches and even less attention paid to their relative effectiveness or economic efficiencies.[16]

Major content owners typically require that content distribution services adopt approved digital rights technologies as a condition of granting content licenses, while smaller "indie" content owners do not. The best way to explain this dichotomy is to note that content from major studios often comes from "brand name" creators and thus already has a market; studios seek direct revenue from such content. In contrast, indie content owners seek exposure and are thus predisposed to trade off revenue in favor of technologies that maximize exposure. Another source of the dichotomy is the desire of some indie content owners to avoid DRM precisely because of its association with "big media."

The consumer electronics industry's primary incentive, meanwhile, is to design new gadgets to sell to the public quickly. Consumer electronics products have short "half-lives" in the market: they start out with high profit margins, but margins shrink rapidly to virtually nothing as competition destroys uniqueness and newer, cooler products appear on the horizon. CE vendors must constantly refresh their product lines in order to preserve their overall profitability, and refresh cycles tend to get shorter and shorter every year.

For consumer electronics products that handle media content, CE vendors must secure cooperation of content owners so that brand-name content can be available on the new devices. At the risk of oversimplification,[17] the bargain that the two industries have struck has been: we (the media industry) will let you (CE vendors) distribute our content on your products only if we are comfortable that your products won't allow consumers to misuse our content. Therefore you must demonstrate that your products are going to curb misuse to our satisfaction.

This has led to a situation where the CE industry has been given responsibility for designing DRM systems and thus has taken the lead –through companies acting on their own (Microsoft, Sony), companies licensing technology from third parties (Apple), or via intra-industry partnerships (DVD), consortia (SVP, Marlin), or standards bodies (OMA). The media industry has declined to share in the cost of such systems[18] and has only recently started participating in their design in any meaningful way.

As a result, DRM schemes tend to be designed with low cost of implementation as a primary consideration. This has been especially true of the CSS encryption built into DVDs (designed by Matsushita and Toshiba) and Apple's FairPlay. The law that makes hacking DRM illegal – the DMCA,[19] bolsters this situation by deflecting liability for weak DRM from the technology vendor to the hacker.[20]

In other words, CE vendors generally view DRM as a necessary evil to get content licenses. In most other respects, DRM is antithetical to their business: it costs them money to implement, yet it limits their products' functionality.[21]

CE vendors' focus on costs – based on an assumption that their products should all become low-cost blockbusters, like the ubiquitous $50 DVD player – and leads them to favor DRM schemes that have minimal functionality, both with respect to their security strength and their inclusion of consumer-friendly features.

An admitted exception to this is the AACS (Advanced Access Content System) and BD + DRM schemes for Blu-ray high-definition optical discs, which are far more sophisticated than the CSS scheme for DVDs with respect to both security strength and features for consumers (such as "managed copy"). Two major content owners, Warner Bros. and Disney, have even contributed to AACS's design.

Yet even this is an exception that proves the rule. CE vendors invented these high-def formats to enable them to sell high-margin players to consumers instead of those $50 DVD players. They feared that both consumers and movie studios would need further motivation to support the new disc formats, so they felt compelled to introduce features that appealed to both parties. Furthermore, there have been disputes over implementation of certain content protection features in players for the new formats.[22]

Currently, the CE industry sees the Digital Home as its next great opportunity to sell new products to consumers. Unfortunately, "digital home" is a far more complex and ambiguous paradigm than previous CE paradigms such as "portable media player" or even "home theater." The value propositions –reasons why consumers should buy equipment and services for home digital media networking – are still relatively unclear. That is one reason why Apple's approach has been more cautious and focused than those of the other axis of power described above: Apple can be said to be waiting for compelling value propositions to emerge before it fully embraces the digital home.

Many CE products for home networking paradigm have been introduced and then quickly abandoned. Current market uncertainty leads to excess fragmentation among the axis of power. Cost of DRM implementation will certainly play a part in determining which axis, if any, ends up as the dominant one when relevant technologies converge.

The third participant in the DRM tug-of-war is consumers. The AACS example above is evidence of indirect influence that consumers have had on the design of DRM schemes in digital media. Yet it must be said that consumers have had no direct influence, no seat at the table when DRMs are designed. Consumers may enjoy new content business models, but while consumer acceptance of DRM is slowly increasing, consumers still generally dislike DRM.[23]

Thus, consumers' most effective influence on DRM design is through market forces. Advocacy groups that purport to represent consumer interests, such as the Electronic Frontier Foundation (EFF) and Public Knowledge, have influenced DRM-related legislation and litigation, but their influence on market forces has been strictly limited as well.[24]

Some scholars[25] have pointed to consumers' lack of a seat at the DRM table as *prima facie* evidence of a copyright system that has been effectively hijacked by industry interests – in this case media and electronics. Yet market forces can be powerful, especially when bolstered – as in this case – by easy availability of content through illegal means.

For example, major music companies recently decided to eliminate DRM from most paid permanent Internet music downloads – with the notable exception of Apple's iTunes.[26] One could say that this was primarily the result of market jockeying between record labels and online retailers – specifically, the labels' efforts to destabilize Apple's dominance of the online music market; elimination of DRM was the only significant way they could attract both retailers (such as Amazon.com) and users to alternate sites. But the ultimate objective is to get users to pay for copyrighted works, and the design or absence of DRM thus affects that outcome.

Precious little unbiased analysis has been done on effects of digital rights technologies on large-scale economics of media and electronics industries. Therefore it is premature to say how consumers' merely indirect influence on DRM and related issues influences the balance of economic interests in the copyright system. Only time will tell.

Notes

1. Proceedings still available at http://www.cni.org/docs/ima.ip-workshop/.
2. For example, Twentieth Century Fox refers to "download-to-own" Internet video distribution as "electronic licensing" rather than the more standard industry term "electronic sell-through" because the latter connotes sale of a copyrighted work, which could be interpreted as subject to copyright law.
3. Einhorn, M. and Rosenblatt, B. *Peer-to-Peer Networking and Digital Rights Management: How Market Tools Can Solve Copyright Problems.* Cato Institute Policy Analysis No. 534, 2005. http://www.cato.org/pub_display.php?pub_id=3670
4. A technology called Broadcast Monitoring emerged during the first Internet Bubble that used digital watermarks to track music plays on radio. After some limited experimentation, this technology did not succeed in the market. Instead, traditional inaccurate methods of compensating music rights holders for radio airplay, such as statistical proxies, survive, while at this writing new attempts are being made to revive broadcast monitoring, this time with video content.
5. See generally Shapiro, C. and Hal R. Varian, *Information Rules.* Cambridge, MA: Harvard Business School Press, 1999.
6. See for example Rosenblatt, B. et al., *Digital Rights Management: Business and Technology.* New York: Wiley, 2001, Chapter 5.
7. Some watermarks are meant to be visible or audible in order to act as a deterrent to misuse. For example, samples of digital images that are not meant to be used in production typically contain visible marks identifying their sources.

8. Napster and Relatable Enter into Agreement, Relatable Inc. press release, April 20, 2001, http://www.relatable.com/news/pressreleases/010420.release.html. Napster never did launch its paid service and thus never put Relatable's audio fingerprinting technology into production. The service called "Napster" today has the same brand name but completely different technology.

9. Assuming that the content has not been altered so much that watermark detection becomes difficult or impossible.

10. As measured by the length of time it takes for a signal to roundtrip from the control center to the device and back; this allows for wireless network connections.

11. One major content owner, Twentieth Century Fox, is also a member of SVP. However, this could be viewed as an extension of NDS's involvement: Fox and NDS are siblings in the News Corp. family.

12. More specifically, Marlin uses standard concepts from directed graph theory.

13. See generally Moore, Geoffrey A., *Crossing the Chasm*. New York: HarperCollins, 1991. In his terminology, these vendors are "gorillas" and "chimps" respectively.

14. By law, specifically 17 USC 512 in the United States, network service providers are obligated to remove content on receipt of takedown notices that contain the required information.

15. http://www.ugcprinciples.com/.

16. Rosenblatt, B. *Paying for DRM*. In: Proceedings of BUMA/IViR Symposium: Copyright and the Music Industry: Digital Dilemmas, Amsterdam, Netherlands, July 2003; available at: http://www.ivirbumaconference.org/docs/thefutureofdigitalrightsmanagementformusic1.doc

17. For example, this argument does not take into account the instances where the media industry is actively interested in reaching a new market enabled by new consumer electronics technology; however, such cases are in the minority.

18. On the contrary, the money has flowed in the opposite direction in a couple of instances. For example, some CE vendors pay to license DRM patents from ContentGuard, a firm that is part-owned by Time Warner.

19. 17 USC 1201, known informally as "DMCA" because it was included in the Digital Millennium Copyright Act of 1998. There are equivalent anticircumvention laws in other countries, such as those occasioned by the European Union Copyright Directive of 2001.

20. Federal district court judge Lewis Kaplan in *Universal v. Reimerdes* (2000) affirmed that the law should apply regardless of the strength or weakness of the protection technology. See http://w2.eff.org/IP/Video/MPAA_DVD_cases/20000817_ny_opinion.pdf, p. 34.

21. Clashes between Consumer Electronics Association CEO Gary Shapiro and media industry trade associations have become more frequent and public in recent years. See for example: CEA: RIAA refuses to cooperate, carries out "thinly veiled attack" on fair use. Ars Technica, August 10, 2006, http://arstechnica.com/news.ars/post/20060810-7472.html. Or, @ MidemNet: MPAA, RIAA, CEA Execs Clash Over DRM & Hardware Controls. PaidContent.org, January 20, 2007, http://www.paidcontent.org/entry/midemnet-mpaa-riaa-cea-execs-clash-over-drm-hardware-controls/.

22. Hollywood and CE Makers Stall on HD Protection. DRM Watch, May 25, 2006, http://www.drmwatch.com/standards/article.php/3609096.

23. See for example the survey results in the In-Stat report *Digital Rights Management Update*, July 2007, http://www.instat.com/Abstract.asp?ID=212&SKU=IN0703584CM.

24. One exception to this is the EFF's successful efforts to eliminate the use of copy protection technologies for audio CDs in the United States. In late 2005, a Microsoft Windows internals expert found that one of the three CD copy protection technologies used by the major music companies introduced so-called "rootkit" security vulnerabilities into users' PCs. The EFF capitalized on the ensuing public outcry by inducing a series of events that led to the withdrawal of all three technologies from the US market.

25. See for example: Litman, Jessica, *Digital Copyright*. Amherst, NY: Prometheus Books, 2001. Or, Gillespie, Tarleton, *Wired Shut: Copyright and the Shape of Digital Culture*. Cambridge, MA: MIT, 2007.

26. EMI, one of the four music majors, chose to offer DRM-free tracks on iTunes as well.

Index

About the Editor

 **Darcy Gerbarg** is a Senior Fellow at the Columbia Institute for Tele-Information (CITI), Columbia University Business School. Her consulting company, DVI, Ltd., provides management for technology nonprofits. At present she is the Director Operations for the nonprofit startup, CineGrid, Inc. Ms. Gerbarg previously served as an Executive Director of the Marconi Society, Inc. at Columbia University. Prior to that, she was the Director of Business Development for the startup, Everest Broadband Networks, Inc. She was the first artist in residence at Courant Institute for Mathematical Science, New York University and at Magi SynthaVision. Before that Ms. Gerbarg was at the Computer Graphics Laboratory, New York Institute for Technology. She has been an adjunct faculty member and consultant at many universities including the Interactive Telecommunications Graduate Program, the Film and Television Departments, and most recently the McGhee Center at New York University, as well as at the State University of New York at Stony Brook where she started their first computer graphics courses and built their multimedia laboratories. Ms. Gerbarg started and directed both the graduate program in Computer Art and the Computer Institute for the Arts at the School of Visual Arts in New York City.

Ms. Gerbarg is a pioneer computer artist. Her work has been exhibited in galleries and museums internationally. She was the Chairman of the first Computer Art Show for the Special Interest Group in Graphics (SIGGRAPH) of the Association for Computing Machinery (ACM). She has lectured, organized, and conducted panels, workshops, and presentations for industries, companies, and universities.

Conferences she has organized include: The Future of Digital TV (1997), Venture Capital in New Media (1999), World Wide Web Redux: Trends, Obstacles and Potential (2002), Moore's Law: Consequences and Future (2005), Unleashing the Potential of Communications (2006), Business Models for Rural Broadband (2006), and Digital Television: Beyond HD & DTV (2007).

Ms. Gerbarg's edited publications include *The Economics, Technology and Content of Digital TV* (Kluwer, Boston, Dordrecht, London, 1999), *Internet TV*

(Lawrence Erlbaum, Mahwah, NJ, London, 2003), and *The Marconi Century* (Marconi Society, Inc., New York, NY, 2004 and 2005). Ms. Gerbarg holds a B.A. from the University of Pennsylvania and an M.B.A. from the New York University.

About the Contributors

Bill Battino serves as the Managing Partner of the media and entertainment, telecommunications, and utilities consulting practices for IBM Global Business Services. Mr. Battino has 24 years of consulting experience in the areas of strategic planning, transformation, acquisition, market assessment, financial analysis, and organizational assistance in the media and telecommunications sectors. In addition to being a frequent speaker at industry conferences and events, Mr. Battino has led and authored media and telecommunications studies, including "Cable/Telco at the Crossroads," "Electronic Marketing, Electronic Shopping," "Fine Tuning Cable Television," and "Electronic Access." Bill can be reached at william.battina@us.ibm.com.

Dr. Saul J. Berman is a Partner and Global Executive of IBM Global Business Services. Renowned for his expertise in media and entertainment, Dr. Berman leads the IBM worldwide Media and Entertainment Strategy practice and serves as the IBM Global Services Leader for the Strategy and Change practice for all industries. Dr. Berman has over 25 years of consulting experience with senior management and has published multiple articles on the future of media and entertainment and strategy, including "The End of Television as We Know It," "Navigating the Media Divide," and "Beyond Access." Dr. Berman is a frequent keynote speaker at major industry conferences and was named one of the 25 most influential consultants of 2005 by *Consulting Magazine*. Saul can be reached at saul.berman@us.ibm.com.

John Carey is a Professor of Communications and Media Industries at Fordham Business School and Director of Greystone Communications, a media research and planning firm. Previously, he taught at Columbia Business School and New York University. He has more than 25 years of experience in conducting research on new media, consumer behavior, and telecommunication policy. Recently, he has conducted studies on consumer use of mobile video technologies, online video, the impact of HDTV on viewing behavior, and the media habits of 18–34 year olds. Clients include A&E Television Networks, Cablevision, The Markle Foundation, NBC Universal, *The New York Times*, PBS, Real Networks, and XM Satellite Radio, among others. John is a board member of the Donald McGannon Communication Research Center and on the Advisory Board of the Annenberg School for Communications. He holds a Ph.D. from the Annenberg School for Communication at the University of Pennsylvania and has more than 100 publications about new technology adoption and consumer use of media.

Tom Coughlin, President, Coughlin Associates, is a widely respected storage analyst and consultant. He has over 30 years of experience in the data storage industry with multiple engineering and management positions at companies such as Ampex, Polaroid, Seagate, Maxtor, Micropolis, Syquest, and 3 M. Tom has over 60 publications and six patents to his credit. Tom is also the author of *Digital Storage in Consumer Electronics: The Essential Guide* which was published by Newnes Press in March 2008. Coughlin Associates provides market and technology analysis (including reports on several digital storage technologies and applications and a newsletter) as well as Data Storage Technical Consulting services. Tom is active with IDEMA, the IEEE Magnetics Society, IEEE CE Society, and other professional organizations. Tom was the Chairman of the 2007 Santa Clara Valley IEEE Section and currently chair of the IEEE Region 6 Central Area. He was the former Chairman of the Santa Clara Valley IEEE Consumer Electronics Society and the Magnetics Society. Tom is the founder and organizer of the Annual Storage Visions Conference, a partner to the annual Consumer Electronics Show as well as the Creative Storage Conference that was recently held during the 2008 NAB. He is also an organizer for the Flash Memory Summit and the Data Protection Summit He is also a Leader in the Gerson Lehrman Group Councils of Advisors. For more information go to www.tomcoughlin.com.

Gali Einav is currently the Director of Digital Technology Research at NBC Universal where she oversees strategic and consumer research across various digital technologies such as VOD, Mobile, and online media. Building on her work at Columbia University's Interactive Design Lab, Gali specialized in researching the use and content of interactive media, focusing on the state of interactive television in the USA and the UK. She is the author of "Producing Interactive Television" and "The Content Landscape of Internet Television", published in "Television over the Internet: Network Infrastructure and Content Implications." Gali has worked as a senior producer and journalist for the second television channel in Israel where she produced, researched, and brought to air numerous investigation reports, documentaries, and in-depth interviews. She also taught television and media studies at the New School of Communications in Tel-Aviv. Gali holds an M.A. in Communications and Journalism from Hebrew University and a Ph.D. in Communications from Columbia University's School of Journalism. She is a member of NATAS and its New York Chapter Advanced Media Committee. Since 2003 she has been serving as Judge for the Advanced Media Technology Emmy Awards.

Liz Gannes is the editor of GigaOM's NewTeeVee.com blog. She has made NewTeeVee the premier publication for news and analysis in the online video world. Liz still contributes to GigaOM.com; prior to joining the company, she was a reporter for Red Herring. She graduated from Dartmouth with a degree in linguistics.

Monisha Ghosh is a Principal Member of Research Staff and Project Leader in the Wireless Communications and Networking department at Philips Research where she is currently working on cognitive and cooperative radio networks. She is actively involved in the White Space Coalition as well as in IEEE 802.22 working on developing sensing and cognitive protocols for the TV bands. She received her B.Tech. in Electronics and Electrical Communication Engineering from the Indian Institute of Technology, Kharagpur, India, in 1986, and M.S. and Ph.D. in Electrical Engineering in 1988 and 1991, respectively, from the University of Southern California, Los Angeles. From 1991 to 1998 she was a Senior Member of Research Staff in the Video Communications Department at Philips Research, where she was primarily involved in developing the ATSC 8-VSB standard for digital television broadcasting. From 1998 to 1999 she was at Lucent Technologies, Bell Laboratories, working on OFDMA-based wireless cellular systems. She has also participated in IEEE 802.11n developing multiple-antenna communication methods. Her research interests include multiple-antenna systems, equalization, estimation theory, error-correction, and digital signal processing for communication systems.

Jon Gibs is the Vice President, Media Analytics for Nielsen Online. He specializes in research methodology design and development using their wide array of media measurement and market research products. With 10 years of market research experience, Mr. Gibs previously managed the US-based survey group for Nielsen Online. Using their suite of MegaPanel products, he has in-depth experience in helping clients develop surveys and methodologies to meet their strategic and tactical needs. Prior to Nielsen Online, Mr. Gibs was an analyst and analytics director at Jupiter Research. During his time there, he developed numerous client reports based on primary survey analysis. He specialized in developing analyses merging behavioral and survey analysis to develop further insight into a wide array of online consumer markets. He received a Master's Degree in Geography, specializing in spatial statistics, from the State University of New York at Buffalo. His Bachelor's Degree is from Clark University in Geography. Mr. Gibs' expertise has been sought out by many news outlets including MSNBC, CNBC, the Investor's Business Daily, and CBS MarketWatch.

Ellen Goodman is a Professor of Law at Rutgers University at Camden, specializing in information law. Professor Goodman's scholarship probes the appropriate role of government policy, markets, and social norms in supporting a robust information environment. Her recent law review articles include "The First Amendment at War with Itself," "Peer to Peer Marketing," "Stealth Marketing and Editorial Integrity," "Media Policy Out of the Box: Content Abundance, Attention Scarcity, and the Failures of Digital Markets," "Spectrum Rights in the Telecosm to Come," and "Bargains in the Information Marketplace: The Use of Government Subsidies to Regulate New Media," all available at: http://papers.ssrn.com/sol3/cf_dev/AbsByAuth.cfm?per_id=333377. Professor Goodman has spoken before a wide range of audiences around the world and has consulted with the US government on media policy. Prior to joining the Rutgers faculty in 2003, Professor Goodman was a partner at the Washington, DC, law firm of Covington & Burling where she practiced in the information technology area. A 1988 graduate of Harvard College, magna cum laude, and a 1992 graduate of Harvard Law School, cum laude, Professor Goodman was a law clerk for Judge Norma Shapiro on the federal court for the Eastern District of Pennsylvania. She lives near Philadelphia with her husband and three children.

Jeffrey Hart is a Professor of Political Science at Indiana University, Bloomington, where he has taught international politics and international political economy since 1981. His first teaching position was at Princeton University from 1973 to 1980. He was a professional staff member of the President's Commission for a National Agenda for the Eighties from 1980 to 1981. Hart worked as an internal contractor at the Office of Technology Assessment of the US Congress 1985–1986 and helped to write their report, *International Competition in Services* (1987). His books include *The New International Economic Order* (1983), *Interdependence in the Post Multilateral Era* (1985), *Rival Capitalists* (1992), *Globalization and Governance* (1999), *Managing New Industry Creation* (2001), *The Politics of International Economic Relations*, 6th edition (2002), *Technology, Television, and Competition* (2004), and he has published scholarly articles in *World Politics*, *International Organization*, the *British Journal of Political Science*, *New Political Economy*, and the *Journal of Conflict Resolution*.

Laurin Herr is the President of Pacific Interface, Inc., an international consulting company, and organizer of the CineGrid International Workshop. He was previously the vice president for strategic development within Pinnacle Systems' Professional Media Division, where he played an integral role in the integration of the Truevision and Pinnacle Systems desktop product lines. Herr brings more than 25 years of experience as a product strategist, consultant and programmer to Pinnacle Systems. Previously, Herr held senior management positions at Truevision, Radius and SuperMac Technology during periods of rapid growth of the desktop publishing and desktop video markets. He has also worked in the television production industry for 20 years as a producer/director of broadcast and industrial programs in Japan and the USA. Herr wrote, produced, and hosted a series of five critically acclaimed video reports about computer graphics technology and market trends published in the ACM SIGGRAPH Video Review between 1987 and 1992. Laurin Herr has spoken in front of international audiences on topics such as HDTV, desktop production of digital media, applications of image-intensive informatics, digital archiving, computer graphics, and immersive virtual reality. He is the author of several in-depth market studies, most recently on the topic of digital cinema. From 1982 to 1992, Herr was the official ACM SIGGRAPH liaison to Japan and served on the board of directors of the National Computer Graphics Association (NCGA) from 1988 to 1989. After receiving his Bachelor of Arts degree from Cornell University in 1972, Herr – who is fluent in Japanese – pursued additional graduate studies at Cornell and in Tokyo at Sophia University.

Kas Kalba is the president of Kalba International, Inc., a communications investment advisory firm, and the author of numerous studies on mobile and video communications. His mobile advisory and research assignments have taken him to more than 30 countries on five continents. Currently, he is completing a cross-national study of the factors underlying the adoption of mobile phones at Harvard's Program on Information Resources Policy and has recently taught a seminar on the globalization of communications media at Yale. Dr. Kalba received his M.A. (Annenberg School for Communication) and Ph.D. (Communications Planning) from the University of Pennsylvania.

Mr. Satoshi "Phil" Kono has over 15 years of experience in advertising, specializing in media planning and buying for a number of global brands. He has a thorough knowledge of current circumstances surrounding media and changes in consumer communications due to the rise of Internet and Mobile. His role at Dentsu requires him to be well versed in conventional mass media and emerging interactive media in Japan and Asian markets such as China, India, Taiwan, and Thailand.

Andreas Neus is the Leader of IBM Institute for Business Value European Media and Entertainment. He focuses on innovation and disruptive changes in the media industry and has spearheaded IBM's primary research on media consumer behavior in Europe. Mr. Neus has authored more than 20 articles and book chapters on innovation and change and regularly speaks at conferences and for postgraduate programs. Andreas can be reached at andreas.neus@de.ibm.corn. He is the Vice President of Media Analytics at Nielsen Online.

Eli M. Noam Professor of Economics and Finance at the Columbia University Business School since 1976. Director of the Columbia Institute for Tele-Information, a research center focusing on strategy, management, and policy in communications, mass media, and IT. Served for three years as a Commissioner for Public Services of New York State. Appointed in 2003 by the White House to the President's IT Advisory Committee. A regular columnist for the *Financial Times* online edition. He has published about 400 articles and 27 books, including those relating to Europe: *Telecommunications in Europe;*

Television in Europe; The International Market in Film and Television Programs; Asymmetric Deregulation: The Dynamics of Telecommunications Policies in Europe and the United States; Interconnecting the Network of Networks; Internet Television; and *Mass Media over Mobile Networks.* His forthcoming books include *Media Concentration in the United States* (Oxford, 2008). He served as Board Chairman of TPRC. His academic, advisory, and non-profit board and trustee memberships include the Oxford Internet Institute, Jones International University (the first accredited online university), the Electronic Privacy Information Center, the Minority Media Council, and several committees of the National Research Council. He served on advisory boards for the governments of Ireland and Sweden. Noam received the degrees of BA, MA, Ph.D (Economics) and JD from Harvard University, and honorary doctorates from the University of Munich (2006) and the University of Marseilles (2008).

A. Michael Noll is a professor emeritus at the Annenberg School for Communication at the University of Southern California. He has published over 90 professional papers, has been granted six patents, and is the author of 11 books on various aspects of telecommunications. Prof. Noll was dean of the Annenberg School for an interim period from 1992 to 1994. He is a Senior Affiliated Research Fellow at the Columbia Institute for Tele-Information at Columbia University's Business School and has been an adjunct faculty member of the Interactive Telecommunications Program at New York University's Tisch School of the Arts. Prof. Noll has a Ph.D. in Electrical Engineering from the Polytechnic Institute of Brooklyn, an M.E.E. from New York University, and a B.S.E.E. from Newark College of Engineering. Prof. Noll has been a regular contributor of opinion pieces to newspapers and periodicals and is quoted frequently on telecommunications by the media. He has lectured to various industry groups, consulted on the social impacts of new technology, and advised new venture firms in the telecommunications field. Before joining the Annenberg School, Prof. Noll had a varied career in basic research, telecommunication marketing, and science policy. He worked in the AT&T Consumer Products and Marketing Department where he performed technical evaluations and identified opportunities for new products and services. Prof. Noll spent nearly 15 years performing basic research at Bell Labs in Murray Hill, NJ in such areas as the effects of media on interpersonal communication, three-dimensional computer graphics, human–machine tactile communication, speech signal processing, and esthetics. He is one of the earliest pioneers in the use of digital computers in the visual arts, in force-feedback systems, and in raster-scan displays. In the early 1970s, Prof. Noll was on the staff of the President's Science Advisor at the White House and was involved in such issues as computer security and privacy, computer exports, scientific and technical information, and educational technology.

Bill Rosenblatt is the president of GiantSteps Media Technology Strategies, a management consultancy focused on the content industries that helps its clients achieve growth through market intelligence and expertise in business strategy and technology architecture. Clients include technology and media companies ranging from early stage to Global 500. Bill also advises on public policy related to digital copyright and technology issues in the USA and Europe, provides industry insight into investment firms, serves as a testifying expert witness in commercial litigation, and lectures at leading universities and law schools. He is the managing editor of the Jupitermedia newsletter DRM Watch (www.drmwatch.com) and the author of *Digital Rights Management: Business and Technology* (Wiley) as well as several technical books for O'Reilly & Associates. Before founding GiantSteps, Bill was the chief technology officer of Fathom, a knowledge destination Web site for lifelong learners backed by Columbia University and other scholarly institutions. He served as the VP of technology and new media for McGraw-Hill's vertical industry publishing division and the director of publishing systems at Times Mirror Company. At Sun Microsystems, Bill was a technology strategy consultant to media and publishing customers and did business development work for Sun's video server product line; then, as the market development manager for media, entertainment and publishing, he defined Sun's market strategy for the industry and built alliances with software vendors who serve it. He holds a B.S.E. in electrical engineering and computer science from Princeton University and an M.S. in computer science from the University of Massachusetts, and he has had executive education from Harvard and University of Southern California business schools.

Louisa Shipnuck is the Leader of IBM Institute for Business Value Global Media and Entertainment. She has worked with leading companies on wide-ranging strategy and operation projects, including market-entry strategies, merger and acquisition planning, and content distribution. Ms. Shipnuck frequently speaks at industry conferences and has coauthored other IBM publications, including "The End of Television as We Know It," "Navigating the Media Divide," and "Beyond Access." Louisa can be reached at louisa.a.shipnuck@ us.ibm.com.

Printed in the United States of America